ASCETICISM AND THE EUCHARIST

Exploring Orthodox Spirituality with
METROPOLITAN JOHN ZIZIOULAS

MAXYM LYSACK

DARTON·LONGMAN✠TODD

In loving memory of

Maxym Martynovych Lysack
1921-2021

Memory eternal!

For if we believe that Jesus died and rose again, even so
God will bring with Him those who sleep in Jesus.
(1 Thessalonians 4:14)

First published in 2024 by
Darton, Longman and Todd Ltd
1 Spencer Court
140 – 142 Wandsworth High Street
London SW18 4JJ

ISBN: 978-1-913657-88-8

Material in Chapter 9 is adapted from "The Ascetic and Sacramental Dimensions in
Metropolitan Hierotheos (Vlahos) of Nafpaktos' Theological Work" Greek Orthodox
Theological Review 44 (1999): 1-4 is being used with the permission of Greek Orthodox
Theological Review, Brookline, MA.

Cover image: Details from *The Communion of the Holy Apostles* by Alexandre Sobolev,
icon in Christ the Saviour Orthodox Church, Ottawa. Used by permission of the artist.
A catalogue record for this book is available from the British Library.

Printed and bound in Great Britain by Bell & Bain, Glasgow

TABLE OF CONTENTS

FOREWORD   9

INTRODUCTION   13
The Structure of the Book   19

SECTION A: METROPOLITAN JOHN ZIZIOULAS: PRECURSORS, THE THEOLOGIAN, ADMIRERS AND DETRACTORS   23

CHAPTER 1: THE BACKGROUND: THREE SIGNIFICANT PRECURSORS   25
The Debate   25
Archbishop Basil Krivocheine   27
Father Dumitru Staniloae   31
Paul Evdokimov   35

CHAPTER 2: METROPOLITAN JOHN ZIZIOULAS' UNDERSTANDING OF THE SPIRITUAL LIFE: AN OVERVIEW   44
First Main Facet of Metropolitan John Zizioulas' Spirituality:
    Historical-Eschatological Dimension   46
Second Main Facet of Metropolitan John Zizioulas' Spirituality:
    Christological-Ecclesiological Dimension   46
Third Main Facet of Metropolitan John Zizioulas' Spirituality:
    The Limited Anthropological Dimension   50

CHAPTER 3: RESPONSES TO METROPOLITAN JOHN ZIZIOULAS   59
Petros Vassiliadis   59
Stavros Yangazoglou   64
Father Calinic Berger   66
Aristotle Papanikolaou   68
Jean-Claude Larchet   69
Father Nikolaos Loudovikos   71

SECTION B: SAINT MAXIMOS THE CONFESSOR AND HIS SUCCESSORS — 75

CHAPTER 4: THE MYSTAGOGY OF SAINT MAXIMOS THE CONFESSOR — 77
Introduction — 77
Structure and Character of the Mystagogy — 78
Prologue — 79
The Church and Man as Images — 79
The Commentary on the Divine Liturgy — 82
The Application of the Divine Institutions to the Perfection of the Soul — 84
The Recapitulations and Exhortations — 85
Two Levels of Spiritual Life — 88
Conclusion — 89

CHAPTER 5: THE EUCHARIST IN THE ETHICAL DISCOURSES OF SAINT SYMEON THE NEW THEOLOGIAN — 92
The Life and Witness of Saint Symeon — 92
Saint Symeon on the Eucharist — 93
Basic Themes — 94
The Nuptial-Ecclesial Theme and the Eucharist — 94
Saint Symeon's Ecclesiology — 95
A Eucharistic Reading of the Fifth Chapter of Ephesians — 95
Incarnation and Eucharist — 96
The Creation of Man, the Incarnation, and the Eucharist — 97
The Pneumatological Theme — 98
The Eternal Good Things — 99
The Eucharist and Asceticism — 100
Perceiving the Eucharist with Spiritual Eyes — 101
Baptism, Eucharist and Deification — 102
Orthodox Spirituality and the Human Soul — 104
Double Perception — 105
The Goal of the Eucharistic Life — 106
Unity between Asceticism and the Eucharist — 107

CHAPTER 6: BAPTISM AND THE EUCHARIST IN THE HOMILIES OF SAINT GREGORY PALAMAS — 108
The Importance of Saint Gregory Palamas in Contemporary Orthodox Theology — 108

CONTENTS

The Homilies   110
Baptism   112
Baptism as Healing   113
Baptism, Chrismation and Eschatology   115
Ascetic Preparation for the Eucharist   116
The Eucharist as Entrance into Heaven   117
The Eucharist as Union   118
Christ as Brother, Father and Mother   119
Two Twentieth-Century Commentators   121

CHAPTER 7: THE WITNESS OF THREE IMPORTANT AND
INTER-RELATED FATHERS   124

SECTION C: TWO REPRESENTATIVE
CONTEMPORARY ORTHODOX
THEOLOGIANS   133

CHAPTER 8: FATHER ALEXANDER SCHMEMANN
ON THE SPIRITUAL LIFE   135
Introduction   135
Reservations: What Spirituality Is Not   136
Spiritualities of Capitulation or Retreat   138
What Spirituality Is   139
Conclusion   151

CHAPTER 9: METROPOLITAN HIEROTHEOS OF
NAFPAKTOS ON THE SPIRITUAL LIFE   152
Introduction   152
Spirituality Both Sacramental and Ascetic   153
Ascetic Practice Before and After Baptism   154
The Role of Deacons, Priests and Bishops in the Baptismal
    Celebration   155
Asceticism as a Means to Rekindle the Grace of Baptism   156
Baptism as a Source of the Ascetic Life   158
Eucharist as a Source of the Ascetic Life   160
Orthodox Spirituality and Pietism   163
Metropolitan Hierotheos's More Recent Works   163
Conclusion   166

CHAPTER 10: TWO IRRECONCILABLE EXTREMES
OR TWO REPRESENTATIVES OF ONE GREATER
THEOLOGICAL ENTERPRISE?   167

SECTION D: METROPOLITAN JOHN OF
PERGAMON: SPIRITUALITY AND ITS
UNDERPINNINGS   175

CHAPTER 11: METROPOLITAN JOHN OF PERGAMON
ON THE SPIRITUAL LIFE: AN ANALYSIS   177
The Antecedents in Orthodox Theology   177
Metropolitan John Zizioulas' Earlier Work: Being as Communion   179
Metropolitan John Zizioulas' Later Work: Communion and
    Otherness   181
Transferring Evil from the Other to the Self   182
Kenotic Asceticism: Saint Sophrony Sakharov   184
Metropolitan John Zizioulas and Saint Sophrony Sakharov on
    Spirituality: A Comparison   185
Metropolitan John Zizioulas on Asceticism, Theosis, and the
    Eucharist   190
Metropolitan John Zizioulas' Fundamental Assumptions   191
The Exclusive Primacy of the Eucharist in Metropolitan John
    Zizioulas' Thought   192
Metropolitan John Zizioulas' Understanding of Asceticism   194

CONCLUSION   197
Chalcedonian Principles not Fully Applied to Spirituality and
    Ecclesiology   197
The Synthesis of the Mystagogy not Fully Retained   199
The Utility of the Maximian Synthesis   199
The Limits of the Maximian Synthesis   200
Monasticism as the Enduring Problem?   200
The Intrinsic Weaknesses of Eucharistic Spirituality   203
The Synthesis of the Ascetic and the Eucharistic Dimensions
    Must be Safeguarded   208
What is Orthodox Spirituality?   209

BIBLIOGRAPHY   211
INDEX OF AUTHORS   223

FOREWORD

Some books are marked by subjectivism, highlighting the acumen and quirks of their authors. Others are consistently coy concerning self-disclosure, and instead point only to their subject matter. Then there are those rare works in which the subject matter entrances the reader, without muting the compelling voice of the author, who befriends us as we share a common fascination. *Asceticism and the Eucharist: Exploring Orthodox Spirituality with Metropolitan John Zizioulas* is of the third kind. The Very Rev. (Protopresbyter) Dr. Maxym Lysack takes readers on an absorbing journey into the area of Orthodox spirituality, fastening on the twin importance of asceticism and the Eucharist, and speaking both with academic depth and pastoral insight.

Anyone who knows the author would expect nothing less. In the years when first I met Father Maxym, he served not only as the priest of a multi-cultural Orthodox parish in downtown Ottawa, Canada, but also as an astute and nurturing chaplain at University of Ottawa. At his recommendation, I opened the luminous volumes of Father Alexander Schmemann, where I was startled to find a friend alongside answers to the large questions that I had about Orthodoxy—and indeed, about the world. Father Lysack's own book similarly weds the theological and the spiritual, reminding us to take seriously Vladimir Lossky's "disarmingly simple definition of Orthodox spirituality." In *Asceticism and the Eucharist*, too, we find a radiant Orthodox "spirituality that expresses a doctrinal attitude." Those who know Father Maxym Lysack as a homilist and pastor have been enriched by words that are both invigorating and strengthening, as have his students at Saint Paul University, Ottawa (where he also served as Director of Eastern Christian Studies). Now, we have from his hand (and heart), a tome that will introduce some to the main streams in the field of Orthodox spirituality, while challenging those who know this field better to reassess the importance of integration, through a probing analysis of the celebrated work of Metropolitan John Zizioulas.

In the following pages, we are expertly led into an exploration of Orthodox spirituality, centering on the key themes of the Eucharist and asceticism, which the author insists should be seen in complementarity rather than as alternative approaches. More fundamentally, the question broached is the relationship between the corporate and the personal in Orthodox spirituality, a matter that Father Lysack notes has "received much attention in the last two generations of Orthodox theologians"— to the extent of becoming a point of contention. Metropolitan Zizioulas is well known for highlighting the eucharistic life of communion, and for his concomitant suspicion of private interiority as the way to theosis. (As a newcomer to Orthodox ecclesiology, I myself found the Metropolitan's emphasis on communion refreshing as I emerged from the rather claustrophobic individualism of my Protestant formation. At the same time, I worried that personal piety got rather short shrift in his portrait of the Church). Rather than simply affirming or critiquing Metropolitan Zizioulas, Father Lysack allows the questions of the Metropolitan to lead the reading pilgrim on this quest for clarity. Frequently the Metropolitan's moves are explicated and confirmed, even while some weaknesses or under-developed points are registered, so that we can move forward in our pilgrimage of the Christian spiritual life.

En route, because of the synthetic nature of the Metropolitan's work, and due to the broad interests of the author himself, we are immersed in the work of a wide variety of Orthodox thinkers, both ancient and contemporary. The spiritual and intellectual trek through this terrain involves examining the nature of the synthesis between the ascetic life and the Eucharist that was put forward by Saint Maximos (whom the Metropolitan holds up as exemplary). It also requires coming to grips with the Metropolitan's precursors, placing Zizioulas amidst his contemporaries, and taking advantage of what seems to have been his later movement towards a more positive assessment of the monastic life.

Both briefly and extensively, as necessary to move us towards a fuller understanding, the reader is exposed to: the precursive thought of Archbishop Krivocheine, Father D. Staniloae, and Paul Evdokimov; the various responses to the Metropolitan by Jean-Claude Larchet,

Vassiliadis, Father Berger, Papanikolaou, and Father Loudovikos; the three giants in ecclesial and personal spirituality, Saints Maximos, Symeon the New Theologian, and Gregory of Palamas; and the more recent work of Father Alexander Schmemann and the lesser-known Metropolitan Hierotheos of Nafpaktos, some of whose work has not yet been translated. Interpreted to us with both concision and care, these theologians and pastors are deftly placed in Father Lysack's argument. All along we see that, with their differences in approach, these thinkers uphold the twin truths of our faith regarding the human person and the Church, and the glory to which God's people are called.

Merely listing this host of witnesses unfortunately gives this work a "heavy" feel that is not characteristic of its tone. Even while we are captivated by the close analysis of each section, we are also charmed by the wry humor and deeply pastoral voice of the one who is helping us to navigate the terrain. He laments, for example, that "non-eucharistic asceticism is quietly suspicious of marriage," gently suggests that "monasticism does not need to be seen as a threat" to the communal life, and regrets that in some renderings of spirituality "the altar of the heart has been rendered superfluous." Moreover, we never lose the forest for the trees, as Father Lysack continually brings us back to the symmetry and significance of the two streams of Orthodox spirituality, the personal and the ecclesial. His work is also marked by a modesty and subtlety that recognizes the danger of overstating one's case. While acknowledging that Metropolitan Zizioulas is correct in identifying the Maximian synthethesis of the two strands in Orthodox spirituality, he shows how "Zizioulas has not applied the Maximian synthesis to his own work in a way that would produce a balance." He further indicates that even the Maximian synthesis, rightly discerned, cannot tell us everything about ecclesiology or spiritual theology.

C. S. Lewis once remarked that "no man who bothers about originality will ever be original: whereas if you simply try to tell the truth (without caring twopence how often it has been told before) you will, nine times out of ten, become original without ever having noticed it" (*Mere Christianity*). Here is a book on the most personal yet universal of subjects that demonstrates the truth of this judgment. Clearly, the author of *Asceticism and the Eucharist* has been compelled to construct,

11

so far as he can, a truthful account of these topics, as handled by Church fathers and contemporary theologians who were seeking an authentic and balanced Orthodox spirituality. What emerges is a sparkling (and challenging!) introduction to Orthodox spiritual theology seen through the lens of contemporary Orthodox theology, grounded in the great fathers of the past, and manifestly rejoicing in the Trinity and the God-Man who died and rose again. It provides an essential intervention in the current debate among scholars concerning the contours of Orthodox spiritual theology. More than that, it is pastorally useful for instruction of the faithful, calling us to celebrate the "liturgy of the Eucharist" and the "liturgy of the heart," without playing off one against the other.

Edith M. Humphrey
William F. Orr Professor Emerita of New Testament
Pittsburgh Theological Seminary

INTRODUCTION

I n his Introduction to the now-classic work *The Mystical Theology of the Eastern Church*, Vladimir Lossky wrote the following words:

> It is our intention, in the following essay, to study certain aspects of eastern spirituality in relation to the fundamental themes of the Orthodox dogmatic tradition. In the present work, therefore, the term "mystical theology" denotes no more than a spirituality which expresses a doctrinal attitude.[1]

Lossky could not have imagined that his words would find their way into the Introduction of another work on Orthodox spirituality of considerably less renown. While I will not use the term "mystical theology" in this book, I will certainly avail myself of Lossky's disarmingly simple definition of Orthodox spirituality: spirituality that expresses a doctrinal attitude. Indeed, Lossky is quick to point out that all the struggles of the Church to express true doctrine can be understood collectively as an effort to safeguard the possibility of attaining to the fullness of union with God.[2] This leads us to another important definition: the process of attaining union with God is what we call the spiritual life or, quite simply, spirituality.

So far, so good, but what shall we make of "asceticism" and "Eucharist" and their connection to union with God, or spirituality? Here we make an important distinction: asceticism is that effort or discipline which we apply to the spiritual life in order to receive the grace of God to attain to full union with Him; Eucharist is that celebration that makes us one with God *as Church*. While asceticism can certainly be practised corporately, it normally points to a *personal* effort. Eucharist, on the

[1] Vladimir Lossky, *The Mystical Theology of the Eastern Church*, (Crestwood, NY: St. Vladimir's Seminary Press, 1976), 7.
[2] *Ibid.*, 9-10.

other hand, is the *corporate* experience *par excellence* for the Christian. We see, therefore, that spirituality has two distinct but inseparable aspects, the personal and the corporate.

All of Orthodox spirituality includes the two aspects of the personal and the corporate and therefore acknowledges the importance of both asceticism and the Eucharist. Certain Orthodox theologians, however, have placed a greater or a lesser emphasis on one or the other aspects, leading to a lively discussion and occasionally hot debate between them. The tendency to place greater emphasis on the Eucharist as a constituent aspect of Orthodox spirituality characterizes theologians who embrace what is often called 'eucharistic ecclesiology.' Metropolitan John Zizioulas is likely the most prominent representative of this tendency among contemporary theologians. Important theologians holding similar convictions about eucharistic ecclesiology came before him: Father Nicholas Afanasiev, Father Kiprian Kern, Father Alexander Schmemann, to name a few. We might place Father Georges Florovsky among the aforementioned theologians as well, although he developed a model of eucharistic ecclesiology in only a seminal form and did not pursue its development as vigorously as did the others. Other Orthodox theologians place a strong emphasis on the ascetic dimension of Orthodox spirituality. We might, with care, place Vladimir Lossky in this group, and we certainly could place Father John Romanides there. Metropolitan Hierotheos Vlachos is likely the most prominent of these theologians, although, as we shall see later in the book, he also acknowledges the indispensable place of the Eucharist in the spiritual life. Other theologians, such as Paul Evdokimov and Father Dumitru Staniloae, embrace both the eucharistic and ascetic dimensions carefully and deliberately, although the former embraces the basic premises of eucharistic ecclesiology, while the latter does not. To be sure, it is rather perilous to attempt to place the Orthodox theologians of the twentieth century and our time into two simple categories. The most important thing is to realize that the corporate and personal aspects of spirituality have received much attention in the last two generations of Orthodox theologians, and it seemed appropriate to produce a study of Orthodox spirituality focusing on these two aspects explicitly.

This leads us to the next question: Why choose Metropolitan John Zizioulas among contemporary Orthodox theologians as the point of departure and reference point for a study of Orthodox spirituality? It is a valid question, since the Metropolitan's name is more frequently associated with ecclesiology, Trinitarian theology, ecumenism, and more recently with the relationship between theology and ecology, than it is with spirituality. While renowned for his contribution to these areas, Zizioulas nevertheless articulates the contours of Orthodox spirituality without always explicitly naming his endeavour. In other words, he discusses spirituality at length. We need to add, however, that Zizioulas has distinguished himself as a theologian of the history of spirituality. His groundbreaking article "The Early Christian Community," in which he lays out his hypothesis that there were two dominant types of spirituality in the early Church – monastic spirituality and the spirituality of the eucharistic community – represents an important contribution to the history of Christian spirituality in general, patristic spirituality in particular, and, by implication, for Orthodox spirituality. Furthermore, Zizioulas' thesis that a synthesis of the two was effected by Saint Maximos the Confessor immediately places the Metropolitan into the middle of a lively discussion of a number of theologians about the spiritual and theological legacy of the Confessor. Here is how Zizioulas summarizes his position:

> The most important attempt to arrive at a healthy reconciliation of these two types of spirituality – the eucharistic and the monastic (to describe them in general terms) – is to be found in the person and the writings of a Greek father of the late sixth and early seventh century, Maximus the Confessor. Maximus not only corrected Origenism and purified Evagrianism from the dangers they involved for spirituality, but, in a way that remained unique in the entire history of the church, he recovered and synthesized the old biblical and early patristic eucharistic approach to existence with monastic experience.[3]

While the Metropolitan's admiration for Saint Maximos is clear, we will come to see that the former will not view the synthesis forged by

[3] John D. Zizioulas, "The Early Christian Community," *Christian Spirituality: Origins to the Twelfth Century,* Bernard McGinn *et al.* (eds.) (New York: Crossroad, 1997), 42.

Saint Maximos as a union of two elements joined on an equal basis, but rather as the subordination of the monastic type of spirituality to the eucharistic type of spirituality. Indeed, the Metropolitan's choice of the word "reconciliation" reveals his contention that the monastic and eucharistic types of spirituality were to some extent in conflict with each other and that the only proper course of action was the absorption of monastic spirituality into eucharistic spirituality. Zizioulas' contention is exactly what we would expect to find in the work of a proponent of eucharistic ecclesiology. What makes him particularly interesting for our purposes, however, is that he not only articulates a position on Orthodox spirituality, but that he is prepared to support his position with a specific theology of the history of Christian spirituality.

There is another important reason for having Metropolitan John as our guide to Orthodox spirituality: he is a theologian who synthesizes broadly. The scope of Zizioulas' theology is expansive. Zizioulas continues in some respects the tradition of the neo-patristic synthesis of Father Georges Florovsky. He includes Lossky and Afanasiev in his thought, locating lacunae in their work and addressing them. He relates to Roman Catholic and Protestant theologians. He is constantly in dialogue with modern philosophy. He is clearly one of the important theologians of the twentieth and twenty-first centuries. Many have praised or critiqued him, but few have allowed him to be their guide for exploring spirituality, which is precisely what I propose to do in this book. Enlisting him as our guide does not mean that I do not critique him; it will, in fact, mean the exact opposite. I do, however, propose to critique him from the vantage point of someone who appreciates his work. Zizioulas needed to deepen his appreciation of asceticism, as several theologians have observed.[4] Few, however, have pointed to the exact places in his work that could have benefitted from further development. I will attempt to point to these places in this book,

---

[4]   Nicholas Loudovikos, "Person Instead of Grace and Dictated Otherness: John Zizioulas's Final Theological Position." *The Heythrop Journal*, XLVIII (2009), 1-16; Aristotle Papanikolaou, "Integrating the ascetical and the eucharistic: current challenges in Orthodox ecclesiology." *International Journal for the Study of the Christian Church*, 11: 2-3 (2011); Alexis Torrance, "Personhood and Patristics in Orthodox Theology: Reassessing the Debate." *The Heythrop Journal*. LII (2011), 700-707.

but I propose also to let Metropolitan John Zizioulas ask the fundamental questions about spirituality and lead us through the Tradition to key moments for theological and spiritual reflection. We are about to embark on a journey with him through several Fathers and toward our own time.

Finally, there is a certain approach or method that I use in the book that I should make explicit as we begin. I believe that every contemporary Orthodox theologian has contributed something important to the legacy of Orthodox theology. There needs to be a way to receive their works critically while noting the fundamental strengths and insights of their work. There also needs to be a way to compare them to other contemporary theologians that allows us to make sense of contemporary Orthodox theology as an enterprise. We ought not to see theologians in isolation either from each other or from Orthodox theology in general or, especially in our time, from theology in the so-called "West." Zizioulas is a case in point. His eucharistic ecclesiology represents a refinement of Afanasiev's ecclesiology. His Pneumatology emerged in response to Lossky's thought. At the same time, the Metropolitan integrates insights from Yannaras, Tillich, Levinas, Buber, and a number of Roman Catholic theologians. Zizioulas does not theologize in isolation. He would not be the theologian he is without either his predecessors or his contemporaries. We generally consider him a successor to Florovsky, but he approaches the Fathers differently. We want to acknowledge his contributions to theology, and we need to receive them with critical openness. We need to do the same with all other contemporary Orthodox theologians. I have included the work of several theologians in this book and have tried to approach them much as I did Zizioulas. I gave the Metropolitan a privileged position inasmuch as I allowed him to be our guide. At the same time, precisely because he has a privileged position, I also critique him more. My hope, however, is to present a broader picture of the efforts of contemporary Orthodox theologians to articulate a theology of the spiritual life.

I tried earlier to position a number of Orthodox theologians on the map of contemporary theology by discussing how they approach the ascetic and eucharistic dimensions of the spiritual life. While I think that this is an entirely legitimate approach and absolutely indispensable to the understanding of spirituality, I also realize that there are other questions of importance to theology, questions that define a theologian in equally important ways. One is the question of personalism. In Zizioulas' case, it is central to his work. Yet another question is the recovery and use of patristic thought in contemporary theology. Not all Orthodox theologians approach the Fathers in the same way. This particular question becomes especially acute but also gratifyingly revelatory when we turn our attention to how an individual theologian approaches Christology. It is precisely here that we can see *how* a theologian theologizes. Some believe that humanity is created in the "image of an image," that is to say, in the image of Christ. This conviction informs their whole theological work. Others, like Zizioulas, take their inspiration from Trinitarian relations and see deification as an entrance into the filial relationship that the Son enjoys with the Father. This understanding of deification is determined in part by the Metropolitan's personalist convictions.

These questions help us to understand contemporary Orthodox dogmatic theology as both diverse and cohesive: diverse, because of the differences between theologians over questions such as personalism, the relationship between the Eucharist and asceticism, and the approach to the Fathers; cohesive, because there is not an endless list of questions that define contemporary Orthodox theologians. With what I have just said in mind, we can begin to compare theologians more meaningfully. Sometimes this means that two theologians who were thought to be very similar are revealed as quite different. Other times we can see that there is not as much space between theologians as we might have thought. Zizioulas and Lossky are both personalists, but the former places a great emphasis on the Eucharist for ecclesiology and spirituality, while the latter, without devaluing the Eucharist in any way, is indebted to the ascetic tradition. Zizioulas, as I mentioned, is often presented as a successor to Florovsky, but the two do not share a common approach to Christology. More specifically, Florovsky is inspired by Saint Augustine and draws from him heavily for his understanding of Christology. Zizioulas is no supporter of Augustine and embraces the notion of corporate personality in Christology. Is Zizioulas the successor of Florovsky? Perhaps not to the extent he is thought to be. If I have included chapters on Father Alexander Schmemann and Metropolitan

Hierotheos Vlachos in this book, not to mention substantial sections on Paul Evdokimov and Father Dumitru Staniloae, it is not simply because they were prominent theologians of the twentieth century or, in the case of Metropolitan Hierotheos, the twenty-first century; rather, it is to allow us the opportunity to compare the positions of these theologians on the spiritual life and to permit us to see both the unity and complexity of contemporary Orthodox dogmatic theology.

THE STRUCTURE OF THE BOOK

In the first section of the book, I sketch out a map of the landscape of contemporary Orthodox theology as it pertains to the relationship between the ascetic and eucharistic dimensions of spirituality. I begin by explicating the position of three Orthodox theologians: an Archbishop, a priest, and a layman. These three are Archbishop Basil Krivocheine, Father Dumitru Staniloae, and Paul Evdokimov. All three theologians understood Orthodox spirituality to have both ascetic and eucharistic or liturgical dimensions. I continue with the theological work of Metropolitan John Zizioulas. I demonstrate that his spirituality is a product of his ecclesiology. I raise certain questions about his assumptions and conclude that he is presenting Orthodox spirituality in a new key. Next, I review the pertinent articles of six contemporary Orthodox theologians who respond to Zizioulas in various ways: Professor Petros Vassiliadis of the Aristotle University of Thessaloniki, Professor Stavros Yangazoglou of the National and Kapodistrian University of Athens, Father Calinic Berger, a parish priest and scholar, Professor Aristotle Papanikolaou of Fordham University, Jean-Claude Larchet, a lay theologian and prolific author, and Father Nikolaos Loudovikos, Professor of the University Ecclesiastical Academy of Thessaloniki. The first affirms Zizioulas, while the fifth and sixth critique him. The third assesses his ecclesiology through the lens of Father Staniloae's work. The second and fourth call for a full integration of the ascetic and eucharistic currents in contemporary Orthodox ecclesiology.

In the second section of this book, we allow Metropolitan John to take us on a journey to the Fathers, specifically Saint Maximos the Confessor, Saint Symeon the New Theologian and Saint Gregory Palamas. I address several questions: Is Zizioulas correct in his assessment of the *Mystagogy* of Saint Maximos the Confessor as a work of synthesis of the monastic and eucharistic dimensions of Christian spirituality? If so, to what extent is the Metropolitan faithful to the paradigm that emerges from the *Mystagogy*? Can the synthesis allegedly forged by Saint Maximos be observed in the *Ethical Discourses* of Saint Symeon the New Theologian and the *Homilies* of Saint Gregory Palamas? In this section, I do not investigate these questions as an historian, but as a student of Orthodox spirituality. I have selected only three Fathers of the Church for this study. Saint Maximos needs to be included among them, for obvious reasons, since Zizioulas relies on him so heavily in his work. The other two Fathers, Saint Symeon the New Theologian and Saint Gregory Palamas, are among the most prominent expositors of the spiritual life in the Orthodox Church and are included in all the standard manuals of Orthodox spirituality. In addition, a recent analysis of patristic theology has revealed that there is a significant relationship among the three: the importance of Saints Maximos, Symeon the New Theologian, and Gregory Palamas for Orthodox dogmatic theology and spirituality has been explicated in an in-depth study by Father Nikolaos Loudovikos recently published in English, in which the author argues that they are the most important patristic theologians after Saint Dionysios the Areopagite for the articulation of a genuinely Christian understanding of the self, a self that Loudovikos describes as an analogical identity beyond spirituality.[5] Not insignificantly for our own study, Metropolitan John opines that Saint Gregory Palamas should be understood primarily as a eucharistic theologian and, in addition, calls for a study of Saint Symeon the New Theologian with a view to explicating his eucharistic theology.[6] I have selected for analysis only one significant work or body of work of each Father. Although the sample is limited, the works included are nevertheless entirely representative of each patristic author and rich in material pertaining to the spiritual life in the Orthodox tradition. Furthermore, the prominence of all three Fathers included

---

[5] Nikolaos Loudovikos, *Analogical Identities: The Creation of the Christian Self: Beyond Spirituality and Mysticism in the Patristic Era* (Turnhout, Belgium: Brepols Publishers, 2019), 264-265.

[6] Zizioulas, *Lectures in Christian Dogmatics*, Douglas H. Knight (ed.). (London: T&T Clark, 2008), 124.

in this study and the sheer weight of their contribution to Orthodox theology and spirituality allow for some significant conclusions about Orthodox spirituality to be drawn.

In the third section of this book, we will turn to the theological work of two contemporary Orthodox theologians: Father Alexander Schmemann and Metropolitan Hierotheos Vlachos. The first shares with Metropolitan John a clear commitment to the Eucharist as a major source of theology, whereas the second has a long experience of monastic spirituality and is known for his many works steeped in the ascetic tradition. Furthermore, Father Schmemann was identified by Metropolitan John explicitly as a representative of eucharistic ecclesiology,[7] while Metropolitan Hierotheos has been identified as a proponent of therapeutic, or what I have termed *ascetic*, spirituality.[8] I thought it appropriate to include an identified representative of each tendency in Orthodox spiritual theology and to carry out a critical evaluation of their understandings of the spiritual life using the synthesis of Saint Maximos identified by Zizioulas as a point of reference for analysis. Thus, while the choice of proponents of each tendency is limited, it nevertheless gives a good representation of twentieth-century Orthodox theological thought. More importantly, it gives us the opportunity to compare Father Schmemann with Metropolitan Hierotheos. The comparison reveals that they do not represent two extremes in Orthodox theology and are not irreconcilably different from each other.

In the fourth and final section of the book, I return to Metropolitan John to complete a critical appraisal of his work in the area of spirituality and ecclesiology in the light of my previous investigations and conclusions. It seems fitting to apply to his work the paradigm that he himself identified and that he describes as normative for Orthodox theology: the synthesis of Saint Maximos. Is there a balance between the ascetic and eucharistic dimensions in his work? Does the Metropolitan really value the ascetic tradition? To what extent is his understanding of

[7] John D. Zizioulas, *Eucharist, Church, Bishop,* trans. Elizabeth Theokritoff (Brookline, MA: Holy Cross Orthodox Press, 2001), 17.
[8] Petros Vassiliadis, "Eucharistic and Therapeutic Spirituality." *The Greek Orthodox Theological Review* 42 (1997), n. 87.

asceticism determined by his theology of personhood and communion? I argue that there are certain ambiguities in his theology of asceticism that need to be addressed. I contend that eucharistically based spirituality needs a sound ascetic foundation in order for the volitional dimension of Christian anthropology to be protected. Finally, I assert that asceticism and spirituality, together with the Eucharist, should be constitutive of Orthodox ecclesiology.

A NOTE FROM THE AUTHOR

The manuscript for this book was completed before Metropolitan John Zizioulas left this world on February 2, 2023. I had written the entire manuscript in the present tense, and had noted that the Metropolitan was still writing, still responding to criticism of his work, and still revising his position. I had even proposed that he might consider generating a new synthesis that would give a meaningful place to personal prayer and asceticism within the context of his ecclesiology. Alas, we will no longer hear from him in this life, but we shall certainly now hear much about him, as the process of evaluating his considerable theological legacy has already begun. I changed a few sentences in the book to reflect the fact that Zizioulas' theological work had ended. On the other hand, I found it appropriate to keep the vast majority of the references to the Metropolitan in the present tense, both to allow the manuscript to read smoothly and to recognize the reality that Zizioulas' voice is still being heard by the Church and the next generation of theologians.

Section A:
Metropolitan
John Zizioulas:
Precursors,
The Theologian,
Admirers and
Detractors

CHAPTER ONE

THE BACKGROUND: THREE SIGNIFICANT PRECURSORS

THE DEBATE

Metropolitan John (Zizioulas) of Pergamon is one of the best-known contemporary theologians of the Orthodox Church and a recognized ecclesiologist. His doctoral thesis and first major work, *Eucharist, Bishop, Church*, was a major contribution to the field following in the tradition of Father Nicholas Afanasiev, a key architect of eucharistic ecclesiology in the Orthodox diaspora, who was himself keenly interested in the history and structure of the early Church. While Zizioulas acknowledges his debt to Afanasiev, he chooses to distance himself from some of the latter's conclusions.[9]

Despite his attention to history, Zizioulas has distinguished himself more properly as a dogmatic theologian than as a historian. He is clearly more of a theologian of history than a historian of theology. Zizioulas' theological thought represents a refinement of the previous categories of eucharistic ecclesiology developed by Fathers Afanasiev and Schmemann. He views Orthodox theology as a series of syntheses. It is not surprising, then, that he analyzes the history of early Christian spirituality as the convergence of two poles or orientations: monastic and eucharistic. His search for a synthesizer of the two expressions led him to Saint Maximos the Confessor, whose theological legacy Zizioulas

---

[9]   John D. Zizioulas, *Being as Communion* (Crestwood, NY: St. Vladimir's Seminary Press, 1993), 23-25.

25

values very highly. To synthesize, in Zizioulas' view, is not necessarily to reconcile: Maximos, according to the Metropolitan, synthesized Greek philosophy with biblical notions of time and eschatology precisely by wrecking the categories of the former.[10] Analogously, in Zizioulas' perception, Saint Maximos's synthesis of the monastic and eucharistic approaches to spirituality was not a simple combining of these two types, but represented instead a recovery of the eucharistic community as the great source of spirituality.[11] Thus, while taking the ascetic tradition into account, the Maximian synthesis propounded by Zizioulas clearly prioritizes the eucharistic dimension.

Metropolitan John is not the first contemporary Orthodox theologian to speak of a sacramental pole and an ascetic or monastic pole in Orthodox spirituality. Indeed, such a concept was already present, as we shall see, although not necessarily widely articulated in Orthodox theology. What is new in Zizioulas' view, as expounded in his article "The Early Christian Community," is the explicit identification of Saint Maximos the Confessor as the one responsible for achieving a *synthesis* of the two poles in patristic theology. Also unique to Zizioulas is the introduction of a very strong relational emphasis from eucharistic ecclesiology as well as a related stress on corporate personality in Christology, which Zizioulas presents as hallmarks of early Christian spirituality. We will explore these dimensions of his thought at a later point in this chapter. What concerns us for the moment is the context in contemporary Orthodox theology for Zizioulas' thesis that Orthodox spirituality turns around a sacramental and specifically eucharistic pole, in addition to a therapeutic one.

A detailed analysis of all of contemporary Orthodox theology lies beyond the scope of this book, but the names of several twentieth-century Orthodox theologians come to mind as representatives and as an appropriate sample: Archbishop Basil Krivocheine, Father Dumitru Staniloae, and Paul Evdokimov. All three theologians reject any attempt to split the sacramental from the ascetic. They speak instead of a spirituality that is shaped by both dimensions. Archbishop Basil writes

[10] Metropolitan John of Pergamon, "The Eucharist and the Kingdom of God," trans. Elizabeth Theokritoff. *Sourozh* 58 (1994), 5-7.
[11] Zizioulas, "The Early Christian Community," 43.

explicitly about a sacramental or liturgical pole as well as a mystical or devotional pole in Orthodox spirituality.[12] He does not spend much time developing this notion; he simply takes it for granted in his writing. Father Dumitru Staniloae treats of the question of the two dimensions in Orthodox spirituality in greater detail. What is remarkable in his work is the way in which he demonstrates the integration of the two in the context of the classic manual of Orthodox spirituality, the *Philokalia*.[13]

Paul Evdokimov also works with the sacramental and ascetic dimensions of Orthodox spirituality, demonstrating a robust and creative synthesis of the two. Also notable in his case is the fact that he explicitly identifies himself as an exponent of eucharistic ecclesiology.[14] His strong identification with this trend in Orthodox ecclesiology nevertheless does not impede him from insisting on the absolute integration of the sacramental and the ascetic in Orthodox spiritual theology. Zizioulas is clearly less of an integrationist than the three aforementioned theologians, although he does acknowledge the indebtedness of Orthodox spirituality to the ascetic tradition. In the paragraphs that follow, we will elaborate the theology of the three important Orthodox theologians and then turn to the theology of Metropolitan John Zizioulas.

ARCHBISHOP BASIL KRIVOCHEINE

Archbishop Basil Krivocheine was a monk, a patrologist, and a much-loved bishop of the Russian Orthodox Church in Western Europe. His translations of Saint Symeon the New Theologian for *Sources Chrétiennes* earned him a place in twentieth-century patristic scholarship, especially in the area of patristic spirituality. He wrote on various topics in Orthodox theology, both in patristics and outside of the area of his specialization. He also represented the Orthodox Church in ecumenical dialogue. His life as a monk on Mount Athos and his intimate knowledge

---

[12] Archevêque Basile Krivochéine, "La spiritualité orthodoxe," trans. Nikita Krivochéine *et al. Dieu, l'homme, l'Église*. (Paris: Les Éditions du Cerf, 2010), 166.
[13] Dumitru Staniloae, "The Liturgy of the Community and the Liturgy of the Heart from the View-point of the Philokalia." *One Tradition*, No. 4 (1980).
[14] Paul Evdokimov, "Eucharistie – Mystère de l'Église." *La Pensée orthodoxe*, 1968 (2).

of the writings of Saint Symeon and Saint Gregory Palamas allowed him to gain a deep knowledge of the Orthodox spiritual life. In his article on Orthodox spirituality, the Archbishop states:

> In the traditional current of Orthodox spirituality (past and present), we can discern two distinct aspects, even two poles of ecclesial piety. One of them can be characterized as sacramental and liturgical, the other as mystical and devotional. Both have an important place in Orthodox spirituality; to ignore or to minimize either one would result in a historically inaccurate and distorted picture of the religious life of Eastern Christians.

Archbishop Basil recognizes that there is a possible tension between the sacramental and the mystical poles in Orthodox spirituality. He understands that the former points to the *corporate*, while the latter expresses the *personal*. This for him does not suggest any contradiction. The mystical presupposes the sacramental.[15] One might even say that the sacramental is already present in the mystical since, according to the Archbishop, the sacraments are the source of Orthodox spiritual life.[16] The mystical-devotional pole is essential for Orthodox spirituality because it allows the personal appropriation of the grace of God given in the sacraments. It is the experiential dimension of the spiritual life that engenders an ever-deepening awareness of sacramental grace.[17]

Archbishop Basil sees the Eucharist as the sacrament of sacraments, the one that perfects all the others. He relies on Saint Dionysios the Areopagite and Saint Nicholas Cabasilas for this insight.[18] Contemporary eucharistic ecclesiologists, and Metropolitan John Zizioulas in particular, would likely find such a definition wanting, since there is no explicit reference here to the direct relationship between the Church and the Eucharist. There is, nevertheless, a dynamic understanding of the Eucharist, one that suggests something more than a simple

[15] *Ibid.*
[16] *Ibid.*
[17] *Ibid.*
[18] *Ibid.*, 167-168.

entrance into the past, namely an eschatological event with a profound Pneumatological character.[19]

Later in his article, Archbishop Basil returns to theme of the devotional-mystical pole. Calling this pole "ascetic-mystical" this time, he states that, while the sacraments are the source of the spiritual life, their personal appropriation requires a free ascetic effort that must itself be consciously felt.[20] Here the emphasis is both on the free act of the will and on awareness. The Archbishop posits that this ascetic approach finds its roots in the monastic tradition and notes the extent to which it has been integrated into Orthodox spirituality.[21] He suggests that Orthodox spirituality is basically contemplative and demonstrates a preference for seclusion over involvement in the world. This, he says, reveals the Orthodox conviction that contemplation results in true knowledge of self and real knowledge of God.[22] He stresses the fact that this tradition is essentially Christian in character and does not represent a simple recapitulation of Greek philosophical thought. The Christian underpinnings of this contemplation are based rather on the biblical notion of the image of God in humanity.[23] The contemplative aspect, therefore, is based on a Christian anthropology. Asceticism in Orthodox spirituality, according to Archbishop Basil, has a strong Christocentric character.[24] It is neither abstract nor purely moral in nature. Its goal is the acquisition of Christ-likeness.[25]

The Archbishop names *prayer* as the main and most essential aspect of Orthodox spirituality.[26] He distinguishes two movements in it: an ascent of man to God and the descent of God to man.[27] He takes care to describe the *Jesus Prayer* in great detail and sees it as being the most important expression of prayer in the Orthodox tradition.[28] He notes

[19] Archevêque Basile Krivochéine, "La spiritualité orthodoxe," 168.
[20] *Ibid.*, 173.
[21] *Ibid.*
[22] *Ibid.*, 174.
[23] *Ibid.*
[24] *Ibid.*, 176.
[25] *Ibid.*
[26] *Ibid.*
[27] *Ibid.*, 176-178.
[28] *Ibid.*, 177-178.

the importance in the tradition of the rejection of all images in prayer. He contends that this sobriety is a hallmark of Orthodox spirituality.[29]

The last aspect of Orthodox spirituality to be described by Archbishop Basil is the entrance into a heavenly experience in this life. He ties this experience to a vision of the uncreated light of Christ.[30] Here he bases his presentation on the witness of both Saint Symeon the New Theologian and Saint Gregory Palamas.[31] The author, of course, knows the writings of both intimately. What is of great importance for our study, however, is the Archbishop's conviction that both Fathers are authoritative exponents of the Orthodox spiritual tradition.

Summarizing his position, Archbishop Basil states that the Orthodox spiritual tradition, characterized by a great emphasis on prayer, asceticism, interiority, sobriety and the vision of Christ, is nevertheless firmly rooted in the life of the Church. The relationship between it and the liturgical life of the Church may seem somewhat dialectical, especially at first glance. The two, however, are completely integrated. Analogously, the personal and the corporate dimensions also find their integration here. The Archbishop explains: "Personal spiritual life is always understood as a part of our supernatural life, in the Body of Christ which is his holy Church."

The Archbishop is quick to point out that Saint Symeon the New Theologian, whom he regards as the greatest mystical theologian of the Orthodox Church, taught extensively on the Eucharist in his writings.[32] Saint Gregory of Sinai described prayer as a manifestation of Baptism, thus linking the mystical dimension with the sacramental.[33] Finally, the conviction that life in heaven begins here on earth finds its inspiration equally in the mystical and in the liturgical dimensions of the ecclesial life.[34]

What we find in Archbishop Basil is a complete balance between the mystical-ascetic and liturgical-sacramental aspects of the tradition. Furthermore, he presents this balance while maintaining a full

[29] Archevêque Basile Krivochéine, "La spiritualité orthodoxe," 177.
[30] *Ibid.*, 179.
[31] *Ibid.*, 179-180.
[32] *Ibid.*
[33] *Ibid.*
[34] *Ibid.*, 180-181.

appreciation of the ascetic dimension. Nothing in Orthodox spirituality is ignored or treated as marginal to the tradition. Instead, the ascetic-mystical dimension is explicated in all its richness and power. At the same time, the sacraments are identified as the source of the spiritual life and the Church as its context. In this way, Archbishop Basil does violence to neither dimension; he retains each in its full integrity while guarding their interdependence.

FATHER DUMITRU STANILOAE

According to the dogmatic theologian Father Boris Bobrinskoy, it is Father Dumitru Staniloae, the celebrated Romanian Orthodox theologian and confessor of the Faith, who located the synthesis of the hesychastic tradition and the Eucharist in the *Philokalia*.[35] The work to which Father Boris is referring is a short but remarkable article by Father Dumitru.[36] In this article, Father Staniloae draws upon the resources of the *Philokalia* to explain the relationship between the Eucharist and inner prayer. Inspired by the teaching of Saint Mark the Ascetic on *prayer of the heart*, he calls the latter "the liturgy of the heart." In selecting the *Philokalia* as a source of teaching on the *liturgy of the community* and the *liturgy of the heart*, Father Staniloae is making an important point: the Orthodox mystical tradition, as represented by the neptic Fathers, contains within it an integration of the sacramental and the ascetic, the *corporate* and the *personal*.[37] Here he refers to the ascetic work *Centuries* by Saints Kallistos and Ignatios Xanthopouli. Summarizing the implications of their work, Father Staniloae writes: "One can say that the personal spiritual life does not develop in isolation from the eucharistic community. In turn, the eucharistic community does not stand outside the influence of the spiritual state of those persons who compose it...."[38]

---

[35] Boris Bobrinskoy, *The Compassion of the Father*, trans. Anthony P. Gythiel (Crestwood, NY: St. Vladimir's Seminary Press, 2003), 110.
[36] Dumitru Staniloae, "The Liturgy of the Community and the Liturgy of the Heart from the View-point of the Philokalia," *One Tradition* No. 4 (Crawley Down, West Sussex: The Community of the Servants of the Will of God, 1980).
[37] *Ibid.*, 1.
[38] Staniloae, "The Liturgy of the Community," 1.

Commenting further on Kallistos and Ignatios, Staniloae remarks that the eucharistic body of Christ is a source of our deification.[39] Deification is understood here as an intimate union with Christ, such that Christ becomes the subject of our operations and we become the subjects of Christ's operations in us.[40] This intimate union nevertheless does not result in any confusion of the subjects. Describing the mode of this union in greater detail, Father Staniloae writes:

> I am united with Christ, but united in the paradoxical mode of a dialogue which at the same time unites and distinguishes the partners. Christ speaks, feels, thinks in my words, in my feelings, in my thoughts. He supports, nourishes and raises up my operations within me. Nevertheless I rejoice in Him as from Him, not from myself. The union does not suppress the distinction and difference.[41]

Uniting and distinguishing simultaneously is an idea that will be reiterated later by Metropolitan John Zizioulas in his book *Communion and Otherness*. What is of importance here is Father Staniloae's use of the word dialogue, which denotes an ongoing reciprocity. It is not simply that a distinction of the subjects is maintained, but that neither the distinction nor the unity is in any way imposed. Significantly, the proper articulation of the mode of union of the believer with Christ and *vice versa* requires an entrance into Christology and, by extension, ecclesiology. This is implicit in the argumentation set forth in Father Dumitru's entire article. Attentive to the implications for both areas of dogmatic theology, Father Staniloae explains that the mode of relationship between the believer and Christ does not suggest exclusivity in any absolute sense: "The members of the personal Body of Christ do not become exclusively my members, but our members in common."[42] Furthermore, the union that a believer has with Christ is also a union with other Christians. In this union, all Christians remain

[39] *Ibid.*, 2.
[40] *Ibid.*, 3.
[41] *Ibid.*, 4.
[42] *Ibid.*

distinct persons. Father Dumitru characterizes the relationship as a gift that is freely brought and freely offered.[43] Here again, the freedom and reciprocity of the relationship are protected.

Father Dumitru advances his case by presenting a basic tenet of Christian anthropology: a human person is both body and soul. Because of this, the believer who receives the Body of Christ receives Him not into his body only but into his soul as well. In addition, when we receive the Body of Christ, we receive Him together with His soul and His divinity.[44] In this way, the whole Christ enters the soul of the Christian, sanctifying and spiritualizing it and the rational and sensible roots of our body, which, as Father Staniloae notes, are found within the soul.[45] This enables the soul to resurrect the body at the end of the age. Christ becomes "the eternal and ultimate ground of our hypostases."[46] Father Staniloae is not endorsing a dualism of soul and body; on the contrary, he understands that, as the human person is spiritualized, the union between soul and body increases as both are drawn closer to Christ.[47] Indeed, dualism is overcome in the saints. In any case, the dualism experienced by human beings is, according to the theologian, functional and not substantial.[48] Father Staniloae emphasizes the Pneumatological dimension of this eucharistic union with Christ, stating that, through the body of Christ, the entire person is nourished by the Holy Spirit.[49]

Father Dumitru sees the Eucharist as the source of spiritual growth both of the community and of each Christian who participates in it. The indwelling of the eucharistic Christ in each Christian therefore has, in his understanding, a distinctly liturgical character. Christ acts as the High Priest, Who enters the inner sanctuary of the human person to

receive there the sacrifices of the person with whom he is concerned, and to offer them with His own proper sacrifice to

[43] Staniloae, "The Liturgy of the Community," 5.
[44] *Ibid.*, 5.
[45] *Ibid.*, 6.
[46] *Ibid.*
[47] *Ibid.*, 7.
[48] *Ibid.*
[49] *Ibid.*, 8.

God the Father. The Liturgy of the community is thus continued in a personal liturgy, as though the latter were the second part of the former. Its action is extended in the work of spiritualising the life of the believer.[50]

The relationship between the Eucharist and the interior liturgy is very close indeed. Father Staniloae goes on to cite Saint Mark the Ascetic, who describes an interior temple, an interior altar, and an interior sacrifice.[51] The sacrifice is comprised of the first-born thoughts of the noetic faculty (the *nous*). Christ, acting as the High Priest, offers those thoughts as a sacrifice so that they are consumed by the divine fire.[52] Father Staniloae observes that, just as we eat the body of Christ in the Divine Liturgy, so also Christ "eats" our minds in the interior liturgy.[53] The mind is made ready as food for Him precisely through participation in the Eucharist. While we receive Christ in the Eucharist, Christ also assimilates our minds to Himself, so that the union between Him and us is complete.[54] Christ's Archpriestly ministry therefore has two aspects: the offering of Himself to us, and the assimilation of us to His own sacrifice.[55] Citing other patristic sources, Father Dumitru notes that the sacrifice offered to Christ and assimilated by Him to His own sacrifice includes not only our thoughts, but also our whole lives. Christ offers both of these to God the Father.[56]

In Father Staniloae's thought, the integration between the Eucharist and the interior or mystical life is complete. What is notable is that the theologian's argumentation does not follow the contours of eucharistic ecclesiology. This becomes especially clear in his magisterial work *Orthodox Spirituality*.[57] In this substantial study, Father Staniloae begins

[50] Staniloae, "The Liturgy of the Community," 8.
[51] Mark the Ascetic, "Reply to Those Who Have Doubts about Holy Baptism", PG 65, c. 996, cited in Staniloae, *op. cit.*, 9.
[52] *Ibid.*, 9-10.
[53] Staniloae, "The Liturgy of the Community," 10.
[54] *Ibid.*
[55] *Ibid.*, 11.
[56] *Ibid.*, 13.
[57] Dumitru Staniloae, *Orthodox Spirituality*, trans. Archimandrite Jerome (Newville) and Otilia Kloos. (South Canaan, PA: Saint Tikhon's Seminary Press, 2002).

by setting out his basic assumptions: that union with God is possible and that the basis for spirituality is a sound Trinitarian theology. Next he establishes the tight connection between Pneumatology, Christology, and ecclesiology. This connection we will also see later in Metropolitan John Zizioulas. Next he launches into a detailed presentation of three stages of the spiritual life: *purification, illumination,* and *deification*. In the process, he elucidates the teaching on the passions, the virtues, and Christian anthropology taken directly from the ascetic tradition. Here again he refers to Saint Mark the Ascetic's teaching on the interior liturgy.[58]

Clearly, Father Staniloae has assimilated all the basic perceptions of Orthodox ascetic theology. At the same time, as demonstrated in his article, he sees the complete unity between the ascetic tradition, as it has been received by the Church, and the Eucharist. Rather than going outside of the ascetic tradition to develop a hypothesis, he has demonstrated the intrinsic compatibility of the latter with eucharistic life. In Father Dumitru's thought, the two are revealed as sources of each other, demonstrating an inherent interdependence.

Paul Evdokimov

Paul Evdokimov was one of the outstanding Orthodox theologians of the twentieth century. He was a professor, a prolific author, a spokesman for the Orthodox Church in the ecumenical movement and, in his own special and dynamic way, a shepherd of souls. He exercised his "priesthood of the baptized" through service to the poor, by protecting those persecuted by the Nazi regime and, after the war, working among refugees and displaced persons. The combination of his deep commitment to *diakonia* and extraordinary intellectual abilities made Evdokimov one of the most remarkable representatives of the Orthodox Church in the diaspora.

Evdokimov was the author of a number of books and many articles on Orthodox dogmatic and spiritual theology. Perhaps his best-known works are *Les âges de la vie spirituelle*, in which he articulates a theology of the ascetic life, and the magisterial *L'Orthodoxie*. The latter contains an extensive section on Orthodox ecclesiology, and it is one

---

[58] Staniloae, *Orthodox Spirituality*, 283.

of the major sources for his work on eucharistic ecclesiology. Another major source is his article "Eucharistie–Mystère de l'Église," which appeared in the journal *La Pensée orthodoxe*. This article appeared in a modified form in Evdokimov's book *La prière de l'église d'orient*. Finally, the book *Le Christ dans la pensée russe* includes short but important sections on eucharistic ecclesiology and on Father Nicholas Afanasiev. Evdokimov's writings on eucharistic ecclesiology indicate that he was committed to this particular way of understanding the Church. What is especially interesting, however, is the way in which he integrates his ecclesiology into a much larger picture of Orthodox spiritual life.

Evdokimov's reasons for embracing eucharistic ecclesiology are connected to his conviction that this was the ecclesiology of the ancient Church. Comparing eucharistic ecclesiology to universal ecclesiology, Evdokimov states that the former is more ancient, more biblical, and more patristic than the latter. In fact, he suggests that universalist ecclesiology has no New Testament basis whatsoever.[59] Of course, he shares this presupposition with Father Afanasiev, whom he cites frequently in his writings on ecclesiology.

Commenting on the worship and doctrine of the ancient Church, Evdokimov states that, in early Christianity, *all sacraments were an organic part of the eucharistic liturgy*.[60] Referring to Saint Dionysios, he asserts that the Eucharist is not one sacrament among others, but rather the Sacrament of Sacraments.[61] Here he agrees with Archbishop Basil Krivocheine who, as we have already seen, cites the same patristic source to make the same point. Evdokimov insists that this definition is the starting point of all Orthodox ecclesiology: "This fundamental definition goes to the source of Orthodox ecclesiology. It means that the Eucharist is not a sacrament *in the Church*, but the sacrament *of the Church* itself ... [62] The presupposition that the Eucharist is the sacrament of the Church is certainly one of the assumptions of Orthodox eucharistic

---

[59] Paul Evdokimov, *Le Christ dans la pensée russe* (Paris: Cerf, 1986), 211; Paul Evdokimov, *L'Orthodoxie* (Paris: Desclée de Brouwer, 1979), 129-130.
[60] Paul Evdokimov, "Eucharistie–Mystère de l'Église," *La Pensée orthodoxe*, 1968 (2), 53.
[61] *Ibid.*
[62] *Ibid.*

ecclesiology. Evdokimov is saying, however, that this presupposition is normative for Orthodox ecclesiology in general.

Orthodox eucharistic ecclesiology has, in Evdokimov's view, several important implications for Orthodox theology. The *first* implication is anthropological. Evdokimov states that the Eucharist makes man "a liturgical being" and "a living Eucharist."[63] Man finds his greatest fulfilment, his healing, and indeed his salvation in the eucharistic celebration. He is called, of course, to be profoundly "liturgical" in whatever context he finds himself, but is ultimately most at home in the Liturgy. *Second*, the Eucharist also has implications for cosmology. Evdokimov states: *"En vérité, le monde est créé pour le Repas messianique ...."*[64] If the world was created for the Eucharist, then it necessarily finds its completion in and through the Eucharist. No doubt Evdokimov has in mind here references from the Liturgy of Saint John Chrysostom in which we see that the Eucharist is offered "on behalf of all and for all" and that Christ's life was given "for the life of the world." *Thirdly*, Evdokimov states that the Eucharist embodies the synthesis of the dogmatic definitions of the Councils and the teachings of the Fathers.[65] Citing Saint Irenaeus, he calls the Liturgy "the cup of the synthesis,"[66] meaning, of course, that the Liturgy re-presents the entire plan of salvation. *Fourthly*, the Eucharist has implications for Christology, just as Christology has implications for the Eucharist and ecclesiology. Evdokimov draws out these implications in the following passage:

> So it is quite natural that the Eucharist finds itself right at the heart of the Church, and reveals itself as engendering the unity proclaimed, offered and lived....Eucharistic communion effects a real participation in the whole Christ, and this work, which is by its very essence unifying, makes of the communicants, according to Saint Athanasios, "Christified beings transformed into the Word."[67]

[63] Evdokimov, "Eucharistie," 53.
[64] *Ibid.*, 54.
[65] I*bid.*
[66] *Ibid.* St. Irenaeus of Lyons, *Against the Heresies*, III, 16, 7.
[67] Paul Evdokimov, *Les âges de la vie spirituelle* (Paris: Desclée de Brouwer, 1995), 74.

Evdokimov uses the term "Christ total" or in Latin, *totus Christus*, an expression taken originally from Saint Augustine that indicates the totality of Christ as the Head of the Church together with His body. What we are meant to infer from Evdokimov's use of this term is that ecclesiology is nothing less than an extension of Christology, and this, in fact, is one of the main operating assumptions of Metropolitan John Zizioulas. The implications of the term *totus Christus* were also explored in great detail by several noted Roman Catholic theologians writing in the middle part of the twentieth century, such as Émile Mersch and Henri de Lubac, both of whom are cited by Zizioulas in his work.[68]

Paul Evdokimov has a specific approach to eucharistic ecclesiology. *Firstly*, he emphasizes deification as the common goal of both the eucharistic and the ascetic lives. *Secondly*, he shows how asceticism can provide a deeper experience of the Eucharist. *Thirdly*, he shows how the spiritual life results in the interiorization of the Eucharist, which, *fourthly*, is lived out concretely in the lives of the saints.

Evdokimov highlights the deifying impact of the Eucharist on the faithful. He notes that Saint Maximos the Confessor places a great emphasis on the effect of the *epiklesis* on the eucharistic community. We should note here that, in the Orthodox Liturgy, the priest asks God the Father to send the Holy Spirit upon *both* the eucharistic assembly and the Holy Gifts. It is therefore not only the Gifts that are deified, but the faithful together with them. This is a key point in the teaching of Saint Maximos on the Divine Liturgy, and Evdokimov brings it to the forefront of his own teaching.[69] He also relies heavily on Saint John Chrysostom, Saint Nicholas Cabasilas, and Saint Cyril of Jerusalem, all of whose teaching points very much in the same direction. For Evdokimov, then, part of the "fullness" that the local

---

[68]   For an in-depth study on the affinities between John Zizioulas and Henri De Lubac, see Paul McPartlan, *The Eucharist Makes the Church: Henri de Lubac and John Zizioulas in Dialogue* (Edinburgh, Scotland: T & T Clark, 1993). Zizioulas relies on some of Émile Mersch's work for building his own presentation of the corporate personality of Christ in his Christology. See *Communion and Otherness*, pp. 290-291.

[69]   St. Maximos the Confessor, *Mystagogy*, 21; Evdokimov, "Eucharistie," 68.

church of God enjoys is the experience of deification.

The eucharistic and ascetic lives are very much linked, according to Evdokimov, because they both have deification as their objective: "A life of asceticism leads to *theosis* by means of a gradual ascent, by climbing the rungs of the "heavenly ladder" (Saint John Climacus). By contrast, the sacramental life offers the grace of deification instantaneously."[70]

One may get the impression from this quotation that Evdokimov accepts asceticism but sees it as separate from, and inferior to, the sacramental life. This is not at all the case. Commenting further on their relationship, he writes: "It may be said that the ascetic and mystical life is a deeper and deeper awareness of the sacramental life. The identical nature of the two is indicated by the image that is used to describe them both, that of the mystical marriage."[71] Here the author makes his point clear: the ascetic and sacramental lives are both necessary, and the former provides a deepening of the experience of the latter. By describing the two as "identical," Evdokimov rejects the possibility of divorcing one from the other.

Asceticism plays a very special role in preparing the Christian for participation in the Eucharist. It allows the believer and, indeed, the entire worshipping community to enter into a state of deep reverence for the great eucharistic mystery, and in this way to discern the Body of the Lord (1 Cor. 11:29). Evdokimov agrees with Father Afanasiev that this verse from First Corinthians has been misinterpreted to mean that a state of moral readiness is required before a Christian can receive the Eucharist. Since no one is ever completely ready from the moral point of view, the tendency, tragically, has been in the direction of reduced eucharistic participation.[72] The idea here is not that the moral condition of the worshipper is irrelevant, but that to interpret readiness for the Eucharist in an *exclusively* moral sense is to do violence both to the scriptural text in question and to the Orthodox understanding of asceticism. The Eucharist, asserts Evdokimov, is not

[70] Paul Evdokimov, *Woman and the Salvation of the World* (Crestwood, NY: St. Vladimir's Seminary Press, 1994), 74.

[71] *Ibid.*

[72] Evdokimov, *L'Orthodoxie,* 129; Paul Evdokimov, *La prière de l'Église d'Orient* (Paris: Desclée de Brouwer, 1985), 69.

a reward for good behaviour, but the medicine of immortality without which the Christian dies spiritually.[73]

In his article "Eucharistie – Mystère de l'Église," Evdokimov begins his section on eucharistic ecclesiology (Section V) by stating that the patristic liturgical norm is the participation of the entire Body of Christ in the Holy Eucharist on every Lord's Day.[74] He starts with this premise because it is vital to the experience of lived eucharistic ecclesiology. Given that a wrong understanding of eucharistic readiness and consequently of Orthodox asceticism is a major factor in the reduced liturgical participation in the contemporary Church, it follows that a recovery of true Orthodox asceticism is indispensable for the renewal of liturgical life and thus of the manifestation of eucharistic ecclesiology on the practical level. Evdokimov has the following to say about the character of Orthodox asceticism:

> Asceticism and moralism are of differing natures. Moralism attempts to regulate behavior by subjecting it to moral imperatives .... In Eastern spirituality, "works" do not refer to moral actions (in the sense of the Protestant contrast between "faith and works") but to the theandric energy, the acting of man within the acting of God.[75]

The Orthodox understanding of asceticism comes from a particular anthropology that differs essentially from the anthropology embraced by late Western Christendom:

> The Western anthropology is thus essentially a moral anthropology .... Orthodox anthropology is not "moral" but ontological; it is the ontology of deification. It is centered not on overcoming this world, but on "seizing the Kingdom of God" (cf Lk 16:16), on the inner transformation of the world into the Kingdom .... The Church, then, is viewed as the place

[73] Evdokimov, *La prière*, 70.
[74] Evdokimov, "Eucharistie," 65.
[75] Evdokimov, *Woman*, 86.

where this metamorphosis occurs through worship and the sacraments, and is revealed as being essentially eucharistic ....[76]

The ontology of deification, which is at the root of Orthodox anthropology and therefore of Orthodox asceticism, is the ontology of the eucharistic assembly and, by extension, of true eucharistic ecclesiology. Here we see the truth of Evdokimov's words that the ascetic and sacramental lives in the Orthodox Church are "identical."

The experience of the Eucharist should not, according to Evdokimov, remain exterior to the life of a Christian. With time, the Eucharist can be internalized. This is the interpretation that Evdokimov applies to the verse "Behold, I stand at the door and knock; if anyone hears my voice and opens the door, I will come in to him and eat with him, and he with me," (Rev. 3:20, RSV).[77] Commenting on this passage, Evdokimov writes: "This text is of a clearly eucharistic nature; this aspect, which makes it a liturgy, even an 'interiorized Eucharist,' should be emphasized."[78] The interiorization of the Eucharist is the desired and expected result of an ascetic and eucharistic spiritual life. Evdokimov states that this interiorization is directly connected to ecclesiology.[79] This interiorized Eucharist is the *liturgy of the heart* described in detail by Father Dumitru Staniloae. It is a significant point of convergence in the thought of the two theologians. Perhaps it also represents the best way in the patristic tradition to establish the connection between the eucharistic and ascetic dimensions of the spiritual life.

This interior Eucharist is not something purely in the theoretical realm, but is revealed concretely in the lives of the saints. Evdokimov refers specifically to Saint John of Kronstadt, who is well known in the Orthodox Church as a proponent of asceticism, the practice of the *Jesus Prayer*, and frequent communion.[80] One might even conclude from Evdokimov's presentation that saints such as Saint John are the living proof of the truth of the fundamental unity between the eucharistic

---

[76]   *Ibid.*, 72-73.
[77]   Evdokimov, *Woman*, 90.
[78]   *Ibid.*
[79]   *Ibid.*
[80]   *Ibid.*; "Eucharistie," 68; *Pensée russe*, 208.

and ascetic aspects of the one life in Christ. In his book *Le Christ dans la pensée russe*, Evdokimov traces what he sees as the development of a living eucharistic ecclesiology from Saint Nikodemos the Hagiorite (who defended the practice of frequent communion) to Saint Païsiy Velychkovskyy (a kindred spirit to Saint Nikodemos, who translated the *Philokalia* into Slavonic and popularized it in Slavic lands) to the fathers of the Optina Hermitage (who put into practice the teachings of Saint Païsiy) to Saint Theophan the Recluse (who articulated and systematized their teachings) and finally to Saint John of Kronstadt (who inherited all of the fruits of this ascetic and eucharistic renewal in Slavic lands and lived it out in his own life and ministry). Of great significance in this spiritual genealogy are also Saint Tikhon of Zadonsk and Saint Seraphim of Sarov.[81] Significantly, every spiritual figure mentioned by Evdokimov was a great ascetic.

There is, of course, nothing theoretical about all the saints whom Evdokimov has called to mind. Theirs is the practical eucharistic ecclesiology of holiness, which embodies the unity of the Eucharist and asceticism. The strength of Evdokimov's presentation is that he moves it from the level of a theological enterprise to the level of sanctity. He presents Saint John of Kronstadt as perhaps the first twentieth-century "representative" of eucharistic ecclesiology who lived out his ecclesiological witness through the daily celebration of the Divine Liturgy, during which so many miracles were witnessed by the faithful.[82] Evdokimov writes: "It is in the Eucharist that the mystery of the Church is fully accomplished, and Father John is the promoter of a eucharistic ecclesiology. The twentieth century receives it as its spiritual inheritance."[83] Evdokimov's presentation of eucharistic ecclesiology leads us to Saint John of Kronstadt's statement about his inner life on the days when he could not celebrate the Divine Liturgy: "The days when I do not celebrate the Eucharist I feel myself dying ...."[84]

Evdokimov's ecclesiology contains within it basic presuppositions that are common to the ecclesiological thought of Father Afanasiev

81 Evdokimov, *Pensée russe*, 206-208.
82 *Ibid.*, 208.
83 *Ibid.*
84 Evdokimov, "Eucharistie," 68.

and other proponents of eucharistic ecclesiology. What makes his argument so compelling, however, is the way in which he is able to present eucharistic ecclesiology as an integral part of a larger whole. His emphasis on deification as an important aspect of the Church's eucharistic experience and as a common goal of both asceticism and sacramental participation provides a solid grounding for his thought in patristic theology. In addition, Evdokimov's insistence on the need for a lived eucharistic ecclesiology of holiness refers his theology to the concrete reality of ecclesial life. His is not the ecclesiology of the armchair theologian but of the committed member of Christ's Body struggling to live the ascetic and sacramental dimensions of the one spiritual life. Finally, one cannot help but be struck by Evdokimov's ability to raise his theological enterprise from the level of discussion to the level of experience by locating the essence of his ecclesiology in the life and witness of contemporary saints. This gives his theology an empirical character that, in turn, connects it organically to the Orthodox spiritual tradition.

CHAPTER TWO

METROPOLITAN JOHN ZIZIOULAS' UNDERSTANDING OF THE SPIRITUAL LIFE: AN OVERVIEW

As we turn to Metropolitan John Zizioulas' theological work, the first question we might pose is: How does Metropolitan John understand the spiritual life? Here we must recall that the Metropolitan began his theological enquiries as an ecclesiologist. His understanding of the spiritual life emerges in this context, so the term *ecclesial spirituality* could be used to describe his position accurately. Furthermore, his adherence to the basic premises of eucharistic ecclesiology is clear. This means two things: firstly, that the Church is the *locus* of the spiritual life and, secondly, that the Eucharist is its primary event. Put simply, Zizioulas' spiritual theology is, to a great extent, an extension of his ecclesiology. His ecclesiology, on the other hand, is an extension of his Christology. With time, Zizioulas expanded his theology to include a developed understanding of communion, personhood, and otherness.

Zizioulas' understanding of the spiritual life has, in my view, three main facets: 1) a historical-eschatological dimension, 2) a Christological-ecclesiological dimension, and 3) a limited anthropological dimension. The historical dimension is based, as we have already noted, on the assumption that the history of Christian spirituality revolves around two poles: monastic and eucharistic.[85] The synthesizer of these two strands of spirituality is identified as Saint Maximos the Confessor, who

[85] Zizioulas, "Early," 42.

not only combined the two expressions of spirituality successfully, but also recovered the biblical dimension of eschatology.[86] This, according to Zizioulas, was a watershed in the history of Christian spirituality, and the resulting synthesis became, we are led to believe, normative for spirituality from that point forward. Zizioulas summarizes it in this way:

> Spirituality in this approach becomes a matter of participation in the eucharistic community as a way of overcoming individualism through the purification of the heart from all passions, but also through the actual gathering of the Eucharist, which places creation in the movement – in space and time – toward its proper eschatological end.[87]

Several important points emerge from this description. The *first* is that the *locus* for spirituality is the eucharistic community. There is nothing here to say how or if one engages the spiritual life outside the eucharistic community. *Secondly*, the challenge of the spiritual life is *to participate* in this community. *Thirdly*, the stated goal is *to overcome individualism*. The reference to the purification of the heart seems to be taken from the ascetic tradition, but it has been placed in a new context that is entirely relational. *Fourthly*, the *eucharistic gathering* itself becomes the means of reaching the objective of the spiritual life, which is to join the great cosmic movement towards the *eschaton*. This is an impressive statement indeed. What is not entirely clear, however, is the extent to which this spirituality accurately reflects what Saint Maximos had in mind when he wrote the *Mystagogy*, which Zizioulas references in his text. In any case, this is how Zizioulas envisions the synthesis of the monastic and eucharistic dimensions of the spiritual life. Gone are the references to sin and the devil with which the classic ascetic texts are replete. The new sin in this instance, and perhaps the new devil, is individualism.[88] The

---

[86] *Ibid.*, 42-43.

[87] Zizioulas, "Early," 43.

[88] In *Communion and Otherness*, Zizioulas describes sin as a form of idolatry, more specifically as "an *ekstasis* of communion with the created world alone." See John D. Zizioulas, *Communion and Otherness*, p. 228. For Zizioulas' understanding of the devil, whom the theologian sees as an "extra-human factor" tempting humanity to the possibility of non-existence, see *ibid.*, 245-246.

resultant spirituality is relational, dynamic, and cosmic. Spirituality is being presented in an entirely new key.

FIRST MAIN FACET OF METROPOLITAN JOHN ZIZIOULAS' SPIRITUALITY: HISTORICAL-ESCHATOLOGICAL DIMENSION

As we noted above, the historical dimension for Zizioulas is intimately connected to eschatology. Christianity distinguished itself from paganism in its early years by being focused on history and not cosmology.[89] Its orientation towards history is precisely what permitted it to have an eschatological outlook. This outlook, according to Zizioulas, was the most important factor in the shaping of its spirituality in early times.[90] Because of this, "Christian spirituality had to be experienced as a dialectic between history and eschatology...."[91] Since Saint Maximos was the one, in Zizioulas' understanding, who restored this dialectic to Christian spirituality in the seventh century, his synthesis is of great importance.

SECOND MAIN FACET OF METROPOLITAN JOHN ZIZIOULAS' SPIRITUALITY: CHRISTOLOGICAL-ECCLESIOLOGICAL DIMENSION

The second dimension of Zizioulas' spiritual theology represents a combination of *a)* a particular Christology with *b)* a highly relational ecclesiology. We shall take them in turn. Zizioulas' Christology has something in common with the *totus Christus* understanding embraced by Evdokimov. Zizioulas, however, bases his Christology on a hypothesis of corporate personality in Christ, which is not a feature of Evdokimov's thought.[92] Christ in this Christology is never an individual, but a corporate Person. The "One" is always also the "many."[93] Zizioulas embraces this particular Christology to the point that he is able to speak of the community as praying not only in and through Christ, but *as*

---

[89]   Zizioulas, "Early," 23.
[90]   *Ibid.*
[91]   *Ibid.*
[92]   *Ibid.,* 28.
[93]   *Ibid.*

Christ.[94] This is a rather daring statement, but Zizioulas insists that this is the *only* way to understand early Christian spirituality, in which spiritual life was practised exclusively in the community. Individualistic forms of spirituality were, in Zizioulas' view, non-biblical.[95] Not surprisingly, the ecclesiology that emerges from this type of Christology is very relational. Zizioulas, in fact, goes as far as defining the Church as a set of relationships.[96] Spirituality was therefore about acquiring new relationships, and with them, a new identity.[97] If we add to this that Christ is revealed as a corporate Person "in the Spirit,"[98] then the picture is complete: Zizioulas has integrated Christology with Pneumatology, ecclesiology with Christology, and spirituality is simply the expected product of that integration. The rest of what Zizioulas has to say on this theme is totally predictable and reflects the inner logic of his synthesis. He states the corollary in these terms:

> Christian spirituality, therefore, could not be experienced outside the community.... Individualism is incompatible with Christian spirituality. None can possess the Spirit as an individual, but only as a member of the community. When the spirit blows, the result is never to create good individual Christians, but members of a community.[99]

In Zizioulas' view, Christian spirituality is always corporate. If individualism in the spiritual life is to be understood as the stubborn refusal to relate to the community and the insistence on a kind of privatized spirituality, then Zizioulas' comments can be accepted without further qualification. *But what exactly constitutes individualism in the spiritual life?* Does all spiritual practice outside of liturgical prayer fall into that category?

A similar problem arises with the Metropolitan's contention that

---

94 *Ibid.*, 27.
95 *Ibid.*, 28.
96 *Ibid.*
97 *Ibid.*, 29.
98 *Ibid.*
99 Zizioulas, "Early," 27.

the Holy Spirit is received by members of the community. This seems to be a fair statement of an underlying assumption of baptismal theology, but what does it really mean? Does it mean, for example, that the Spirit is received in the sacraments but not in the context of personal prayer? *Do all members of the community continue to possess the Spirit simply by continuing to be members, or is something else required?* These questions point in the direction of asceticism, and it is precisely the ascetic dimension that has been displaced here.

If Saint Maximos effected a *synthesis* of the eucharistic and monastic-ascetic dimensions, *where is the latter dimension in Zizioulas' presentation?* It would seem that the synthesis espoused by Zizioulas in this instance entails the subordination of the ascetic to the eucharistic to the point where the ascetic dimension is eclipsed by the corporate-eucharistic dimension.

Metropolitan John, as mentioned earlier, not only sees the Church as the *locus* for Christian spirituality, he sees the Eucharist as its primary event. Specifically, he calls it "the spiritual event par excellence, because it was the eschatological reality manifested and foretasted in history."[100] The Eucharist is the great source of Christian spirituality, and this spirituality has an ontological and not simply moral or psychological character.[101] Spirituality does not pertain to the moral improvement of the person, neither is it based on subjective experiences; instead, it manifests itself on the level of being. Zizioulas summarizes his position in this way:

> Since the old biological identity is based on natural necessity, it leads to death; whereas the new identity given in the Eucharist – based on free and undying relationships, above all on the eternal filial relationship between the Father and the Son, which was "lent" to the Christian in Baptism – gives eternal life. The Eucharist is life eternal, primarily because it offers this set of relationships, which involves an eternal identity. Belonging to the community of the Eucharist is, therefore, tantamount

[100] Zizioulas, "Early," 29.
[101] *Ibid.*

to acquiring eternal life. Spirituality in this eucharistic context acquires an ontological and not simply a moral or a psychological context.[102]

Zizioulas' reasoning is internally consistent. In his understanding, it is the new and eternal identity acquired by the Christian in Baptism and actualized in the Eucharist that gives eternal life. Because identities emerge from relationships, and since Baptism and most especially the Eucharist provide new relationships, the Eucharist offers eternal life. Identity, of course, is an ontological and not a moral or psychological category. It follows, then, that spirituality is a matter of ontology. This, indeed, would seem to be the logical conclusion to Zizioulas' line of argumentation. It does leave important questions unanswered, however, for spirituality: *Is simple adherence to the eucharistic community enough, in and of itself, to receive eternal life?* Is the decision to adhere to the community and to struggle to continue in it all that is essentially needed in the spiritual life? In addition, while Zizioulas does not use the word "salvation" here, his discussion about spirituality and eternal life clearly has a soteriological character. Not surprisingly, he espouses a radically relational soteriology, which can be seen as both the product and the source of his highly relational ecclesiology. The idea of corporate salvation certainly has its roots in the Old Testament and is developed by Saint Paul in the New Testament. The Orthodox tradition has preserved this notion in its theology. *Did the early Church conceive of soteriology, however, in exclusively relational terms?* Does salvation in Orthodox dogmatic theology turn on the question of relationships and identities? If the answer to these questions is no, then some clarification should be made.

Metropolitan John is free, of course, to develop his own line of reasoning, but it would be helpful if he could find a way to indicate that he is referring to an important theme in the history of spirituality and theology, and not to the entire tradition. There is, for example, a strong current in early Christian theology that locates the defeat of sin, death, and the devil in the Death and Resurrection of Christ. There *is* a biblical and patristic theology of the atonement. These aspects of

[102] *Ibid.*

Christian theology and spirituality can hardly be ignored. It is also highly unlikely that Zizioulas could somehow compact them into his relational framework without doing violence to them.

THIRD MAIN FACET OF METROPOLITAN JOHN ZIZIOULAS' SPIRITUALITY: THE LIMITED ANTHROPOLOGICAL DIMENSION

In *Communion and Otherness*, Zizioulas addresses the topic of anthropology, and it becomes quickly evident that his anthropology has been conditioned by certain reservations. *First of all*, the Metropolitan strongly objects to an anthropology centred on individual consciousness. He posits that Saint Augustine is responsible for introducing this concept into Christian theology.[103] He also accuses modern Orthodox spirituality of being affected by it.[104] *Secondly*, he is uncomfortable with a "fundamentalistic" reading of the anthropology of the early Fathers.[105] This places Zizioulas in a very delicate position. On the one hand, he is arguing against a spiritual tradition in the Christian West that, according to him, has been more or less dominant since the fifth century. He is also arguing against an alleged influence of the latter on the Orthodox spiritual tradition. His argument is based on the assumption that the Greek Fathers do not support this Augustinian innovation in Christian anthropology.[106] On the other hand, he is sensitive to a literal reading of the same Greek Fathers. In other words, he would like to enlist the support of the Greek Fathers against Augustine, but he is aware that not everything in the anthropological thought of the Greek Fathers fits his particular model. *What is it in patristic anthropology and in theology in general that causes Zizioulas to be so apprehensive?*

Metropolitan John Zizioulas' Rejection of the "Self"

Zizioulas' concern about anthropology and its development in Christian

---

[103]   John D. Zizioulas, *Communion and Otherness*, Paul McPartlan (ed.) (London: T&T Clark, 2006), 46.
[104]   *Ibid.*
[105]   *Ibid.* 42, n. 83.
[106]   Zizioulas, *Communion and Otherness*, 52.

theology is tied very much to his critique of the emergence of *the self* in Western thought. It is specifically *the self as a centre of consciousness* that Zizioulas finds so objectionable. In Zizioulas' view, this model came about as the result of the substitution of psychology for ontology.[107] This places the person in a position of evaluating experience rather than living in true communion with the other. Modern Western philosophy up to and including existentialism, in Zizioulas' view, was unable to free itself from this tendency and ended up asserting *the self* over *the other*.[108] This is a fair critique of much of modern Western philosophy, and the word that would prove so useful to Zizioulas in this context comes, ironically, straight out of modern psychology: *narcissism* – the pathological preoccupation with self. Perhaps Zizioulas might not want to dispose of psychology so quickly. A nuanced discussion of "psychology" could strengthen, or at least clarify, his argument here.

Zizioulas finds the final departure from consciousness-centred individualism in two contemporary thinkers: Buber and Levinas. Their thought represents, for Zizioulas, a significant breakthrough in Western thinking. He praises them for shifting the discussion in philosophy away from the previous categories and towards a philosophy and anthropology of communion. While appreciating their creativity, Zizioulas is nevertheless aware of their deficiencies.[109] There is certainly enough here to suggest that Zizioulas draws inspiration from these thinkers without becoming their disciple.

Zizioulas returns then to the Fathers to bring his argument to a potent conclusion:

> The first thing that one must acknowledge with appreciation is the proclamation of the *death of the Self* [my emphasis] by leading thinkers of postmodernism. Certainly, a theology inspired by the Greek Fathers, such as this essay wishes to expound, would welcome the questioning of self-identity, unity of consciousness and subjectivity, in spite of the fact that

---

[107] *Ibid.*, 46.
[108] *Ibid.*, 44.
[109] *Ibid.*, 47-50.

a great deal of modern Orthodox theology and 'spirituality' still operates with similar categories, borrowed from western modernity. *The Self must die* – this is a biblical demand (Mt. 16.25; Lk. 14.26; Jn. 12.25; Gal. 2.20; etc.) – and any attempt to question the Self at a philosophical level should be applauded, together with the rejection of substantialist ontology that supports it.[110]

Zizioulas' point is well taken; the "self" must die, but which one? It seems inconceivable that the Gospel writers and Saint Paul could be speaking about the same "self" as the postmodernists. If indeed Saint Augustine is responsible for introducing a new understanding of the self into Western Christian theology and philosophy, then the self of the New Testament would be another self entirely, *a pre-Augustinian self*, as it were. One could argue that a *substantialist self* existed in the first century as a product of Greek philosophy, but it would seem unlikely that the Lord had that self in mind when He taught about losing oneself for the sake of the Gospel. The appeal to Holy Scripture is impressive, but it does not necessarily result in a consistent argument. What if the self to which the Lord is alluding is simply a person who refuses to submit himself or herself to God? *Must we invest the Gospel passages with all the weight and baggage of ontological discussions?*

Metropolitan John Zizioulas' Charge Against Modern Orthodox Spirituality

Zizioulas charges much of Orthodox theology and "spirituality" with operating on the basis of assumptions borrowed from Western modernity. This is a serious charge, and it can hardly be left without any elaboration. It is serious, not because everything Western is dangerous to Orthodox theology and spirituality, but because it suggests that much of Orthodox theology is not true to its own tradition. Furthermore, the suggestion is that the spirituality associated with it is not true spirituality at all, which is why Zizioulas describes it as "spirituality," placing the word intentionally, it seems, in quotation marks. We are left to infer

---

[110]   *Ibid.*, 51-52.

that this is at best a by-product of Augustinian thought or, worse yet, a cheap imitation of modern Western philosophy and psychology. If this is the case, it would seem to be a generalization. I understand that the Metropolitan wants to be diplomatic in this instance and is therefore avoiding the prospect of naming anyone in particular. Perhaps he could at least identify in greater detail the kind of thought he has in mind? In addition, since postmodernism is also a Western philosophical phenomenon, is it not somewhat disingenuous to champion this particular philosophy just because it represents the disintegration of the previous categories of Western philosophical discourse about the self? What if postmodernism leads eventually to a position that is even further away from patristic thinking than that of Western modernity?

Returning to the Gospel passages regarding the denial of the self, do we not find a dimension that Zizioulas is missing? Is much of the discussion there not about a choice or, better yet, an *invitation* to follow Him on the part of Christ to all who would hear? When the exegesis of the passages turns exclusively on the question of the content and meaning of the self, is the whole dynamic of discipleship not lost? One of the weaknesses of Zizioulas' thought is the lack of attention to the human will on a personal level.[111] Christ's invitation is addressed first and foremost to persons who, upon accepting it, become part of a body. They are not incorporated against their will or even without their active participation. The choice to accept Christ's invitation is deliberate or, as we would say in modern language, conscious. Surely in this case, however, a conscious choice is not the product of a substantialist ontology.

Metropolitan John Zizioulas and Patristic Anthropology

Zizioulas' aversion to the development of the self in Western Christian theology, Western philosophy and, as he opines, in much of contemporary Orthodox theology and "spirituality" – as well as his resistance to a "fundamentalistic" reading of the anthropology of the early Fathers – leads

---

[111] Zizioulas has a developed presentation of freedom in the relationship between the uncreated and the created – in other words, on the corporate and cosmic level. See *Lectures*, 93.

us to an important question: What is it in anthropology that Zizioulas is trying so studiously to avoid? We have already seen some of Zizioulas' objections to the self as a centre of consciousness. Now we need to turn our attention to the Metropolitan's treatment of the theme of the image of God in patristic thought. This, of course, is an entire study on its own and merits a discussion that exceeds the limits of this study. Nevertheless, one can at least get a general idea of how Zizioulas relates to this important theme in patristic literature. It is, of course, a topic of great importance to Christian anthropology in general and to Orthodox spiritual theology in particular.

For Zizioulas, the Fathers either speak about freedom as the primary characteristic of the image or they use the terms 'rationality' and 'self-government' in the same context. Since, in Zizioulas' opinion, the latter two characteristics refer to freedom in any case, there is no real divergence in their understandings. Zizioulas relies especially on Saint Gregory of Nyssa, whose interest in the image of God in humanity is well known.[112]

While Zizioulas is reading the Fathers in a way that supports and enhances his own thought, we can still go along with him; he is certainly not doing violence to Saint Gregory of Nyssa here. There is, however, something missing. There is a whole body of patristic literature in which there is a very extensive discussion of anthropology, the writings of the ascetic or neptic Fathers, which Zizioulas does not even mention. The *Philokalia* is replete with references to anthropology. Then there is *The Ladder* of Saint John Climacus. There is much in this literature to suggest that there are many Fathers who understand the image of God in different, albeit complementary, ways from those who stress freedom or rationality. Could it be the emphasis that these Fathers place on the role of the *nous*, or spiritual intellect, that troubles Zizioulas?

An Aversion to the Nous?

Zizioulas sees the emphasis on the *nous* as a hallmark of Evagrian or Origenistic thought.[113] Origenism, he is quick to point out, was condemned by the Church at the Fifth Ecumenical Council.[114] The Metropolitan is

---

[112] Zizioulas, *Lectures*, 95.
[113] Zizioulas, *Early*, 42.
[114] *Ibid.*

correct, of course, on both counts. He goes on to say that Saint Macarios of Egypt is to be credited with providing a corrective to Origenistic spiritual theology by locating the centre of spiritual activity in the heart instead of the *nous*.[115] Zizioulas concludes: "This was a most important development that saved Christian spirituality in the patristic period from the dangers of Origenism and somehow brought it back to its biblical and early patristic roots."[116] Metropolitan Kallistos Ware suggests much the same thing.[117] He also speaks of the two currents in Orthodox spirituality, Evagrian and Macarian, but he reaches a different conclusion:

> Yet in reality the two 'currents' are less far apart than appears at first. When Evagrius, for example, spoke of the *nous*, he meant not only the reasoning brain but also, and more fundamentally, the apprehension of spiritual truth through direct, non-discursive insight; and Macarius understood by the heart not merely the emotions and affections but the deep centre of the human person. From the fifth century onwards there was a growing convergence of the two 'currents.' This tendency is to be seen already in St Diadochus of Photice, and is continued by St John Climacus and above all by St Maximus the Confessor.[118]

Several important points emerge from Metropolitan Kallistos's text that are germane to our discussion here. *Firstly,* we may agree or disagree with Ware's opinion that the difference between the Evagrian current and the Macarian current is not that dramatic. I can certainly understand Zizioulas' reservations here.[119] *Secondly,* a synthesis between the two currents begins to appear already in the fifth century. Zizioulas may be right that the Macarian

[115] *Ibid.*
[116] *Ibid.*
[117] Kallistos Ware, "Greek Writers from the Cappodocians to John of Damascus: Introduction," *The Study of Spirituality*, Cheslyn Jones *et al.* (eds.) (New York: Oxford University Press, 1986), 160.
[118] *Ibid.*
[119] Loudovikos notes Meyendorff's observation that Evagrius was able to write an entire treatise on prayer with scarcely a reference to Christ. See *Analogical*, p. 96 and John Meyendorff, *Christ in Eastern Christian Thought*, trans. Fr. Yves Dubois. (Crestwood, NY: Saint Vladimir's Seminary Press, 1975), p. 59.

current corrected the Evagrian by displacing it rather than combining with it. *Thirdly*, the synthesis of the two currents continues in ascetic literature up to Saint Maximos the Confessor, who seems to complete the process. The result is that the term *nous* is still used, but the *nous* is placed now in the context of the heart and is no longer the centre of all spiritual activity. The term *nous* can finally be used freely without all of its historically associated implications. Equally important is the assumption that the heretical aspects of Origenistic and Evagrian teaching have now been expunged from the ascetic tradition. If Metropolitan John's point is that they have not been, and that certain representatives of the ascetic tradition are still operating within an Origenistic-Evagrian framework in spirituality, then it would be helpful if he were to explain the situation in detail and provide the necessary correctives from the tradition.

Metropolitan John Zizioulas' Reservations Regarding Ascetic Anthropology

I believe that Zizioulas has reservations with regard to an anthropology rooted in the ascetic tradition because such an anthropology would not be easily integrated into the particular model he espouses. Zizioulas advances an ontology of communion. The emphasis is, as we have seen, on the acquisition of a new identity and, with it, a new relationship. It is therefore the relationship itself and the mode of relationship that are important. Ascetic spirituality turns the attention to the inner life, to what Zizioulas likely sees as dangerously close to the "self." Furthermore, its emphasis on vigilance, the control of thoughts, dispassion, and so forth likely strikes him as reflective of the self functioning as a centre of consciousness.

Here again, I believe that it would be important for the venerable theologian to clarify his identification of much of modern Orthodox spirituality and theology with what he calls "Augustinian" or even modern Western thought. More specifically, we need to know what exactly he means by "Augustinian."[120] There is a real risk of dismissing out

---

[120] The clearest answer to this question in contemporary Orthodox theology is to be found in a magisterial treatment of patristic and modern spirituality by Loudovikos in his aforementioned book (see p. 8 n. 5) *Anagogical Identities*. The significance of this book for the theology of spirituality cannot be overstated.

of hand much of the ascetic tradition by simply calling it "psychological" or "modern" or "Western." On the other hand, the Metropolitan may well have identified a problem in Orthodox spirituality and, if so, we need to hear his voice.

Yet another reservation of Zizioulas to ascetic anthropology seems to be expressed in his identification of the *imago dei* virtually exclusively with freedom. The crux of the matter is that if the image of God in Orthodox anthropology can be confined to the exercise of freedom exclusively, then it can work appropriately in Zizioulas' model. This is because it pertains to the "how" or mode of relations, to an ontology of communion. If, however, the image of God pertains to the "what" in Orthodox anthropology, that is to say to an aspect of human *nature* that is stable and innate, then such an anthropology would not support Zizioulas' model fully. As an example of this, we may refer to the *nous*, which, in classical patristic and Orthodox ascetic literature, is the soul's faculty of spiritual awareness. As a faculty, it is innate and stable rather than acquired. It is, however, darkened, and must be enlightened through participation in the sacraments and through asceticism. What is acquired, then, is an illumined *nous*. Since the *nous* is connected to perception and awareness, it is also related to consciousness. In this case, the proximity of an anthropology that incorporates the *nous* in the heart to an ontology that refers to nature is perhaps what Zizioulas would find objectionable here. This would give rise to the possibility of the person as a perceiving, conscious being rather than, as Zizioulas would no doubt rather see, a person "freed" of the self and able, therefore, to be in relation or communion with the other. To Zizioulas' mind, this would represent a serious regression to individualism.

Yet another moment in Zizioulas' vision of spirituality that reveals a certain reticence in the face of ascetic anthropology is his insistence on identifying the entire dynamic of the spiritual life with the change from a simple biological *hypostasis* to an ecclesial one.[121] For the Metropolitan, the move toward a new identity with the related set of new relationships

In Part 1, Chapter 1 (p.13-62) and Part 3 (p. 207-270), Loudovikos lays out his engaging and detailed analysis of Augustinian "spiritualism."
[121] John D. Zizioulas, *Being as Communion* (Crestwood, NY: SVS Press, 1993), 49-65.

is crucial.[122] *Theosis*, in the Metropolitan's understanding, is precisely the acquisition by human beings of a new identity as sons and daughters of God, together with the relationships that emerge from this identity.[123] In Scripture, this is called adoption. Who could possibly object to such a position? For Zizioulas, however, the biological *hypostasis* is associated with nature, and the ecclesial *hypostasis* with personhood and communion. The transition from the former to the latter seems to be less of a transformation than a translation. The biological *hypostasis*, rather than being refined and purified, is left behind. There is still a reference to asceticism, but this has little to do with combatting the passions.[124] The focus in Zizioulas' spirituality is not on purification, as we see in classic Orthodox spirituality, but on the acquisition of a new identity. While this clearly resonates with certain Pauline themes in the New Testament, such as the new creation in Christ and the acquisition of the mind of Christ, it still leaves one with the impression that Orthodox spirituality has somehow been redefined. The inner life and its accompanying spiritual struggle are absent. The emphasis is not on the transformation of the inner man, but on the transition to a new relational state.

Significantly, in Zizioulas' thought, it is the new relationships that transform the person; it is not the person who transforms the relationships. There is a real paradigm shift here; it is clearly more than a change of emphasis. It is also not difficult to see why the *nous* has no particular role in this vision of the spiritual life. In classic ascetic theology, the discussion would turn around the purification of the heart, the illumination of the *nous,* and the vision of God. In reality, Zizioulas does not need to take any particular position against the *nous*; his approach to the spiritual life simply renders it irrelevant. While the Metropolitan champions the return of the heart as the central organ or *locus* of the spiritual life in the Macarian writings, he does not in fact elaborate on its role at length. Doing so would shift the emphasis away from the relational-ontological dimension back to the inner life of ascetic spirituality.

---

[122]   *Ibid.*, 58. Zizioulas refers here to "a network of relationships which transcends every exclusiveness."
[123]   Zizioulas, *Communion and Otherness*, n. 51, 30-31.
[124]   Zizioulas, *Being as Communion*, n. 66, 62.

CHAPTER THREE

RESPONSES TO
METROPOLITAN JOHN
ZIZIOULAS

Much has been written in response to Zizioulas in the last fifteen years, but the vast majority of it has been in the area of Trinitarian theology, ecclesiology, and patristics. While it can be argued quite legitimately that all three of these areas are sources of Orthodox spirituality, there is still a noticeable dearth of material that pertains directly to the area of spiritual theology. More specifically, relatively little has been written about the Maximian synthesis propounded by Zizioulas. There are, however, several theologians who have responded to the Metropolitan with regard to his understanding of spirituality and issues arising from it. I have selected six. The first, Professor Petros Vassiliadis, enthusiastically endorses Zizioulas' position.

PETROS VASSILIADIS

Petros Vassiliadis, professor emeritus of New Testament at the Aristotle University of Thessaloniki, refers to Zizioulas' article "The Early Christian Community" in an article of his own, in which he champions eucharistic spirituality.[125] Vassiliadis seems somewhat less taken with Saint Maximos than is Zizioulas,[126] and this might explain the former's apparent lack of interest in the Maximian synthesis itself. Vassiliadis

[125]   Petros Vassiliadis, "Eucharistic and Therapeutic Spirituality," *The Greek Orthodox Theological Review*, 42: 1-2 (1997).
[126]   *Ibid.*, 14 and n. 48.

neither tests it nor applies it; he simply takes the conclusion of Zizioulas'
article "The Early Christian Community" as the starting point of his own
article "Eucharistic and Therapeutic Spirituality" by positing that there
are two main expressions of Christian spirituality. Initially, he identifies
them as monastic and liturgical; later, he refers to them as therapeutic/
cathartic and eucharistic/liturgical.[127]

Vassiliadis follows closely the contours of Zizioulas' presentation
of early church history. The premise throughout his whole presentation
is that the original spirituality of the church has been displaced. It is a
premise that could be better defended, and one senses in it the risk of an
oversimplification of the history of Christian spirituality. It is predicated
on the assumption that the therapeutic expression is absent in primitive
Christian spirituality and only makes its first appearance with the rise
of "Alexandrian" theology. The author does make a strong case for the
existence of an early Christian spirituality that had a "dynamic, radical
and corporate character" and had strong roots in the eschatologically
oriented messianic currents of first-century Judaism.[128] According to
Vassiliadis, the messianic eschatological community *par excellence* was
the eucharistic assembly.[129] Not surprisingly for an ardent supporter of
eucharistic ecclesiology, Vassiliadis understands the community to be
the *locus* for Christian spiritual life. He states: "The faithful are called to
be holy, not as individuals, but as a corporate ecclesial reality."[130]

Vassiliadis notes that a shift in emphasis began to occur in the early
Church. The *first* shift is from eucharistic experience to the Christian
message. The *second* is from eschatology to Christology, and then from
Christology to soteriology. The *third* is from the Kingdom as event to
Christ as the centre of the event.[131] In spite of these shifts in emphasis, the
Church, according to Vassiliadis, was still able to retain the Eucharist as
the sole expression of its identity.[132] In Vassiliadis's view, it is Alexandrian
theology that displaced the original spiritual identity of the Church. The

---

[127]   *Ibid.*, 1.
[128]   *Ibid.*, 3.
[129]   *Ibid.*
[130]   *Ibid.*, 4.
[131]   *Ibid.*, 5.
[132]   *Ibid.*

Church ceased to be the icon of the *eschaton* and became rather the icon of the origin of beings. In short, the historical understanding, with its eschatological orientation, was replaced by an almost exclusively cosmological approach. The collective character and self-identity of the Church decreased and gave way to an emphasis on individual salvation.[133] While noting the positive contributions of monasticism and recognizing the original eschatological impetus behind it, Vassiliadis still charges it with driving the movement that brought about the demise of early Christian spirituality.[134] Vassiliadis puts it this way:

The fact remains that the central core of Alexandrian theology, with which monasticism was historically connected, was a departure from the original radical and dynamic horizontal eschatology of the New Testament and of the early post-apostolic Christian tradition, in some cases even in direct opposition to it.

The consequences for Christian spirituality and ecclesiology were immense. The Church's common worship, her offices and institutions lost virtually all meaning as icons of the *Eschaton*. What became the priority was the union of man with the pre-eternal Logos, the return of the soul to its bliss in Paradise before the Fall.[135]

Vassiliadis calls this historical process a defection from early Christian spirituality and suggests that the resulting *ordo*, which is known as the monastic *typikon*, represents not only a reform in the structure of the worship, but a complete change in its underlying concepts.[136] The Eucharist, according to the author, became the tool to achieve continuous prayer.[137] With this, we see the emergence of a new spirituality, in which the emphasis is placed on "*catharsis* (purification) of the soul from passions, and toward *therapy [sic]*, healing of the fallen nature of the

---

[133]   *Ibid.*, 7.
[134]   *Ibid.*, 8.
[135]   *Ibid.*, 3.
[136]   *Ibid.*
[137]   *Ibid.*, 10.

human beings (men/women) [sic]."[138] One can either accept or reject Vassiliadis's thesis on historical grounds, and work by contemporary liturgiologists would seem to call some of his historical assumptions into question, but the point that the theologian wishes to make about two expressions of Christian spirituality functioning in relationship with each other is consistent, as we have seen, with the observations of several Orthodox theologians. Vassiliadis describes the two expressions – therapeutic and eucharistic – as existing in parallel, sometimes in conflict, other times forming a creative unity.[139] He is led to pose the questions:

> Where should one search to find personal wholeness and salvation? In the eucharistic gathering around the bishop, where one could overcome creatively all schizophrenic dichotomies (spirit/matter, transcendence/immanence, coming together/going forth etc.) and social polarities? Or in the desert, the hermitage, the monastery, where naturally the effort for catharsis and for the healing of passions through ascetic discipline of the individual is more effective?[140]

Here Vassiliadis is echoing similar questions posed by Zizioulas in his own article.[141] These are interesting questions, questions that one would have to pose if one were to accept all of Vassiliadis's assumptions regarding the displacement of an original spiritual and liturgical tradition, but they perhaps suggest a false dichotomy. Why would a Christian be obliged to choose *between* two seemingly separate things, if they happened to be complementary aspects of one reality? Vassiliadis does not entertain this possibility in his article, but I should note that the article is more an exploration of a hypothesis than a definitive historical study. Zizioulas is able to come to terms with this possibility by positing that a synthesis was made by Saint Maximos, thereby suggesting that we have inherited an integrated spirituality that represents a synthesis of

138   *Ibid.*
139   *Ibid.*
140   *Ibid.*, 10-11.
141   Zizioulas, "Early," 42.

the monastic and eucharistic tendencies. Zizioulas and Vassiliadis make some intriguing hypotheses, but given the emphasis these theologians place on the historical dimension and its inherent connection with biblical eschatology, it would be of benefit to both of them to develop a more detailed analysis of the history of Christian spirituality and liturgy.

As we have seen, Vassiliadis shares all of the assumptions of Zizioulas regarding the history of early Christian spirituality and theology. In essence, Vassiliadis's article represents a restatement of certain sections of "The Early Christian Community." What is of special interest in Vassiliadis's article, however, are his concluding remarks. These are stated unambiguously, and they give us some insight into what Metropolitan John might be inclined to say were he to take his thesis further. Vassiliadis's first remark reveals his intention: his aim is to reestablish the pre-eminence of eucharistic spirituality.[142] One can only admire the author for his honesty here. While he is open to a "fertile synthesis" between eucharistic and therapeutic spiritualities, he declares himself an unabashed supporter of the former. His position allows for a synthesis, with the understanding that eucharistic spirituality must play the dominant role. *Secondly*, the professor of New Testament takes issue with the fact that "therapeutic spirituality is widely considered to be a distinguishing feature of the authentic Eastern Orthodox tradition."[143] Here he does what Zizioulas does not do: he names the theologians who represent the tendency he is describing. The three partisans of therapeutic spirituality identified by Vassiliadis are Father John Romanides, Professor Georgios Mantzaridis, and Metropolitan Hierotheos Vlachos. The author describes Metropolitan Hierotheos as an "extreme" representative of the therapeutic school.[144]

Father John Romanides is widely recognized as a pioneer in the renewal of a patristic orientation in Orthodox theology. His groundbreaking doctoral thesis, *The Ancestral Sin*, changed forever the way theologians in Greece did theology, challenging (if not actually permanently disabling) the prevailing scholastic tendency in Greek

---

[142] Vassiliadis, "Eucharistic," 21.
[143] *Ibid.*
[144] *Ibid.* n. 87.

Orthodox academic theology. Metropolitan Hierotheos Vlachos is widely seen as a student and successor of Father Romanides, a role he appears to accept willingly and with great satisfaction. Georgios Mantzaridis was himself a pioneer in the renewal of patristic theology in Greece, having contributed a significant monograph on Saint Gregory Palamas to the increasingly rich area of Palamite studies.[145] Indeed, Vassiliadis is very much aware that there is a strong connection between the three theologians he has named and the recent rediscovery of Saint Gregory Palamas by Orthodox theologians. Vassiliadis insists that he sees this rediscovery as a welcome development in contemporary Orthodox theology, but he feels that certain theologians have interpreted Palamas incorrectly, or have been selective in their analysis, with the goal of presenting an anti-Western polemic.[146] This may be an allusion to Vladimir Lossky, Father John Romanides, and Metropolitan Hierotheos. For that matter, he could be thinking of Father Dumitru Staniloae and Georgios Mantzaridis. Vassiliadis is not specific. In any case, it does show that the revival of Palamite studies represents a challenge to those who, like Petros Vassiliadis, wish to present Orthodox spirituality as pre-eminently eucharistic in character.

Stavros Yangazoglou

I could not present the articles pertinent to our topic without mentioning an important paper by Stavros Yangazoglou delivered at the colloquium of the International Academy of Religious Sciences held in Thessaloniki in 2008.[147] The theme of the colloquium was *Eucharistic Ecclesiology,* and Yangazoglou used the opportunity to make an appeal for the elimination of all competition between eucharistic theology and monastic spirituality in Orthodox theological discourse and church

---

[145]   For an excellent overview of contemporary theological studies in Greece, see Athanasios N. Papathanasiou, "Some key themes and figures in Greek theological thought," *The Cambridge Companion to Orthodox Christian Theology,* Mary B. Cunningham and Elizabeth Theoktitoff (eds.) (Cambridge: Cambridge University Press, 2008), 218-231.

[146]   Vassiliadis, "Eucharistic," n. 87.

[147]   Stavros Yangazoglou, "Ecclésiologie eucharistique et spiritualité monastique," *L'ecclésiologie eucharistique,* Jean-Marie Van Cangh (ed.). (Bruxelles: Éditions du Cerf, 2009), 79-95.

life. In his paper, the author outlines the basic premises of eucharistic ecclesiology, highlighting what he perceives as the substantial benefits for Orthodox theology in recent years.[148] He goes on to critique three Orthodox theologians: Vladimir Lossky, Father Theoklitos Dionysiatis and Father John Romanides. Lossky, in Yangazoglou's view, sets the basis for an artificial split between the Eucharist and asceticism by separating the economy of the Son from the economy of the Holy Spirit, and attributing the Eucharist to the former and asceticism to the latter.[149] Dionysiatis divides Orthodox theology and spirituality into cataphatic and apophatic dimensions, associating, analogously to Lossky, the former with the faith and the sacraments, and the latter with the mystical life experienced mostly by monastics.[150] Romanides limits the Church to a kind of spiritual elite, insisting on illumination and the vision of God as a *sine qua non* for any true member of the Church.[151] Yangazoglou rejects what he understands as the elitism of the former two theologians and faults Lossky with creating the dichotomy in Orthodox theology in the first place, a dichotomy which had been emerging principally in the theological discourse of the Russian diaspora.[152] The author's position is simple: the Eucharist and spirituality must be fully integrated, with the latter finding its source in the former.[153] He closes his paper by positing that patristic theology knows no division between the Eucharist and asceticism,[154] a conclusion which I can only applaud. While one may agree or disagree with Yangazoglou's analysis of twentieth-century Orthodox theology, one can hardly find issue with his conclusion. What is most important in Yangazoglou's paper is the premise articulated by him that all separation of asceticism and spirituality from the Eucharist is alien to patristic theology and the mind of the Church. Rather than simply relegating asceticism to the periphery of his theological project, however, the theologian prescribes the correct order and relationship

---

[148] *Ibid.*, 79-84.
[149] *Ibid.*, 86-87.
[150] *Ibid.*, 87-88.
[151] *Ibid.*, 89-91.
[152] *Ibid.*, 86.
[153] *Ibid.*, 88.
[154] *Ibid.*, 92-95.

for the Eucharist and asceticism, esteeming the recent gains made by Orthodox theologians through the study of eucharistic ecclesiology without disparaging the ascetic tradition. We turn now to a third theologian, Father Calinic Berger, who views Zizioulas' theology through the lens of Father Dumitru Staniloae's work and, on the basis of it, offers some correctives.

FATHER CALINIC BERGER

If Petros Vassiliadis's article represents an unreserved endorsement of eucharistic spirituality, and Stavros Yangazoglou's paper an appeal to always hold the Eucharist and asceticism together, the next article for our consideration sounds a note of caution. This article, by Father Calinic Berger, brings all of the wisdom of Father Dumitru Staniloae's ecclesiological work to bear on Metropolitan John Zizioulas' ecclesiology and understanding of the spiritual life.[155] Its title, "Does the Eucharist Make the Church?: An Ecclesiological Comparison of Staniloae and Zizioulas," reveals its ambitious goal: to offer an alternative to eucharistic ecclesiology, based on the theological thought of Father Dumitru Staniloae. The author does not disappoint: he presents a very substantial analysis of the ecclesiology of Staniloae, complete with a summary of the latter's Pneumatology. He describes the relationship of Staniloae's and Zizioulas' thought to the Trinitarian theology of Vladimir Lossky. He then skillfully applies the ecclesiological insights of Staniloae to the thought of Zizioulas, highlighting the differences and presenting a very convincing argument that contemporary Orthodox ecclesiology needs to take Staniloae's position into account. He selects and develops two specific instances where the ecclesiology of Staniloae can counterbalance or perhaps even correct the ecclesiology of Zizioulas. Significantly, Father Calinic draws out the implications of Staniloae's ecclesiology for spirituality and demonstrates the extent to which the spiritual theology of both theologians is conditioned by their ecclesiology.

Father Dumitru, as we have seen, locates the synthesis between the liturgy of the Eucharist and the liturgy of the heart in the *Philokalia*.

[155]   Calinic (Kevin M.) Berger, "Does the Eucharist Make the Church?: An Ecclesiological Comparison of Staniloae and Zizioulas," *St. Vladimir's Theological Quarterly*, 51:1 (2007).

He stresses the pre-eminence of neither the eucharistic nor the ascetic dimension of Orthodox spirituality; instead, he speaks of a completely integrated spirituality in which the two dimensions support and complement each other. He is able to hold such a position primarily because his ecclesiology is broader than Zizioulas'.[156] Specifically, while accepting the importance of the Eucharist in the life of the Church, Staniloae is able to see the Church existing beyond the context of the eucharistic celebration. This, observes Berger, is only natural for Staniloae, given that he "sees the continual abiding of the Holy Spirit in the Church (as the Body of Christ) and in all its members permeating *all* of its activities at *all* times (not just in its sacramental life) ...".[157] Berger contends that Staniloae's broader ecclesiology comes from a particular Pneumatology, and that Pneumatology has its origins in what he terms "a robust synthesis of Christology and Pneumatology within a highly developed Triadology ...."[158]

Firstly, what distinguishes Staniloae from Zizioulas, according to Berger, is that the former develops a complete synthesis between Christology and Pneumatology, while the latter's synthesis remains incomplete and somewhat tentative.[159] *Secondly*, Staniloae articulates his synthesis in relation to the immanent Trinity, while Zizioulas refers to the Son and the Spirit in the economy.[160] *Thirdly*, and very significantly, Zizioulas uses eucharistic ecclesiology as a starting point, while Staniloae works independently of it, or even in contradistinction to it.[161] The implications for their respective understandings of the Church and of the spiritual life are immediately visible: for Zizioulas, it is difficult, if not impossible, to conceive of a developed spiritual life outside of the Eucharist, whereas for Staniloae, it is entirely natural to do so. Put another way, Zizioulas' ecclesiology does not include spirituality as a constitutive element, whereas Staniloae's does.[162] This means that

---

[156] Berger, "Does the Eucharist Make the Church?," 36.
[157] *Ibid.*
[158] *Ibid.*, 26.
[159] *Ibid.*, 28.
[160] *Ibid.*
[161] *Ibid.*, 30.
[162] *Ibid.*, 38, 46.

Zizioulas can only ever acknowledge the ascetic dimension in a very limited sense. Since it is not a constitutive element of his ecclesiology, it follows that it can be of only passing importance to the spiritual life. Father Calinic makes the following point:

> Spirituality and holiness should not be ignored as integral components to ecclesiology. To do so is based on an assumption that personal prayer, good works and ascetic labors (monasticism in particular), lead to individualism. In fact, the opposite is true in Orthodoxy .... From this perspective, holiness and ascetic struggle *enable* interpersonal communion, and influence the Eucharistic celebration of the community of the Church, and vice versa.[163]

Berger's conclusion is that spirituality and holiness "are essential for a balanced ecclesiology."[164] Taking monasticism as an important example of spirituality and holiness, he posits that its basic principles of humility, loving obedience, and trust are essential for ecclesiology.[165] Father Calinic's article represents a significant contribution to the discourse on contemporary Orthodox ecclesiology. Not only does he do us a service by articulating Father Staniloae's understanding of Pneumatology and ecclesiology with great precision, but he also points to the need for a reappraisal of Orthodox eucharistic ecclesiology based on the full breadth of the tradition.

ARISTOTLE PAPANIKOLAOU

It is perhaps Berger's statement about the importance of monastic principles to ecclesiology that leads Aristotle Papanikolaou to conclude in his article "Integrating the ascetical and the eucharistic: current challenges in Orthodox ecclesiology" that Father Calinic is making "an attempt to reassert the primacy of the ascetical and the monastic over the recent Orthodox emphasis on the eucharistic assembly; a kind of monastic

---

[163]   *Ibid.*, 53.
[164]   *Ibid.*, 54.
[165]   *Ibid.*, 54-55.

backlash."[166] However, the operative word for Berger is "balanced," and for him, a balanced ecclesiology is clearly one in which the ascetic dimension is a constitutive element of ecclesiology, not the dominant element that subordinates the eucharistic dimension.[167] While one might suggest that Papanikolaou is overstating things somewhat when he terms Berger's article "a monastic backlash," it is clear that this does not detract from his observations regarding the future of Orthodox ecclesiology. Papanikolaou builds on Berger's article, which he acknowledges as "one of the more important in recent literature on Orthodox ecclesiology."[168] He traces the emergence of eucharistic ecclesiology from Father Georges Florovsky to Metropolitan John Zizioulas. He makes the point that two important Orthodox theologians of the twentieth century, Vladimir Lossky and Father Dumitru Staniloae, took a different approach to ecclesiology than that of their colleagues, although he is careful not to oversimplify the situation. He draws the conclusion that there are two main trajectories of contemporary Orthodox ecclesiology and, restating the primary observations of Berger, calls for an integration of the ascetic and sacramental dimensions through a Trinitarian theology that demonstrates a synthesis of Christology and Pneumatology.[169] The final two theologians chosen for this study are critical of Zizioulas.

JEAN-CLAUDE LARCHET

By far the most substantial critique of Metropolitan John Zizioulas' spiritual thought, both in terms of length and of detail, was crafted by Jean-Claude Larchet, an Orthodox lay theologian of international renown, who included a major section in his book *Personne et nature* critiquing both Zizioulas and Christos Yannaras.[170] Larchet begins his critique of Zizioulas (and Yannaras) by first challenging him in

---

[166]   Aristotle Papanikolaou, "Integrating the ascetical and the eucharistic: Current challenges in Orthodox ecclesiology," *International Journal for the Study of the Christian Church*, 11: 2-3 (2011), 182.

[167]   Berger, "Does the Eucharist Make the Church?," 54.

[168]   Papanikolaou, "Integrating," 182.

[169]   *Ibid.*, 173.

[170]   Jean-Claude Larchet, *Personne et nature* (Paris: Les Editions du Cerf, 2011), 207-396.

the area of dogmatic theology, calling into question a number of key points in the Metropolitan's theology of Trinitarian relations and of nature and person. He ends his critique with a major critical assessment of Zizioulas' understanding of spirituality and explicates the implications for Orthodox spirituality of Zizioulas' thought.

Larchet enumerates ten consequences for the spiritual life.[171] He begins his list with a charge that Zizioulas has a reductionist conception of the Church and the sacraments.[172] He states that the Metropolitan has stressed the horizontal dimension of ecclesiology to the detriment of the vertical.[173] He finds Zizioulas dismissive of the personal experience that each faithful Christian has in the Church.[174] Larchet distinguishes between the communal and the relational, positing that Zizioulas has reduced the former to the latter.[175] He feels also that Zizioulas devalues the sacraments apart from the Eucharist, at least implicitly, if not explicitly.[176] He believes that Zizioulas has changed the traditional notion of the eucharistic experience by disparaging the personal preparation for and grace experienced in the Eucharist.[177]

Larchet moves next to critique Metropolitan John's conception of deification. He highlights the therapeutic approach of the Fathers toward human nature, stressing their positive assessment of restored human nature in Christ. He insists that Zizioulas' failure to embrace the communion of divine nature with human nature by way of the uncreated energies (the teaching championed by Saint Gregory Palamas) results in an essentially negative appraisal of human nature on Zizioulas' part.[178] He states that the Metropolitan's conception of deification as adoption is too narrow.[179] Larchet returns to some of the points articulated in his magisterial study on Saint Maximos the Confessor to show that the Confessor actually distinguished between deification and adoption,

171   *Ibid.*, 364-396.
172   *Ibid.*, 364-372.
173   *Ibid.*, 365.
174   *Ibid.*
175   *Ibid.*
176   *Ibid.*, 366.
177   *Ibid.*, 370.
178   *Ibid.*, 373-374.
179   *Ibid.*, 374.

seeing the latter as the precursor to the former.[180] He observes that Zizioulas' position on the question is remarkably similar to that of the Roman Catholic theologian Marie-Joseph Le Guillou and his students.[181]

Larchet opines that Zizioulas minimizes the grace of God by identifying it exclusively with the person.[182] He further characterizes Zizioulas' conception of asceticism reductionist and finds that he ignores its dynamic potential for moving human nature towards God, a nature that has already been gifted by God with an innate thirst for the divine.[183] Larchet states that Zizioulas has effectively removed the human pole from ascetic synergy and that he disparages the inner warfare of asceticism as a form of pietism.[184] The theologian accuses the Metropolitan of undervaluing both the reality of sin[185] and the importance of virtue.[186] He analyses and evaluates Zizioulas' overall approach to spirituality in the following words:

> The opposition established by Zizioulas between the eucharistic perspective and the ascetic perspective is totally artificial, since the Christian life is indivisibly eucharistic and ascetic; in the same way, it is inseparably communitarian and personal/individual. In both perspectives, it is the union with Christ (and in Him with other men) that is the goal, and both perspectives contribute to making this union a reality.[187]

FATHER NIKOLAOS LOUDOVIKOS

Recently, a theologian from Greece has challenged a number of points in Metropolitan John's writings, including the latter's anthropology. The theologian in question, Professor of Theology and Philosophy at the University Ecclesiastical Academy of Thessaloniki, Father Nicholas

[180] *Ibid.*, 382.
[181] *Ibid.*, 375-376.
[182] *Ibid.*, 383.
[183] *Ibid.*, 385.
[184] *Ibid.*, 386.
[185] *Ibid.*, 391-393.
[186] *Ibid.*, 393-394.
[187] *Ibid.*, 391.

Loudovikos, is intimately acquainted with Zizioulas' theological work. In his article titled "Person Instead of Grace and Dictated Otherness: John Zizioulas' Final Theological Position," Loudovikos provides a substantial analysis of nature and personhood in *Communion and Otherness* and critiques Zizioulas' position using patristic sources. He suggests that Zizioulas' model of personhood is drawn from Western idealism.[188] He charges Zizioulas with disparaging the dimensions of the gnomic will and consciousness in his anthropology. Commenting on Zizioulas' understanding of the person, he states: "The Zizioulian subject is thus pre-modern; it possesses no interiority (a place where *gnomic will* and *prohairesis* lie), no instincts, and of course no unconscious." [189] He further posits that implicit in Zizioulas' theology of personhood is a "dictated otherness."[190] The charges are serious because they suggest, at best, a failure on the part of Zizioulas to engage the whole person in his theology or, at worst, the creation of a new Zizioulian construct for the notion of person. The implications for spirituality, at least potentially, are immense. If the charge of "dictated otherness" is true, it would suggest that the kind of communion with God envisioned by Zizioulas leans somewhat in the direction of absorption by the Divine, a kind of monophysitism on the level of anthropology. If the charge of "a self possessing no interiority" is true, we have a self that cannot engage actively in the spiritual life. Asceticism in this case would become immediately irrelevant. Loudovikos summarizes the situation this way:

> The problem is again that the nature of the Zizioulian *pre-modern* subject remains passive. Relationality tends to become automatic, as the subject refuses to acknowledge his unconscious, his inner conflicts and contradictions, his *passions* – and he refuses *to work with them*. This is precisely the core of subjective ecstatic idealism as, for example Nietzsche defines it: 'Not to know yourself: this is the cleverness/prudence of the idealist.'[191]

---

[188] Nicholas Loudovikos, "Person Instead of Grace and Dictated Otherness: John Zizioulas's Final Theological Position," *The Heythrop Journal* XLVIII (2009), 3.
[189] *Ibid.*, 5.
[190] *Ibid.*, 5-11.
[191] *Ibid.*, 14.

To be fair to Zizioulas, I should point out that he does discuss asceticism in his work *Communion and Otherness*, but the assertion of Loudovikos is that Zizioulas does not understand the ascetic *struggle* correctly because of a refusal to accept that the self has interiority, "a dark basement of the person" that requires illumination.[192] What is at risk, according to the author, is the loss of "psychosomatic participation in God,"[193] which, in contemporary terms, we might simply call spiritual life. A number of Father Loudovikos's criticisms of Zizioulas were challenged by Alexis Torrance in an article in which the author also respectfully calls upon Zizioulas to deepen his appreciation of asceticism.[194] It should be noted, however, that Torrance did not challenge the majority of Loudovikos's observations that directly pertain to spirituality.

Following on the heels of his article "Person Instead of Grace ...", Loudovikos wrote another pertinent article titled "*Eikon* and *mimesis* eucharistic ecclesiology and the ecclesial ontology of ecclesial reciprocity," in which he explicitly treats of the question of the emergence of eucharistic ecclesiology and therapeutic ecclesiology in contemporary Orthodox theology.[195] This article brought to light in the English-speaking world the author's observations made earlier in his Greek-language book *An Apophatic Ecclesiology of Consubstantiality*, which would be published later in English as *Church in the Making: An Apophatic Ecclesiology of Consubstantiality*[196]. Several points are particularly germane. *The first* is the author's contention that Saint Dionysios the Areopagite was the first to correct the artificial split between the institutional and the spiritual introduced into Christian theology (allegedly) by Origen. This the Areopagite did, according to Loudovikos,

---

[192]   *Ibid.*, 5.
[193]   *Ibid.*, 15.
[194]   Alexis Torrance, "Personhood and Patristics in Orthodox Theology: Reassessing the Debate." *The Heythrop Journal*. LII (2011), 700-707.
[195]   Nicholas Loudovikos, "*Eikon* and *mimesis* eucharistic ecclesiology and the ecclesial ontology of dialogical reciprocity," *International Journal for the Study of the Christian Church*, 11:2-3, (2011), 124.
[196]   Nikolaos Loudovikos, *Church in the Making: An Apophatic Ecclesiology of Consubstantiality*, trans. Norman Russell. (Crestwood, NY: St. Vladimir's Seminary Press, 2016).

by approaching ecclesiology from an ontological perspective.[197] It is thus Dionysios, and not Maximos the Confessor, who effected the first synthesis between the eucharistic and therapeutic dimensions in ecclesiology and, by extension, in spirituality. This adds something significant to Zizioulas' account of the history of early Christian spirituality. *Secondly*, Loudovikos posits that Saint Maximos corrected the deficiencies in Saint Dionysios's synthesis, developing a more nuanced variant.[198] Significantly, here we have a scholar who is critical of Zizioulas' ecclesiology who nevertheless affirms the latter's thesis that Saint Maximos did achieve a synthesis between the eucharistic and monastic dimensions in Christian spirituality. This affirmation adds credibility to Zizioulas' hypothesis. *Thirdly*, Loudovikos opines that contemporary Orthodox ecclesiologists, including Zizioulas, have either misunderstood or inadequately understood key terminology in Maximos, particularly the latter's use of *eikon*.[199] This misappropriation of Saint Maximos's terminology, according to Loudovikos, is the reason why a *new* split has occurred in contemporary Orthodox ecclesiology.[200] The theologian insists that Maximos had a far more dynamic understanding of the word *eikon* than that of contemporary ecclesiologists, and that he made use of the word *mimesis* to further clarify an "ontology of dialogical reciprocity" by providing it with a clearly active and participational orientation.[201] Father Loudovikos points us in the direction of Saint Maximos the Confessor for an authority among the Fathers who would prove formative for contemporary Orthodox ecclesiology. Clearly, other Fathers have proven influential in Orthodox spiritual theology even though they were not noted ecclesiologists. If, however, Saint Maximos is, as Loudovikos says, the *greatest* ecclesiologist among the Fathers,[202] then his magisterial ecclesiological, liturgical and spiritual work the *Mystagogy* can hardly be ignored in any serious discussion of the eucharistic and ascetic dimensions in Orthodox spirituality. It is to this work that we turn our attention in the next chapter.

[197] Loudovikos, Eikon, 123-124.
[198] *Ibid.* 125.
[199] *Ibid.*
[200] *Ibid.*
[201] *Ibid.*, 125-130.
[202] *Ibid.*, 135.

SECTION B:
SAINT MAXIMOS THE CONFESSOR AND HIS SUCCESSORS

CHAPTER FOUR

THE MYSTAGOGY OF SAINT MAXIMOS THE CONFESSOR

For Maximus there is a deeply ecclesial structure and character in the world as a whole and in humanity in particular. Existence is eucharistic, and spirituality makes no sense if it is not an expression of this "cosmic liturgy," which gives meaning to everything.

Metropolitan John Zizioulas

INTRODUCTION

Saint Maximos the Confessor was a sixth and seventh-century Father. He was of noble parentage and was a man of great erudition and singular ability. He served briefly as First Secretary at the Imperial Court of King Heraclius before entering the monastic life.[203] He was a prolific author and is recognized as one of the great Fathers of the Church.[204] As suggested by his title, the Church sees Saint Maximos first and foremost as a defender of the faith. Indeed, the contribution of Saint Maximos to the Church's confession of Orthodox Christology, particularly over and against the monothelitist position, is so well known that it hardly requires an introduction. Saint Maximos was, however, deeply interested

[203] Protopresbyter George Dion. Dragas, "The Lord's Prayer: Guide to the Christian Life According to St. Maximos the Confessor." *Ecclesiasticus II: Orthodox Icons, Saints, Feasts and Prayer* (Rollinsford, NH: Orthodox Research Institute, 2005), 210-211.
[204] *Ibid.,* 209.

in many areas of Christian theology. A closer examination of his work shows that his theological interests were not disparate but focused on several important themes. Important among them is the theme of man's salvation in Christ as deification. Fortunately, the last few years have seen the appearance of a *magnum opus* on Saint Maximos's theology of deification that convincingly demonstrates the great importance of this theme in his theological thought.[205]

STRUCTURE AND CHARACTER OF THE MYSTAGOGY

Saint Maximos also had an enduring commitment to and interest in the Divine Liturgy, which led him to write his short but important work the *Mystagogy*. The *Mystagogy* is not simply another commentary on the eucharistic liturgy; rather, it reveals Saint Maximos's grand vision of the Church in creation. Father George Dragas notes: "In this *Mystagogy*, Saint Maximus presents us, above all, the total mystery of the Church, which embraces all reality in its totality and its parts and gives it an eternal significance.[206]

Father Dragas understands the *Mystagogy* to be divided into three sections together with an extensive prologue and a substantial epilogue. The three major sections include: 1) a presentation of the Church as a series of images; 2) the commentary on the Holy Synaxis, also known as the Divine Liturgy; 3) a section in which the divine institutions of the Church are applied to the soul for its perfection.[207] Here I adopt the same assumption regarding the structure, except that I include two subsections of recapitulations and exhortations in the section that pertains to the application of the institutions of the Church to the perfection of the soul. The proposed schema is as follows:

---

[205] Jean-Claude Larchet, *La divinisation de l'homme selon saint Maxime le Confesseur* (Paris : Les Editions du Cerf, 1996).
[206] Protopresbyter George Dion. Dragas, "What is the Church? Saint Maximus' Mystagogical Answer." *Ecclesiasticus I: Introducing Eastern Orthodoxy* (Rollinsford, NH: Orthodox Research Institute, 2004), 31.
[207] *Ibid.*, 32.

1   Prologue.
2   The Church and man as a series of images.
3   The commentary on the Divine Liturgy.
4   The application of the ecclesial institutions to the perfection of the soul.
4a First recapitulation and exhortation.
4b Second recapitulation and exhortation.
5   Epilogue.

PROLOGUE

Saint Maximos draws upon older mystagogies in order to construct his own synthesis. In his Prologue, he explicitly makes reference to Saint Dionysios the Areopagite[208] and another "blessed old man" who, it appears, contributed quite significantly to Saint Maximos's own spiritual formation.[209] For all of his insistence in the Prologue to the *Mystagogy* that he was not producing anything new, it is certain that Maximos's synthesis of older sources and his development of certain particular themes are unique to him.[210]

THE CHURCH AND MAN AS IMAGES

The second section of the *Mystagogy* includes several chapters in which Saint Maximos presents the Church as an image of four realities: God, the world, man, and the soul. Father Schmemann suggests that Maximos

[208]   In some areas, Saint Maximos is in agreement with Saint Dionysios and simply integrates the teachings of the Areopagite into his own *Mystagogy*. In others, Saint Maximos departs significantly from the teachings of Saint Dionysios, giving the *Mystagogy* a radically different orientation from that of *Ecclesiastical Hierarchy*. For an excellent discussion of the similarities and significant differences between the teachings of Saint Maximos and of Saint Dionysios by an Orthodox theologian, see V. M. Zhivov, "The Mystagogia of Maximus the Confessor and the Development of the Byzantine Theory of the Image," trans. Ann Shukman, in *St. Vladimir's Theological Quarterly*, 31(4), 1987, 349-376.

[209]   (Saint Maximos the Confessor), "The Church's Mystagogy." *Maximus Confessor: Selected Writings*, trans. George C. Berthold (Mahwah, NJ: Paulist Press, 1985), 185.

[210]   Alexander Schmemann, "Symbols and Symbolism in the Orthodox Liturgy." *Orthodox Theology and Diakonia*, Demetrios J. Constantelos (ed.) (Brookline, MA: Hellenic College, 1981), 95.

uses the terms image, type, and symbol more or less interchangeably.[211] In the first place, the Church can be considered an image of God; the Church brings all different kinds of people into Christ in the same way that God brings unity out of disparity. Saint Maximos writes:

> To all in equal measure it gives and bestows one divine form and designation, to be Christ's and to carry his name. In accordance to faith it gives to all a single, simple, whole and indivisible condition which does not allow us to bring to mind the existence of the myriads of differences among them, even if they do exist, through the universal relationship and union of all things with it.[212]

The Church is also a type of the world. In the Orthodox temple, the sanctuary is the image of the spiritual world, while the nave is the symbol of the sensible world. Through the Church's temple, the two "worlds" are revealed as one even as the full integrity of their identities is maintained.[213] When considering the sensible world by itself, Saint Maximos sees the sanctuary as the type of heaven and the nave as the symbol of the earth.[214]

Saint Maximos understands the Church to be the image of man. Referring still to the Church's temple, he identifies the sanctuary as the type of the soul, the altar as the image of the mind, and the nave as the symbol of the body.[215] The temple reveals the unity of the human person as it also discloses the oneness of the world. In a highly detailed discussion of the soul and its powers, Saint Maximos puts forward a symbolic relationship between the sanctuary and the mind on the one hand, and the nave and reason on the other. The sanctuary is also the type of the contemplative power and the nave of the active power.[216] A word should be said here about the Saint's use of the terms "image" and

---

[211] Schmemann, "Symbols," 96.
[212] Mystagogy, 187.
[213] Ibid., 188-189.
[214] Ibid., 189.
[215] Ibid., 189-190.
[216] Ibid., 190-195.

"symbol." For the Confessor, the image or symbol always leads to the archetype.[217] This means that the symbol is filled with the reality that it represents, or more precisely, mediates. Therefore the word "symbol" itself engenders anticipation and hope, since it suggests the possibility of an encounter.

Returning to the text of the *Mystagogy*, we find that Saint Maximos continues his discussion of what we might term ecclesial anthropology. Saint Maximos writes that the Church is a spiritual man and that man is a mystical church.[218] In a spiritual person, Church and humanity are not discrete categories; the Church is internalized by humanity, but the latter is also incorporated into the Church. This idea is certainly in keeping with Saint Maximos's theological thought in general, in which we see a strong emphasis on the movement from multiplicity to unity and from complexity to simplicity.

Next Saint Maximos explores the relationship between man and the world. He writes that the world is a man, and man is a world. The world has invisible and visible aspects that can also be presented as the intelligible and the sensible.[219] Each of these two couplets can be compared to the soul and the body in a human person. Reiterating, apparently, the teaching of the "blessed old man," Saint Maximos writes:

> Intelligible things are the soul of sensible things, and sensible things are the body of intelligible things; that as the soul is in the body so is the intelligible in the world of sense, that the sensible is sustained by the intelligible as the body is sustained by the soul; that both make up one world as body and soul make up one man, neither of these elements joined to the other in unity denies or displaces the other according to the law of the one who has bound them together.[220]

[217] V. M. Zhivov, "The Mystagogia of Maximus the Confessor and the Development of the Byzantine Theory of the Image," trans. Ann Shukman. *St. Vladimir's Theological Quarterly*, 31(4), 1987, 361-362.

[218] Mystagogy, 195-196.

[219] Mystagogy, 19.

[220] *Ibid.*

Saint Maximos describes a situation in which two elements are brought together in a relationship of union. Neither element is subordinated to or absorbed into the other. Both remain what they are by nature. The retention of their natural distinctiveness, however, neither impedes their union nor compromises the expression of their fundamental oneness.

Saint Maximos's teaching on ecclesial anthropology highlights the special role of deified humanity in the relationship of the Church, the world, and humanity. Since a person is both a world and a mystical church, he has the potential to become the place of encounter between the Church and the world. In addition, a deified person can, in a sense, offer the world to the Church, since he is simultaneously a communicant of the Church and a little world. These are things that we can infer from the text of the *Mystagogy*, but we can be certain that Saint Maximos's intention is to express the interrelatedness of Church, humanity, and world. His teaching allows us to speak of the ecclesial aspect of humanity, the anthropic aspect of the Church, the cosmic aspect of humanity, and the anthropic aspect of the *cosmos*. The Church as an image of God, humanity, the world, and the soul; the participation of a symbol in the reality it represents; the possibility of union without confusion or extinction; the interrelatedness of Church, humanity and world – these are all the theological realities with which we must at least acquaint ourselves, if not apprehend, before Saint Maximos allows us to proceed to his explanation of the Divine Liturgy. The Church and its worship need to be understood on the cosmic level, and they have the most profound implications for anthropology.

THE COMMENTARY ON THE DIVINE LITURGY

The commentary on the Divine Liturgy shows how the Liturgy initiates the worshipper into the mystery of salvation in Christ, including the heavenly experience of the Church in the *eschaton*. Since deification is such an important aspect of salvation and the experience of the *eschaton*, it comes as no surprise that Saint Maximos makes reference to it several times. In fact, the entire movement of the commentary is directed toward deification, which Saint Maximos presents as the final experience of the Liturgy. Appropriately, therefore, deification is the subject of the conclusion of the commentary. Because deification embraces both the mystery of God's plan for our salvation and the mystery of the human will, there is a strong ascetic flavour to the commentary.

Saint Maximos begins the commentary by speaking of two entrances by the bishop: the first into the holy temple for the holy *synaxis,* and the second into the sanctuary to take his place on the throne. The former is an image of the incarnation, and the latter of the ascension.[221] The entrance of the people with the bishop is a type of conversion.[222] Through the Divine Liturgy, we participate in the plan of salvation and humanity's response to it.

Saint Maximos then turns his attention to the ascetic aspect of the Liturgy. The divine chants symbolize the delights of divine blessings, and the salutations of peace the divine favours imparted by the holy angels. Both are given to assist us in combatting sin and struggling for the virtues.[223]

Having reached the part of the Liturgy that follows the Gospel, Saint Maximos turns his attention toward the theme of eschatology. The descent of the bishop from the throne after the Gospel reading is a type of the second coming of Christ.[224] The closing of the doors after the dismissal of the catechumens is an image of the last judgment and of the passage from the material to the spiritual world.[225]

The entrance into the holy mysteries initiates the worshipper into the heavenly experience of the *eschaton.* The liturgy of the faithful is first and foremost for Saint Maximos the entrance of the Church into the heavenly realm. All of the elements of this second part of the Divine Liturgy reveal a different aspect of the heavenly experience in which the Church now participates through the eucharistic celebration. The entrance into the mysteries symbolizes the disclosure of the mystery of our salvation in the heavenlies.[226] The divine kiss reveals the unity we will have with each other and the intimacy we will have with the Word

---

221 *Ibid.,* 198.
222 *Ibid.,* 198-199.
223 *Ibid..* 199-200.
224 *Ibid.,* 200-201.
225 *Ibid.,* 201.
226 *Ibid.,* 201-202.

of God in the Kingdom.[227] The symbol of faith is an image of mystical thanksgiving.[228]

The singing of the thrice-holy hymn marks the entrance of the Church into union and harmony with the angels.[229] Here we recall the Lord's statement that, in the resurrection, we shall be *like* the angels.[230] Characteristically, and of course in obedience to Scripture, Saint Maximos speaks of a union with and an equality to the angels, and not of an absorption into the angelic state. The singing of the "Our Father" is a symbol of our full adoption and the elimination of all human particularity.[231] Here we see one of the hallmarks of Saint Maximos's teaching: the movement from complexity to simplicity. Finally, with the reception of the Body and Blood of Christ and the singing of the hymn "One is Holy," the Church enters into union with God and deification.[232] With this, the goal of the Liturgy has been reached. The Church has arrived at its final destination and is at home.

THE APPLICATION OF THE DIVINE INSTITUTIONS TO THE PERFECTION OF THE SOUL

Having completed his commentary on the Divine Liturgy, Saint Maximos proceeds immediately to the topic of the application of the institutions of the Church to the perfection of the soul. This section uses the Liturgy as a point of departure and a model for progression in the life of prayer and asceticism. Its emphasis is almost entirely on the personal and not on the corporate. Metropolitan Hierotheos Vlachos relates the commentary on the Divine Liturgy to this section by designating the former as the "Divine Eucharist and Divine Economy" and the latter as the "Divine Eucharist and the Soul's Perfection by Knowledge."[233] This stresses the unity and connection between these two sections, which is

---

[227]   *Ibid.*, 202.
[228]   *Ibid.*
[229]   *Ibid.*
[230]   Mt. 22:30, Mk. 12:25, Lk. 20:36.
[231]   Mystagogy, 203.
[232]   *Ibid.*
[233]   Metropolitan of Nafpaktos Hierotheos, *The mind of the Orthodox Church* (Levadia, Greece: Birth of the Theotokos Monastery, 1998), 105-113.

of great importance to us here. In essence, Metropolitan Hierotheos is proposing one commentary on the Divine Liturgy with two thrusts. In this section on the soul's perfection by knowledge, the first entrance is an image of the movement of the soul into contemplation.[234] The dismissal of the catechumens is a type of the rejection of the thoughts that come from the senses.[235] The entrance into the mysteries is an image of the movement into the immaterial and the simple.[236]

Some proponents of eucharistic ecclesiology and spirituality might perceive the section on the perfection of the soul as the triumph of "ascetic spirituality" over "eucharistic spirituality," the eclipse of the original liturgical ethos and its replacement by a radically different spiritual approach. When weighing the implications of the two sections, however, we must not lose sight of the fact that we are not dealing with two independent texts. In fact, the section on the application of the divine institutions of the Church is dependent on the commentary on the Divine Liturgy in the sense that the former supplements the latter but does not replace it. Thus the theological assumptions of the commentary on the Liturgy, with its general emphases on the communal and the eschatological, remain normative for the section on the perfection of the soul. In addition, the section on the perfection of the soul is set in a wider context, which is a teaching on the Church and a commentary on its Liturgy. It is only one movement in a much larger symphony. Thirdly, the goal or destination portrayed by this section is the same as that of the commentary on the Liturgy: deification. In general, any attempt to divide the Liturgy as revelatory of the economy of God and the Liturgy as effective for the perfection of the soul would, based on the *Mystagogy*, be entirely artificial.

THE RECAPITULATIONS AND EXHORTATIONS
Further clues to understanding the relationship between the two sections can be found in the movements of the *Mystagogy* that follow them. In the first exhortation and recapitulation, Saint Maximos states that the grace of the Holy Spirit is present in a special way at the holy

[234] Mystagogy, 204.
[235] *Ibid.*, 205.
[236] *Ibid.*

synaxis.[237] His point is that participation in the Eucharist is a *sine qua non* of the Christian life. Eucharistic life and ascetic life complement each other; the latter cannot replace the former. Paul Meyendorff feels that the *Mystagogy* may in fact have been written as a corrective for monks who had no taste for eucharistic piety.[238] Meyendorff has not used the word "Messalian," and perhaps it does not directly apply here, but it would seem that it is the basic tenets of Messalianism, with its emphasis on prayer and asceticism as being of greater importance than the sacramental life, that Saint Maximos wishes to oppose. The Divine Liturgy contains within itself concrete ways of participating in spiritual realities that are given to worshippers to experience now but will be known in their fullness later. Saint Maximos writes:

> Then we shall pass from the grace which is in faith to the grace of vision, when our God and Saviour Jesus Christ will indeed transform us into himself by taking away from us the marks of corruption and will bestow on us the original mysteries which have been represented for us through sensible symbols here below.[239]

Ignoring or undervaluing these "sensible symbols" would therefore represent a great spiritual loss.

Saint Maximos then continues the *Mystagogy* with a second recapitulation and exhortation. The second recapitulation is both a summary and a synthesis of all the previous material. He refers, as he often does, to those at the active stage and those at the stage of knowledge.[240] Referring to a description common to a number of Fathers and spiritual writers, he also speaks of slaves, mercenaries, and sons.[241] The Saint's essential point here is that there is a progression in the spiritual life. Here again asceticism is important, since our position as a slave, mercenary, or son depends not only on the grace of God but also upon our reception of it. This has nothing to do with spiritual

[237]   *Ibid.*
[238]   Meyendorff, "Introduction," 36.
[239]   *Ibid.*, 208.
[240]   *Ibid.*, 209-210.
[241]   *Ibid.*, 210.

elitism; instead, it is connected to the profound freedom of man, who is able to choose how and even if he will receive God's grace.

In his second exhortation, Saint Maximos appears to be addressing two possible problems: a refusal to acknowledge the absolute importance of liturgical worship, and a refusal to engage in the ascetic life. Perhaps this is why he feels the need both to reiterate and to expand on what he has said already elsewhere in the *Mystagogy* and thus to provide us with a second exhortation. Only then, it seems, does he feel the freedom to proceed to his conclusion and bring the work to a close. Turning his attention to the first problem, he writes:

> Let us, then, not stray from the holy Church of God which comprehends in the sacred order of the divine symbols which are celebrated, such great mysteries of our salvation. Through them, in making each of us who conducts himself worthily as best he can in Christ, it brings to light the grace of adoption which was given through holy baptism in the Holy Spirit and which makes us perfect in Christ.[242]

What we see in the first part of this quotation is a reiteration of what we have seen already in the first exhortation.[243] There is, however, a very important addition: the reference to Baptism. With this addition, the appeal to adhere to the Church is strengthened. Through Baptism, we first experience the grace of adoption, which, coupled with the grace received through the celebration of the "divine symbols," brings us to perfection.

Addressing the problem of the refusal to engage in asceticism, Saint Maximos exhorts his readers to fight laziness and zealously practise obedience to the Lord's commands. This, in simple biblical language, is asceticism. The Saint writes: "Who, then, is so slow and lazy with regard to virtue as not to desire divinity when one can acquire it at such small cost and so readily and easily?"[244] He also writes, "Therefore, let us to the best of our ability not be careless in obeying

[242] *Ibid.*, 211.
[243] *Ibid.*, 208.
[244] *Ibid.*, 212.

God ... in time of need."[245] Continuing his call to basic asceticism, Saint Maximos completes his exhortations and recapitulations and begins his concluding remarks.

TWO LEVELS OF SPIRITUAL LIFE

Saint Maximos endeavours always to invite the Christian to greater heights. What Christian would not be stirred to move from being a slave to becoming a son or daughter? Who would choose to remain at the level of activity (*praktikē*) forever? The invitation is implicit on many occasions in the *Mystagogy*. I would like to highlight three of them that can be found in chapter 24 of this work. In all three instances, a particular moment in the Divine Liturgy can be assimilated in two different ways. We begin first with the holy Gospel: "The holy Gospel is in general the symbol of the fulfillment of this world; ... *in the active* [my emphasis], the mortification and the end of the law and thinking according to the flesh; *and in those who have knowledge* [emphasis mine], the gathering and ascent from the numerous and various principles toward the most comprehensive principle ...."[246]

Now we proceed to the dismissal of the catechumens:

> The descent of the bishop from the throne and the dismissal of the catechumens signifies in general the second coming from heaven of our great God and Saviour Jesus Christ .... *Thus for the active ones* [emphasis mine] there results perfect detachment by which every passionate and unenlightened thought departs from the soul, *and for those with knowledge* [emphasis mine] the comprehensive science of whatever is known by which all images of material things are chased away from the soul.[247]

Now, finally, the closing of the doors, the entrance into the holy mysteries, the divine kiss and the recitation of the Creed:

---

[245]   *Ibid.*, 213.
[246]   *Ibid.*, 209.
[247]   *Ibid.*

The closing of the doors and the entrance into the holy mysteries and the divine kiss and the recitation of the symbol of the faith mean in general the passing away of sensible things and the appearance of spiritual realities .... *For those at the active stage* [emphasis mine], it means the transfer from activity to contemplation .... *For those who have knowledge* [emphasis mine], it involves the passing of natural contemplation to the simple understanding according to which they no longer pursue the divine and ineffable Word by sensation or anything that appears and the union with the soul of its powers and the simplicity which takes in under one form by the intellect the principle of Providence.[248]

What we can see here is a very clear pattern of describing how certain liturgical moments or realities are assimilated differently by those who are at the stage of activity and those who are at the stage of knowledge. Thus, while the grace of God is one, it is received differently by Christians according to their spiritual state and ability. This experience cannot be explained by referring to the Eucharist alone; it can be explained only through asceticism.

CONCLUSION

Saint Maximos has presented a profound theology of image, ecclesial anthropology, and union. The Saint is neither exclusively a representative of eucharistic nor of ascetical spirituality; he embodies the full balance and the integration of the two. His is an ecclesiology that has both a corporate and a personal dimension. What we encounter in the *Mystagogy* reveals this balance between the eucharistic and the ascetic, the communal and the particular: the Christian encounters God in the corporate; he enters into the great mystery of salvation through the Church and its sacraments. In the eucharistic celebration, he tastes of the perfection of salvation and is brought gradually to deification. At the same time, the grace of God is active in his life according to the measure of his openness to God and his commitment to the ascetic life.

[248]   *Ibid.*, 209-210.

All the spiritual aspects of the mystery of salvation are appropriated by him personally. He makes the choice to live according to Christ's commandments, to fight spiritual lethargy or even to participate in the eucharistic celebration. Indeed, without some degree of practical asceticism, a Christian would not even be present at the holy *synaxis* to receive the special grace experienced there.

Saint Maximos is presenting a theology of the ascetic life alongside a commentary on the Divine Liturgy. To return, however, to Father Dragas's comments on how the *Mystagogy* reveals "the total mystery of the Church, which embraces all reality," we can say that the Confessor is providing us with a great vision of the Church, which embraces humanity and all creation. Within that great mystery, we have the Divine Liturgy and institutions of the Church that perfect the soul. There is no question that we have a synthesis of the eucharistic and ascetic dimensions here, but it remains to be seen if Saint Maximos ever perceived the two as disparate or in any need of reconciliation. It may simply have been, as Professor Paul Meyendorff opines, that the Saint was addressing certain abuses or rogue tendencies in the monasticism of his time. *Firstly*, if we say that Saint Maximos repositioned monastic spirituality in a eucharistic context, which appears to be what Metropolitan John would have us believe, then it is equally true that Saint Maximos *could never have conceived of the Eucharist outside of an ascetic context*. This then prompts us to ask what, if anything, was repositioned here? Perhaps nothing – in fact, we may never know. The synthesis may have been so innate in Saint Maximos's thinking that he was not aware of effecting a synthesis at all. From a purely theoretical point of view, one might even argue that the *Mystagogy* is, in fact, *an ascetic text* that has been set in a broader ecclesiological framework.

Secondly, we must take stock of the terminology used in the *Mystagogy*. It is steeped in the classic language of monastic spirituality. This language predates Saint Maximos and brings us back to Evagrios, whose negative influence in the history of Christian spirituality, according to the Metropolitan, has been neutralized. Furthermore, this language does not connote a simple choice of vocabulary; *it demonstrates a prevailing ethos and worldview*. To put this in simple terms, Saint Maximos thinks like a monk. To make him anything or anyone else is to ignore a fundamental part of his identity and theological vision.

Thirdly, Saint Maximos reserves a very prominent place in his commentary for the particular. There is a constant movement in his commentary, as Professor Paul Meyendorff observes, between the *general* and the *particular*. This can be observed even in the commentary on the Divine Liturgy itself. *It is my contention that the degree of particularity here exceeds what we can observe in the theological thought of Metropolitan John.* The *person in communion* of Metropolitan John's thought is not, in my opinion, the Christian pursuing *praktikē* or the *gnostic* of the *Mystagogy*. The former is, in my view, quite different from the latter two. The ascetic of the *Mystagogy* appears to have far more interiority. Significantly, he is also interested in different things. When do we ever see the *person in communion* of Zizioulas' thought passing beyond the senses or practising natural contemplation?

Finally, where are the levels of progression in the spiritual life in Metropolitan John's spirituality and ecclesiology? Is there room for slaves, mercenaries, and sons? Do we find practitioners of *praktikē* and *gnostics*? No, we do not. This is not only because the venerable Metropolitan prefers different terminology. There is something more here; there is a difference of substance. The ascetic life and its attendant stages of spiritual development, *praktikē*, *physikē* and *theologia*, as we shall see later on, have no enduring place in his ecclesiology. All of this ascetic activity would shift the dynamics of the spiritual life away from the acquisition of a new relationship and identity, which is the essence of the Metropolitan's ecclesiology, to a far more particular, volitional, and conscious dynamic than the celebrated theologian could likely embrace with any degree of comfort.

Saint Maximos's cosmic vision of the Church and ecclesial understanding of the spiritual life were taken up by his successors. We now turn in the next chapter to one of the best known of these, Saint Symeon the New Theologian.

CHAPTER FIVE

THE EUCHARIST IN THE ETHICAL DISCOURSES OF SAINT SYMEON THE NEW THEOLOGIAN

We are still waiting for studies that will show us where the other significant representatives of the Patristic tradition, in particular Saint Simeon the New Theologian, stand on this issue.

Metropolitan John Zizioulas

THE LIFE AND WITNESS OF SAINT SYMEON

Saint Symeon the New Theologian was an Orthodox monk who lived in the tenth and eleventh centuries. He is called "Theologian" by the Church because of the profound knowledge and experience of God that can be observed in his life and writings. He is known as the "New Theologian" because he follows in the great tradition of Saint John the Apostle and Saint Gregory Nazianzen, who are also called "Theologians" by the Church.

Saint Symeon spent the majority of his life in or near Constantinople. He was abbot of the Constantinopolitan monastery of Saint Mamas for 25 years. Saint Symeon wrote prolifically; his best-known works are likely the *Hymns* and the *Catechetical Discourses*, both of which have been translated into English and published under the titles *Hymns of Divine Love* and *The Discourses*, translated by Father George Maloney, S.J. and Bishop C. J. de Catanzaro respectively.

For this study, I have chosen to limit myself to a body of Saint Symeon's writings somewhat less known than the *Hymns* or the *Catechetical Discourses* and more recently translated into English by Archbishop Alexander Golitzin: the *Ethical Discourses*. This I have done for two important reasons, which arise from the date of the composition of the *Ethical Discourses* and their theological character. Firstly, the *Ethical Discourses* were written towards the end of Saint Symeon's life and represent the fruit of his mature theological reflection. Secondly, the *Ethical Discourses* provide us with Saint Symeon's theological thought in highly concentrated form, rich in biblical references and imagery. Archbishop Alexander perhaps has both reasons in mind when he ventures to call the *Ethical Discourses* Saint Symeon's *summa*.[249]

SAINT SYMEON ON THE EUCHARIST

Saint Symeon the New Theologian's teachings on the Eucharist can be found in First, Second, Third, Tenth, and Fourteenth Ethical Discourses. The Saint does not write as a "professional theologian," and so his teaching on the Eucharist is not presented in a systematic fashion. Rather, his instruction on the Eucharist appears as a critically important part of a larger presentation on the Christian life, a dominant theme that has been integrated into a spirited apologetic for the possibility, indeed necessity, of a full union with Christ in this life, of a vision of His light and glory through the spiritual intellect. What we encounter in Saint Symeon is not a "sacramental theology" as we know it from scholasticism, but a theology of deification in which the Eucharist plays an indispensable role.

In calling attention to Saint Symeon's way of presenting the subject of the Eucharist, I am doing more than describing his literary style or even the particular contexts in which the topic of the Eucharist occurs, although the latter is certainly important. I have in mind, rather, the whole orientation of his thought and the burden of his teaching. If deification is truly the goal of Saint Symeon's instruction, then to

---

[249] Alexander Golitzin, "Introduction." St. Symeon the New Theologian, *On the Mystical Life: The Ethical Discourses, Vol. 1: The Church and the Last Things*, trans. Alexander Golitzin (Crestwood, NY: St. Vladimir's, 1995), 13.

separate his teaching on the Eucharist from that goal is to do violence to his thought and the whole witness of his life. It is for this reason that I have been careful to avoid the temptation of addressing the topic of "Saint Symeon's Eucharistic Theology" in this chapter but have chosen instead to treat the subject of the Eucharist as one facet of Saint Symeon's teaching on deification.[250]

BASIC THEMES

Saint Symeon's teaching on the Eucharist turns around two basic themes that lead to what I would term the dominant theme. The two basic themes are the *nuptial/ecclesial* and the *incarnational*. A third basic theme appears to emerge from the first two, and that is the *Pneumatological*. Whether one counts the basic themes as two, three or more, the important point is that they all lead to what I believe is the dominant theme: deification/vision of God. In addition to the themes already mentioned, which pertain specifically to the Eucharist, there are a number of background themes or assumptions that pervade all of Saint Symeon's writings and can be detected in the *Ethical Discourses* we will be examining. These include intimacy with Christ, the need for a conscious awareness of inner transformation, and the need for asceticism. These form the backdrop against which Saint Symeon develops his argumentation and therefore must not be forgotten.

THE NUPTIAL-ECCLESIAL THEME AND THE EUCHARIST

Turning to the First Ethical Discourse, we encounter what I have termed the nuptial/ecclesial theme. Symeon's remarks on the Eucharist are set in the context of his teaching on the Church as the Body of Christ.

---

[250]   By deification, I do not mean what Loudovikos describes as "the will to power" in his analysis of the history of Christian spirituality. See Loudovikos, *Analogical Identities*, p.2-4, 42-62. Instead, I have in mind union with Christ, or Christification. This union with Christ represents a true ontological change and, as Loudovikos astutely points out, places the person beyond "spirituality," (*Ibid.*, p. 4) if the latter is to be considered mainly a pursuit of the mystical. It is not in the aforementioned sense that I use the word *spirituality* in this book.

Symeon's contention is "that all the saints are members of Christ, are in the process of becoming one body with Him, and that this process will continue indefinitely."[251] This dynamic ecclesiology, which allows for a *process* of *becoming* one body with Christ, sets the stage for Saint Symeon's teaching on the Eucharist. Once we accept that a process is involved, we are already predisposed to discover how the process is furthered. The Eucharist, of course, is the means by which the process is advanced and the Church deepens its experience of becoming the Body of Christ.

SAINT SYMEON'S ECCLESIOLOGY

Before we proceed to Symeon's eucharistic teaching, however, it would be appropriate to say a word about his ecclesiology. The Saint's teaching on the Church is not specifically "his," since many elements of it are common to all the Fathers. That the Church is the *Body* of Christ is an integral part of Scriptural and patristic teaching, but what is peculiar to Symeon is the impassioned way in which he focuses on this point, almost to the exclusion of other aspects of ecclesiology. His is a profoundly non-institutional ecclesiology grounded in the Incarnation, the Eucharist, and asceticism. It finds its truest meaning in deification. It would be a mistake, however, to view Symeon's ecclesiology as marginal to Orthodox theology as a whole. On the contrary, one could take his understanding of the Church as being essentially normative. It is the style of presentation rather than the content that is particularly Symeon's, and the thrust of his argument cannot be dismissed as extreme.

A EUCHARISTIC READING OF THE FIFTH CHAPTER OF EPHESIANS

Returning to Saint Symeon's contention that the saints are members of Christ and are eternally becoming one body with Him, we discover that the author is preparing the way for a eucharistic interpretation of a passage which we have come to know as both nuptial and ecclesial in its meaning: the Epistle taken from Ephesians 5 that is read during the celebration of

[251]   St. Symeon the New Theologian, "First Ethical Discourse." *On the Mystical Life: The Ethical Discourses, Vol. 1: The Church and the Last Things*, trans. Alexander Golitzin (Crestwood, NY: St. Vladimir's, 1995), 44.

the sacrament of marriage. Symeon insists on the legitimacy of an ecclesial interpretation of the passage by highlighting verse 32: "This mystery is a profound one, and I am saying that it refers to Christ and the Church."[252] In using this verse, however, he is defending an explicitly eucharistic interpretation of the passage that he feels is implicit. To do this, he adds little to the passage; he only explores the question of how Christ nourishes and cherishes the Church "because we are members of His body, of His flesh and of His bones."[253] The answer of Symeon is simple: Christ gives us to eat from His flesh and bones "and through this, communion makes us ... one with Him."[254] In the same way that Adam and Eve shared a profound communion since Eve was taken from the flesh and bones of Adam, so also we become one flesh with Christ by communing in His flesh and bones.[255] Of course, Eve was created once, and subsequent to her creation, Adam and Eve could discover the implications of being one flesh. Eucharistic communion has the dynamic quality that Symeon brought to the fore when he described becoming one body with Christ as a process.

INCARNATION AND EUCHARIST

Later in the First Ethical Discourse, Symeon returns to the subject of the Eucharist, but this time using the Incarnation as his point of reference. The same flesh that the Lord received from the Theotokos, He now gives us as food.[256] In the Eucharist, we receive "the entirety of God made flesh, our Lord Jesus Christ, Son of God and son of the immaculate Virgin Mary ..."[257] Here Saint Symeon is stating that the Eucharist is a communion in the whole person of Christ, lest we take the word "flesh" in a crude sense and think that we commune in one aspect of Christ only. Furthering his argument, he says: "He is present in the body bodilessly, mingled with our essence and nature, and deifying us who share His body ...."[258] In saying that Christ is "present in the body

---

[252]   First Ethical Discourse, 48.
[253]   Eph. 5:30.
[254]   First Ethical Discourse, 47.
[255]   *Ibid.*
[256]   First Ethical Discourse, 57.
[257]   *Ibid.*
[258]   *Ibid.*

bodilessly," Saint Symeon is indicating that the Lord is not subject to the physical limitations that normally define a body as we know it. He can therefore achieve a deeper level of intimacy with us by being "mingled with our essence and nature" without, of course, compromising the integrity of His person or our persons. Indeed, Symeon's description of Christ's presence in us captures the strength of the biblical image "flesh of His flesh, bone of His bone."

By stating "deifying us who share His body," Symeon points to the goal of receiving the Eucharist and, one might add, of the Incarnation, which serves as background and point of departure for this passage. He points to an important difference between the Incarnation and our eucharistic participation in Christ: while the Son of God took flesh from the Theotokos in the Incarnation, He takes no flesh from the saints who form His body, but makes them sharers of His own deified flesh.[259] Symeon picks up on this basic theme of the Incarnation in the Second Ethical Discourse and explores it in more detail. What is certainly clear in the First Ethical Discourse is that the nuptial/ecclesial and incarnational themes lead directly to the overarching theme of deification.

THE CREATION OF MAN, THE INCARNATION, AND THE EUCHARIST

Saint Symeon's teaching on the Eucharist in the Second Ethical Discourse includes a recapitulation of the incarnational theme from the First Ethical Discourse, but greatly expanded. In the Old Testament, God removed a rib from Adam and replaced it with flesh of the same nature. The "ensouled" rib was then expanded into woman.[260] Symeon says "ensouled" rib because God did not breathe another soul into Eve, but only formed her from an "ensouled" part of Adam. Symeon's point is that God added nothing to the soul when he created Eve, nor anything save flesh of Adam's same nature when He filled up, as it were, the space in Adam after removing the rib. Put succinctly, the creation of Eve is an extension of creation – it is not a re-creation.

Conversely, in the New Testament, the Word took flesh from the Virgin

---

259   *Ibid.*, 58.
260   Symeon, Second Ethical Discourse, 110.

and replaced it with incorruption and the Holy Spirit.[261] Unlike Adam, the Theotokos received something completely new. In the Incarnation, we have more than an extension of creation – we have a new creation. The impact of the new creation was profound and immediate: deification. Not only was human nature deified when the Word was made man, but the seed of deification was planted already in the Theotokos, who was given the antidote to the corruption that she received from Adam and a new life in the Holy Spirit. The same eternal life and Holy Spirit that were infused into the Theotokos at the Incarnation are now made available to us, according to Saint Symeon, in the Holy Eucharist.[262]

THE PNEUMATOLOGICAL THEME

Commenting on the passage from the Old Testament that is quoted in the New Testament "for this reason a man leaves his father and mother and cleaves to his wife,"[263] Symeon states that a similar movement takes place in the reception of the Eucharist: humanity leaves behind the corruption with which it has been infected, and cleaves to Christ. In this eucharistic union, the two become one flesh.[264] Expanding on this nuptial theme, the Saint writes that the one who unites himself with a prostitute becomes one body with her,[265] but he who is united with the Lord becomes one Spirit with Him.[266] In the Eucharist we receive both the flesh of Christ and the Holy Spirit. The Eucharist thus becomes a primary means to receive the Holy Spirit.

In the Second Ethical Discourse, Saint Symeon develops the incarnational and nuptial/ecclesial themes with which we have already become familiar. From these two themes emerges the Pneumatological theme. Left unanswered, however, is the question of how we become one with Christ or, in other words, what exactly the implications are of becoming one flesh and one Spirit with Him. Symeon anticipates this question and answers it by stating that we become one with Christ in the

---

[261] Ibid., 111.
[262] Ibid., 111-113.
[263] Gen. 2:24.
[264] Second Ethical Discourse, 111-112.
[265] 1 Cor. 6:16-17.
[266] Second Ethical Discourse, 112.

nature of divinity and of humanity.[267] On the one hand, according to the Saint, we are one with Christ in the nature of divinity because we have been made gods by adoption; on the other hand, we are one with Christ in the nature of humanity because we have become His brothers.[268] This oneness with Christ, not surprisingly, is directly connected to deification. The eucharistic passage in the Second Ethical Discourse demonstrates in a clear way how the basic themes that we have been encountering all tend toward the main theme of deification.

THE ETERNAL GOOD THINGS

In his Third Ethical Discourse, Saint Symeon explores in depth the heavenly experience of rapture described by Saint Paul.[269] He poses the question as to how the ineffable speech that Saint Paul heard should be understood and proposes this answer:

> I say that the ineffable speech which Paul heard spoken in Paradise were the eternal good things which eye has not seen, nor ear heard, nor the heart of man conceived. These things, which God has prepared for those who love Him, are not protected by heights, nor enclosed in some secret place, nor hidden in the depths, nor kept at the ends of the earth or sea. They are right in front of you, before your very eyes. So, what are they? Together with the good things stored up in heaven, these are the Body and Blood of our Lord Jesus Christ which we see every day, and eat, and drink. These, we avow, are those good things.[270]

While affirming that the believer will encounter in heaven "eternal good things" that have not been fully understood in this life, Saint Symeon vigorously asserts that access to these things may be obtained now in the Eucharist. In making this assertion, Symeon ties the Eucharist to the experience of the *eschaton*. The "good things" are,

[267] *Ibid.*
[268] *Ibid.*
[269] 2 Cor. 12.
[270] Third Ethical Discourse, 130-131.

after all, "eternal." But "eternal" here does not mean "future," and Saint Symeon is quick to defend this point. The "eternal," on the contrary, is available to us every day through participation in the Eucharist.

Saint Symeon wrote in another age and was not concerned with developing eucharistic ecclesiology, a theology of personhood, or liturgical theology. Instead, he was preoccupied with defending the possibility of a direct, conscious experience of Christ, a vision of God through the spiritual intellect. In a sense, he was presenting an *apologia* for deification. Symeon understood that he had located a point on which his whole argument would stand or fall: if the "eternal good things" could be known in this life, then deification was possible; if not, then it was only a pious hope for the hereafter. By asserting that the "eternal good things" could be experienced by receiving Holy Communion, Symeon was proposing the Eucharist as a kind of guarantee of the viability and legitimacy of deification as the objective of the spiritual life.

THE EUCHARIST AND ASCETICISM

For Saint Symeon, the Eucharist is very much connected to asceticism, and their relationship is described succinctly in the Third Ethical Discourse by one short phrase: "... become holy by practicing God's commandments and then partake of the holy things."[271] The order here is important; *Saint Symeon could never have conceived of a eucharistic life that was not preceded by a serious ascetic life.* Both the ascetic and eucharistic lives are absolutely necessary, according to Symeon, and one would not exaggerate by saying that they represent the core of Christian spiritual experience.

To live the eucharistic life is to be united eternally to Christ or, as we saw in the First Ethical Discourse, to be in the process of becoming one body with Him.[272] In the Third Ethical Discourse, Symeon highlights the part of the eucharistic text in John 6 that suggests the dynamic character of eucharistic life: "Now, He did not say 'Who came down,' because this would indicate that the 'coming down' was a one-time event. What then? He says, 'Who comes down,' clearly because He is always and

---

[271] *Ibid.*, 131.
[272] First Ethical Discourse, 44.

forever descending on those who are worthy, and that this occurs both now and at every hour."[273] By saying "upon those who are worthy," Saint Symeon reminds his hearers again of the importance of asceticism in the eucharistic life. In so doing, he not only maintains the balance between asceticism and the Eucharist in the spiritual life, he also prevents anyone from applying to the Eucharist a magical or mechanical-sacramental interpretation. Anyone who wishes to be engaged in the eucharistic life needs to co-operate actively with Christ; he is not the passive recipient of sacramental grace. Although Symeon does not use the word *synergeia* here, it could certainly be applied appropriately to the type of relationship between the ascetic and sacramental lives that he espouses.

PERCEIVING THE EUCHARIST WITH SPIRITUAL EYES

Saint Symeon asserts that the Eucharist must be perceived with spiritual eyes.[274] Through the physical eyes one sees only the visible or earthly bread. Through the spiritual senses one perceives the heavenly bread.[275] Saint Symeon is suggesting here that it is possible to receive the Eucharist on two levels: one that deifies, and one that does not. An encounter with the earthly bread is a non-deifying participation in the Eucharist. Here again, we are very far from a mechanical understanding of the sacrament. The simple reception of the Eucharist by a baptized Christian in no way guarantees that deification is taking place. If the heavenly bread may be perceived only with spiritual eyes, then it follows that the development of the spiritual faculties of perception is absolutely indispensable. A more than casual analysis of this passage shows us that Saint Symeon is stressing the importance of asceticism yet again. It is the ascetic process that contributes so much to the healing and restoration of the spiritual faculties in man. A deifying participation in the Holy Eucharist is what Saint Symeon also terms "eat[ing] the heavenly bread in the Spirit."[276] Here is how the Saint summarizes his position:

---

[273] Third Ethical Discourse, 133.
[274] *Ibid.*
[275] *Ibid.*, 133-134.
[276] *Ibid.*, 134.

Therefore, if you, yourself a believer, partake of mere bread and not of a deified body when receiving Him, the whole Christ Himself, how do you hope to take life from Him and with full awareness possess within yourself Him, the same Lord Who says: "He who eats the bread which comes down from heaven will live forever" [*cf.* Jn 6:58], and again: "The flesh avails nothing; it is the Spirit Who gives life"? It is the Spirit Who is really the true food and drink. It is the Spirit Who changes the bread into the Lord's body. It is the Spirit Who really purifies us and makes us partake worthily of the body of the Lord.[277]

The deifying participation in the Eucharist is also a reception of the Holy Spirit. On the other hand, it is the Holy Spirit who also prepares us to encounter Christ on the level of deification. It follows, then, that the Holy Spirit is received first through asceticism and then again through the Eucharist. The first reception of the Holy Spirit prepares, and the second deifies.

BAPTISM, EUCHARIST AND DEIFICATION
In the Tenth Ethical Discourse, Saint Symeon explores the place of Baptism and the Eucharist in the spiritual life. Baptism alone is not sufficient for salvation; the Christian must see the glory of Christ.[278] Saint Symeon has already discussed the content of the eucharistic passage in John 6 previously. What is new in the Tenth Ethical Discourse is the link that he forges between the eucharistic passage in John 6 and the prologue to the Gospel in John 1. For Symeon, the Word still becomes flesh and continues "to tabernacle" among us through the Eucharist. It is through this that a Christian may behold the glory of Christ Who has made His dwelling in him.[279] This vision of the glory of Christ is not a pious "extra," but a *sine qua non* of the spiritual life.

The presentation of the Eucharist as a continuation of the Incarnation is by no means unique to Saint Symeon. His way of making this particular

[277] *Ibid.*
[278] Tenth Ethical Discourse, 156.
[279] *Ibid.*

connection is strongly reminiscent of what we see in Saint Justin Martyr centuries before.[280] It is the emphasis on beholding the glory of Christ that is more particular to Symeon. This vision of the glory of God can be understood simply as an aspect of deification. Once again, Symeon is making use of a basic theme, in this case an incarnational–eucharistic one, to reach the main theme, which is that of deification. It is in this context that we can understand the place of Baptism and the Eucharist. Baptism is the introduction into the spiritual life, and the Eucharist embodies the completion or perfection of the spiritual life. Since the whole spiritual life is pointed towards deification, one could certainly not say that the Eucharist is connected to deification and Baptism is not. On the other hand, Saint Symeon is clear in asserting that the Eucharist is a *primary* means of deification. Here is how Symeon explains his position:

> For, once this has happened and we have been baptized spiritually by the Holy Spirit, and the incarnate Word has made His tabernacle as light in us by the communion of His immaculate body and blood, then we have seen His glory, glory as of the Only-Begotten of the Father. Once, He says, we have been born spiritually by Him and from Him, and He has tabernacled in us bodily and we have made our abode consciously in Him, then immediately at that moment, at the hour itself when these things have occurred, we have seen the glory of His divinity, glory as of an Only-Begotten from the Father, glory of such a kind as is clearly possessed by none other, neither angels nor men.[281]

For Saint Symeon, the Incarnation, the Eucharist and deification are so linked that, if the latter is not possible, then both the Incarnation and the Eucharist lose all their significance and power. Symeon already took a stand in the Third Ethical Discourse by insisting on the immediacy and availability of the "eternal good things."[282] In the Tenth Ethical Discourse, he builds upon his earlier position by stating:

---

[280] St. Justin Martyr, *First Apology*, 66.
[281] Tenth Ethical Discourse, 156-157.
[282] Third Ethical Discourse, 131.

> Indeed, if this is not the case and we do not enter into participation and communion with the eternal good things while yet in the body, and if we, the elect, do not receive grace, then Christ Himself is in fact a prophet, and not God. Everything which His Gospel says becomes instead a prophecy about the future and not a gift of grace.[283]

Simply put, if immediate participation in the "eternal good things" is not possible, then the Incarnation did not happen. The relegation of deification (the participation in the "eternal good things" is one of its aspects) to the future is a denial of the gift of grace. Similarly, if in the Eucharist we do not consciously receive another kind of life, then the bread of the Eucharist is mere bread, and not Christ's Body.[284] According to Saint Symeon, if we ourselves are not transformed by participation in the Eucharist, then there must be no transformation of the Holy Gifts in the eucharistic celebration.

ORTHODOX SPIRITUALITY AND THE HUMAN SOUL

In the Fourteenth Ethical Discourse, Saint Symeon emphasizes the necessity of passing beyond the perceptible to commune in the "living bread" and the "blood of God" through the powers of the soul.[285] Here the Saint is recapitulating a theme developed in the Third Ethical Discourse.[286] The Eucharist must be approached properly in order for it to be deifying. A non-deifying participation in the Eucharist is restricted to the level of the perceptible only. The spiritual intellect remains unengaged. The "intellect" and "soul's powers" of the Fourteenth Ethical Discourse are the same as the "spiritual eyes" of the Third Ethical Discourse.[287] We may understand the intellect as the faculty of the soul to consciously and directly perceive God, the *nous* of ascetic literature. As was the case in the Third Ethical Discourse, the theme of asceticism

---

[283] Tenth Ethical Discourse, 165.
[284] *Ibid.*, 166.
[285] Fourteenth Ethical Discourse, 179.
[286] Third Ethical Discourse, 133-134.
[287] *Cf.* 133.

is present here quite explicitly: "If you always drink this worthily, you shall never thirst – only, drink it with perception of soul, with your soul's powers prepared and at peace."[288] Key words here are "worthily," "with perception of soul," and "prepared and at peace." The "worthily" at the beginning of the sentence is explained in greater detail by "perception of soul" and "prepared and at peace." Symeon stresses the importance of perception of *soul*, since to receive the Eucharist with the perception of the senses only is to receive unworthily. However, in order to participate in the Eucharist with perception of soul, the soul's powers must first be prepared and unagitated, and the process of preparation that brings the intellect to a state of preparedness and peace is precisely asceticism.

DOUBLE PERCEPTION

Saint Symeon speaks of a double perception that includes the perceptible and the intelligible.[289] The "intelligible" is the "perception of the soul," which we have seen already. This does not contradict what Symeon says earlier; instead, it is the Saint's way of saying that the entire human person must be engaged for a full and worthy partaking of the Eucharist: body and soul, senses and intellect. Furthermore, this allows the Christian to commune in "both the twin natures of Christ, becoming one body with Him and fellow communicants of His glory and divinity."[290] In short, the entire human person communes in the entire Christ. Although Symeon does not state it explicitly here, it seems reasonable to infer that this complete communion in the total Christ lies at the heart of the Saint's understanding of deification. *Firstly*, deification implies a transformation of the whole person. *Secondly*, this is made possible through a participation in both Christ's Body and His glory.

Having developed his position on the double perception, Saint Symeon heads toward both the climax and the end of the Fourteenth Ethical Discourse. He returns to his emphasis on the intellect, reminding his hearers that "the unapproachable Word, the bread which comes down from heaven, is not held by the senses."[291] He then reasserts the

288 Fourteenth Ethical Discourse, 179.
289 *Ibid.*, 180.
290 *Ibid.*
291 *Ibid.*, 181.

need for the Christian to be "worthy and well prepared," emphasizing yet again the connection between readiness of the soul's powers and ascetic preparation.[292] *Thirdly*, he reiterates that the human person must encounter the glory of Christ through the intellect with full conscious awareness.[293]

Perception through the intellect, ascetic preparation, and conscious awareness are fundamental to Saint Symeon's teaching on the Eucharist. All three points tell us something about the "how" of eucharistic participation. However, it has been my contention throughout this chapter that any presentation of Saint Symeon's eucharistic teaching that does not include the objective of the eucharistic life is tragically incomplete. This objective is deification (or, perhaps more appropriately in Symeon's case, christification), and even if Symeon is not explicitly using the term, this is clearly what he is describing.

THE GOAL OF THE EUCHARISTIC LIFE

At the end of the Fourteenth Ethical Discourse, Saint Symeon describes the goal of the eucharistic life in a succinct and powerful way. It is first of all one single feast, more specifically, one single Pascha.[294] Symeon develops the connection of Pascha with "passage." In this case, the journey is from perceiving by sense to knowing by intellection; it is a passage from shadow, type, and symbol to vision of Christ.[295] Here Saint Symeon has brought us to the point not only of the eucharistic life, but of the Christian life in its entirety: vision of Christ. Since this vision of Christ is realized only through the powers of the soul and not through the senses, the movement from perception by sense to intellection is absolutely essential. This explains why Symeon places more emphasis on intellection than sensory perception, even though he speaks of double perception.

Once we understand the goal of the Christian life in Saint Symeon's theological work, we can begin to see a certain simplicity emerge from the eloquence and apparent complexity of Symeon's teachings:

[292]   *Ibid.*
[293]   *Ibid.*
[294]   *Ibid.*
[295]   *Ibid.*

deification, or vision of Christ, is the objective of the spiritual life, and eucharistic participation is the primary way to get there. However, it is not just any approach to the Eucharist that permits a Christian to reach the desired goal; the eucharistic life must have an ascetic context if it is to be effective at all. Without this context, the passage from sensory perception to intellection does not occur, and the vision of Christ never becomes a reality. It is in this sense that a deifying participation in the Eucharist can be equated with what we might call an ascetic participation in the Eucharist.

UNITY BETWEEN ASCETICISM AND THE EUCHARIST

Saint Symeon is both profoundly ascetic and strongly eucharistic in his life and teaching. He defies any attempt to classify him as either an ascetic or a eucharistic theologian, since the ascetic and eucharistic in Saint Symeon reach such a high level of integration. The apprehension of the ascetic-eucharistic unity, being intrinsic to his theological writings, provides a primary key to their interpretation. A second key is to be found in the overarching theme of deification that permeates all of the Saint's theological work. Without these two keys, any effort to interpret Symeon is reduced to the level of reflection on recurring theological themes – incarnational, nuptial, Pneumatological, and so on – and can provide no real insight into the true ethos and concerns of his life and witness. Saint Symeon does not write out of simple intellectual curiosity but out of conviction, and a failure to engage his convictions means the collapse of any enterprise to interpret him theologically. This is what I had in mind at the beginning of this chapter when I asserted that Saint Symeon is not a professional theologian and does not present us with a "sacramental theology" of the Eucharist. It is also linked to my own contention that a grasp of the deeper spiritual orientation behind the apparent themes in Saint Symeon's work is essential for the discussion of his theological legacy.

In most studies of Orthodox spirituality, Saint Gregory Palamas is featured prominently. It is to him that we turn in the next chapter.

CHAPTER SIX

BAPTISM AND THE EUCHARIST IN THE HOMILIES OF SAINT GREGORY PALAMAS

Saint Gregory Palamas has been commonly portrayed as representative of the ecclesiology in which the divine Eucharist is less important than individual spirituality. Nonetheless, I believe that, taken together, his treatises, doctrinal essays and sermons show that Palamas is in agreement with Maximus in regarding the Eucharist as central.

Metropolitan John Zizioulas

THE IMPORTANCE OF SAINT GREGORY PALAMAS IN CONTEMPORARY ORTHODOX THEOLOGY

Saint Gregory Palamas – monk, theologian, apologist and bishop – was and remains very much today a key figure in the history of Orthodox spiritual and dogmatic theology. His name and writings have become synonymous with Orthodox identity and self-understanding. Indeed, one could argue successfully that the era of the marginalization of Palamas in Orthodox theology – a period which coincides with what Father Florovsky terms the Babylonian captivity of Orthodox theology – reveals a lack of vitality and clarity, a time when Orthodox theology was mimicking a style and form foreign to its very ethos. Conversely, the rediscovery of Palamas, along with that of many other Fathers of great significance to the Orthodox theological tradition, represents

108

a renewal of Orthodox theology itself, a reassertion of a particular spiritual identity, a realignment of its discourse with its very soul. This rediscovery could not but have had profound implications for Orthodox spiritual theology, since it permitted a tradition that is intrinsically empirical to finally express itself in a way consistent with its experience and life.

I do not intend here to trace in detail the development of Orthodox scholarship on Palamas. It is noteworthy, however, that most of the leading Orthodox theologians of the twentieth century were keenly interested in Palamas. Vladimir Lossky, in his now-classic work *The Mystical Theology of the Eastern Church*,[296] relies heavily on the work of Palamas and includes him among the most important Fathers. Nor was the prominence of Palamas among the Fathers lost on Father Georges Florovsky, whose article "St. Gregory Palamas and the Tradition of the Fathers"[297] reveals his sentiments in its very title. Father John Meyendorff began his career as a patristic scholar with a major work on Palamas.[298] Father Dumitru Staniloae established his reputation as a theologian in the same way.[299] The common thread of theological reasoning running through the works of all these authors is that Palamas is a Father of the Church in his own right, and that his teaching is consistent with that of the Fathers who came before him.

The convictions of many contemporary Orthodox theologians reflect the deeper intuitions that Orthodox Christians have held since the Saint was vindicated in a series of councils held during his own lifetime. These intuitions did not set the parameters for Orthodox theological discourse during the time of Orthodox theology's "Babylonian captivity," but they were present in the Orthodox spiritual and therefore theological tradition in other ways. First of all, not only were the teachings

---

[296] Vladimir Lossky, *The Mystical Theology of the Eastern Church*. Crestwood, NY: St. Vladimir's Seminary Press, 1976.

[297] Georges Florovsky, "St. Gregory Palamas and the Tradition of the Fathers." *Bible, Church, Tradition: An Eastern Orthodox View, The Collected Works, vol. 1*. Richard S. Haugh (ed.), Vaduz, Europa: Buchervertriebsanstalt, 1987, 105-120. Reprinted from *The Greek Orthodox Theological Review*, V-2 (Winter 1959-60).

[298] *Introduction à l'étude de Grégoire Palamas*, Paris: Éditions du Seuil, 1959.

[299] Viața și învățătura Sfîntului Grigore Palama : Cu patru tratate, seria Teologica 10, Sibiu, 1938.

of Saint Gregory Palamas accepted by councils convened in Constantinople in 1341, 1347 and 1351, they were upheld as normative expressions of Orthodox teaching. Secondly, Saint Gregory is commemorated on the Orthodox liturgical calendar on the second Sunday of Great Lent. This observance gives Palamas a particular prominence in the Lenten liturgical cycle. The position of his feast, however, is quite significant: it follows the Sunday on which the restoration of icons to the Church is proclaimed to the world. The proclamation is in the form of a *Synodikon*, read by the bishop or, in his absence, the priest, in which the teaching of the Orthodox Church on icons is expounded. The fact that Saint Gregory Palamas is commemorated on the following Sunday suggests that his teachings represent, in a sense, a continuation of the proclamation of the Orthodox Faith read on the previous one. The point here is that the liturgical practice of the Orthodox Church reveals Palamas as an accredited Father and authoritative defender of the Orthodox tradition, and not simply as a great ascetic.

Palamas is best known in the West as an apologist for hesychasm. That he played such a role is certainly undeniable; what the conciliar and liturgical traditions indicate, however, is that what he defended in hesychasm was part of the essence of the tradition. Palamas is thus not a defender of a *movement* within the Orthodox Church, but an apologist *par excellence* of its empirical theology. This is why no study of Orthodox spiritual theology would be complete without him. It certainly justifies his inclusion in this present study.

THE HOMILIES

An important question still remains: what in the corpus of the works of Palamas ought to be chosen as a focus for this study? Here I have made a decision to choose a primary source other than the well-known apologetical and dogmatic treatises the *Triads* and *The One Hundred and Fifty Chapters*. Instead, I have selected Saint Gregory's *Homilies*, which are virtually unknown in the West. In these, Palamas is concerned with the exposition of Scripture and the presentation of the most important aspects of Orthodox spiritual life. This choice of the *Homilies* as a primary text will allow me to concentrate more on Palamas as the spiritual master rather than Palamas as the apologist.

Palamas delivered many of the *Homilies* in his cathedral in

Thessaloniki in his capacity as Archbishop of the city. He is eminently practical in his approach to spiritual questions and very sensitive to the pastoral needs of his community. At the same time, he does not shy away from the most central themes in Orthodox theology and is a master in presenting profound doctrinal truths in uncomplicated language. Palamas was Archbishop of Thessaloniki between 1347 and his death in 1359, and the majority of the *Homilies* were written during that period. The number of *Homilies* that have survived stands at sixty-three. Only recently has a complete collection of the *Homilies* appeared as a critical edition in the Greek original, edited by the scholar and Palamas specialist Panagiotes K. Chrestou.[300] Until very recently, only several homilies were available to the English-speaking world, but this has changed with the appearance of an edition of the *Homilies* translated by Christopher Veniamin, which includes all sixty-three of the homilies.[301]

It is in his *Homilies* that Saint Gregory Palamas gives his most explicit teaching on Baptism and the Eucharist, and for this reason I have turned to them in this chapter, selecting several of the sixty-three Homilies available to us that are devoted entirely to our subject. I have no pretension of presenting a complete "sacramental theology" of Saint Gregory Palamas. To treat Saint Gregory's teachings on the sacraments as a separate department of his theological thought would be to do violence to him, since he has a highly integrated approach to theology in his *Homilies* and tends to weave together a number of themes. Instead, I have chosen the much more modest task of choosing some of the most salient points relating to Baptism and the Eucharist from several of the *Homilies*, principally Homilies Sixteen, Fifty-Six, Fifty-Nine and Sixty, and presenting them in a coherent order. I have also interrogated Saint Gregory's *Homilies* in order to highlight the overarching themes of his sacramental teachings. I have also included in this chapter several relevant insights from two contemporary Orthodox theologians committed to the study of Saint Gregory Palamas: Professor Georgios I. Mantzarides and Metropolitan Hierotheos of Nafpaktos.

[300] Gregoriou tou Palama: Apanta ta Erga. In the series *Ellenes Pateres tes Ekklysias*. P. K. Chrestou (ed.). (Thessaloniki: 1981).
[301] Saint Gregory Palamas, *The Homilies*, trans. Christopher Veniamin (Waymart, PA: Mount Thabor Publishing, 2009).

BAPTISM

In Homily Fifty-Nine, Saint Gregory Palamas sets his discussion of the sacrament of Baptism within the context of repentance.[302] This is hardly unusual, since Saint John the Baptist does exactly the same thing in the Gospel. Saint John refused baptism to those who sought it for the wrong reasons, and required them to produce the "fruits of repentance" first and then to return for baptism.[303] Saint Gregory is clearly following the scriptural tradition when he stresses the key role of repentance before, during, and after Baptism.[304] Of course, Baptism in the Church has a deeper meaning and power than the baptism of Saint John the Baptist, but the basic principles of preparation for its celebration have remained the same.

Continuing in the same Homily, Saint Gregory describes in detail the entire process of preparation for Baptism, beginning from what we might call the pre-catechumenate stage all the way through to the actual celebration of the sacraments of Baptism and Chrismation.[305] The Homily in which we find this presentation and explanation of the catechumenate was preached on the Forefeast of the Theophany.[306] It is well established that Theophany was a baptismal feast, not just in the more obvious sense of its being the commemoration of the Baptism of Christ, but also in that it was a time in the liturgical year when the Church received catechumens as full members of the Body of Christ through Baptism, Chrismation, and participation in the Eucharist. Without a doubt, Saint Gregory had all of this in mind when he wrote his homily, but was there perhaps another motive for his placing such a great emphasis on the catechumenate? I believe that the answer to this question lies in Saint Gregory's understanding of the catechumenate as a period of purification and a school of repentance and *askesis*.

---

[302] Saint Gregory Palamas, *The Homilies*. trans. Christopher Veniamin (Waymart, PA: Mount Thabor Publishing, 2009), 485.
[303] Mt. 3:7-10.
[304] Palamas, *The Homilies*. Homily Fifty-Nine, 485.
[305] Homily Fifty-Nine, 486-489.
[306] *Ibid.*, 485.

BAPTISM AS HEALING

Saint Gregory understood Baptism in terms of purification and restoration.[307] Ordinary water purifies the body only, whereas Baptism is given the potential to purify the entire human person, body and soul.[308] At the same time, Saint Gregory understood that those who had made no effort in *askesis* to struggle with their passions could not participate in the energies and grace of the Holy Spirit.[309] The grace of deification is not imposed on the will; the human person is free to co-operate with it or reject it. Since one of the effects of the energies of God at work in Baptism is purification, it stands to reason that a positive human response to it would manifest itself in ongoing repentance. In repentance, a person expresses his or her desire to turn from sin and be healed from it; it is at the same time a plea for purification and, in the case of a baptized Christian, an acknowledgement of God's purifying action and presence at work.

Saint Gregory Palamas understands Baptism in therapeutic terms. He calls Christ the Healer of Souls[310] and Baptism a cleansing remedy.[311] The illness from which we are cured in Baptism is corruption, and the goal of the treatment is divine regeneration, mystical renewal, and re-creation.[312] This therapeutic understanding of Baptism is clearly quite different from the notion of the sacrament as a washing away of the guilt of original sin. Saint Gregory does not preoccupy himself with the question of guilt, but with the problem of corruption. There is also no hint here of Baptism's being understood as a means of escaping God's wrath. God's anger, according to Saint Gregory, is kindled only against those who through rebellion or sloth refuse to repent.[313]

The therapeutic effects of Baptism are revealed in several other ways. Another therapeutic effect apart from purification is the healing

---

[307] *Ibid.*, 487-488.

[308] *Ibid.*, 488.

[309] St. Gregory Palamas. *The One Hundred and Fifty Chapters.* trans. Robert E. Sinkewicz (Toronto: Pontifical Institute of Mediaeval Studies, 1988), c. 93.

[310] Homily Fifty-Nine, 487.

[311] Homily Sixteen, 121.

[312] *Ibid.*, 122.

[313] Homily Fifty-Six, 462-463.

of the entire human person. When explaining the three immersions in Baptism, Saint Gregory relates them to the three days that the Lord's body lay in the tomb, noting, as Saint Paul teaches, that Baptism is an immersion into the death of Christ.[314] Saint Gregory, however, is equally interested in the three emersions. These embody the granting of the new life of the Resurrection on the third day. They are also, however, the liturgical indication of the return of the intellect, the soul, and the body to incorruptibility.[315] The therapeutic approach that Saint Gregory prescribes is what we would call, in contemporary terms, "holistic;" it does not exclude any dimension of the human person. The return of the intellect, soul, and body to incorruptibility is very closely related to their purification.

It should be stressed that the purification and healing of the intellect, soul, and body are not coterminous with the immersions and emersions in the baptismal liturgy. The implications of this therapeutic movement must be personally appropriated, claimed, and lived out over an entire lifetime. This is quite apparent in Saint Gregory's "Homily for Holy Saturday," in which he describes the spiritual potential of the baptized:

> Even if the heavy burden of mortal flesh still weighs them down so as to exercise, test and correct them, as so that they might forsake the wretchedness of this world, invisibly, however, they have put on Christ, so they can strive to share in His manner of life here and now, and afterwards, when they depart hence, to be partakers of His blessedness, radiance and incorruption.[316]

The above passage provides us with a way to understand Baptism that is clearly ascetical. The baptized have invisibly put on Christ. This clothing in Christ is the gracious gift of God. It is not a reward for completing the time of the catechumenate. The emphasis in the passage then shifts from God's gracious action to the response of the human person: "they can strive to share in His manner of life here and now, and afterwards, when

---

[314] Rom. 6:3.
[315] Homily Fifty-Nine, 488.
[316] Homily Sixteen, 122.

they depart hence, to be partakers of His blessedness, radiance and incorruption." Saint Gregory says "they can" because the choice of every baptized person to respond positively to the baptismal gift he or she has received cannot be taken for granted. The striving to which the Saint refers is the ascetic struggle in which we must engage courageously and energetically so that we reach the goal of incorruptibility.

Saint Gregory's teaching on Baptism allows us to describe the grace of Baptism as both "gift" and "potential." The failure to maintain both elements results in an imbalance that, with time, produces heterodox doctrinal positions. According to Metropolitan Hierotheos, Saint Gregory is a catholic Father of the Church precisely because he presents the whole teaching of the entire Church on dogmatic questions.[317] For this reason, it would be misleading, from the Orthodox point of view, to speak of a Palamite position on Baptism as separate from general patristic teaching. Saint Gregory is not a professional theologian seeking to develop a creative and novel approach to sacramental theology.

BAPTISM, CHRISMATION AND ESCHATOLOGY

In the Orthodox Church, Baptism and Chrismation are normally celebrated together, so some of what Saint Gregory writes about Baptism could apply to Chrismation. He does, however, make a point by referring to Chrismation specifically as "the seal of adoption as sons upon us through anointing with this holy chrism, sealing us by means of the all-holy Spirit for the day of redemption."[318] From this passage we see that to the therapeutic and ascetic aspects of Baptism must be added the dimensions of adoption and eschatology. By receiving the Holy Spirit at Chrismation, we are made sons and daughters of God. We receive "the seal of the gift of the Holy Spirit" that reorients our life toward "the day of redemption" – in other words to the Second Coming of the Lord, when we shall experience salvation in all of its fullness.

Chrismation, according to Saint Gregory's brief but essential description of it, provides an additional dimension to the purifying

[317] Metropolitan Hierotheos of Nafpaktos, *Orthodox Spirituality: A Brief Introduction*, trans. Effie Mavromichali (Levadia, Greece: Birth of the Theotokos Monastery, 1994), 68.

[318] Homily Fifty-Nine, 488.

and therapeutic grace of Baptism: a relationship. We are healed in Baptism in order to become sons and daughters of God. This baptismal therapy allows us to enter a relationship that we would otherwise not be able to enjoy. The sacramental interdependence between Baptism and Chrismation is beautifully described by Father Schmemann, who writes: "In Baptism we are born again of Water and the Spirit, and it is this birth which makes us open to the gift of the Holy Spirit, to our personal Pentecost."[319]

Saint Gregory is able to attribute to Baptism an eschatological orientation by explicating the sacrament of Chrismation and highlighting its close connection to Baptism. We are sealed for "the day of redemption," and yet that day is not an event relegated to the distant future. The Saint tells us that Baptism is "the gate leading those being baptized into heaven," and that indeed, through Christ in the baptismal celebration, "the heavens [open] for us, and they wait for us to enter with their gates flung wide."[320] Baptism and Chrismation in the writings of Saint Gregory have a unifying role with cosmic significance; in them, heaven and earth are united or, more precisely, earth gains access to heaven in the Church. The two sacraments become a kind of Jacob's ladder that provides the baptized Christian with an immediate experience of heaven. This experience is completed, however, with the participation in the Eucharist.

ASCETIC PREPARATION FOR THE EUCHARIST

In Homily Fifty-Six, Saint Gregory Palamas writes in detail about the Eucharist. In a way that runs parallel to his discussion of Baptism in Homily Fifty-Nine, the Saint begins his text by explaining the preparation required for receiving Holy Communion. Once again, he stresses the necessity of repentance, insisting that confession and repentance are both prerequisites for participation in the Eucharist.[321] A key role in the preparation for receiving the Eucharist is played by the spiritual father, who provides the spiritual care that is needed to

[319] Alexander Schmemann, *Of Water and the Spirit* (Crestwood, NY: St. Vladimir's, 1974), 116.
[320] Homily Sixty, 499.
[321] Homily Fifty-Six, 461.

cast out from the soul by the roots those thorns and thistles of sin that each one has nourished through a pleasure-loving life in the grip of passions.[322] Saint Gregory refers to "discerning the Body of Christ" in the Eucharist, a phrase that we recognize from the writings of Saint Paul.[323] He provides an interpretation for it, however, that we might not immediately draw from the original Pauline text but that is completely consistent with it: accepting that Christ's "sinless body will not consent to dwell in a body indulging in sins."[324] "Discerning the Body," for Saint Gregory, is therefore a way of becoming conscious of the need for purification and repentance. It points us directly to the ascetic life.

Saint Gregory refers to the bread of the Eucharist as "a veil concealing the Godhead within."[325] By this, he is certainly not suggesting that the bread is not transformed in the eucharistic celebration. On the contrary, he is exhorting his flock to have a faith that takes them beyond the mere appearances into the deeper spiritual reality of the Eucharist. The divine energies that are "veiled" by the bread are perhaps not immediately perceived by the physical eye, but they are nonetheless present in a powerful way, and we encounter them when we receive Communion, whether we are ready to meet them or not. Preparation for Communion, in the teaching of Saint Gregory, is quite simply preparation for an encounter with God. The implications for the faithful are clear: we must develop the spiritual faculties that make us competent both to perceive and to meet the veiled divinity. This, of course, points to the necessity of ascetic effort, but not to this alone: In referring to the priesthood and to the sacrament of Confession, Saint Gregory is showing us that the grace of God is of paramount importance in the preparation process.

THE EUCHARIST AS ENTRANCE INTO HEAVEN

Saint Gregory teaches that, in the celebration of the Divine Liturgy, "our citizenship is transferred to heaven – for that is where the [eucharistic]

322   *Ibid.*
323   I Cor. 11:29.
324   Homily Fifty-Six, 461.
325   *Ibid.*, 463.

bread is – and we enter into the true Holy of Holies through the offering of the body of Christ in purity."[326] In the celebration of Baptism, the heavens are opened to us. Through the Eucharist, the Church ascends to heaven. Baptism is the gate of heaven, but the Eucharist is the entrance into heaven. Here again we return to the sacramental interdependence we saw earlier: Baptism prepares us to receive the Holy Spirit, and the reception of the Holy Spirit prepares us for the celebration of the Divine Liturgy.[327]

Saint Gregory teaches us that the bread of the Eucharist is to be found in heaven. The Christian must be part of the great liturgical movement of ascension that takes place in every celebration of the Divine Liturgy. If we exclude ourselves from the eucharistic *synaxis,* we cannot expect to encounter the eucharistic Christ. This is why Saint Gregory, in his short treatise on the Ten Commandments called *The Decalogue of the Law According to Christ*, exhorts his flock to be at the *synaxis* every Sunday and to receive Holy Communion frequently.[328] The ecclesial orientation of Saint Gregory's teaching is quite pronounced, and any thought of a full relationship with Christ outside of the Church is absolutely precluded.

THE EUCHARIST AS UNION

In Homily Fifty-Six, we read that, through the Eucharist, we become "one body and one spirit with Christ."[329] Saint Gregory is saying that the Eucharist is the most powerful form of union we will ever experience. Among human persons, Saint Gregory considers the most powerful form of union to be marriage, in which the spouses become one flesh with each other. In the Eucharist, the Christian becomes one body *and* one spirit with Christ – "one with Him not just in spirit but in body, flesh of His flesh and bone of His bone."[330] The eucharistic union in

---

[326]   *Ibid.*
[327]   Schmemann, *Of Water,* 116.
[328]   St. Gregory Palamas, "The Decalogue of the Law According to Christ, That Is, The New Covenant." trans. Soterios Mouselimas. *The Greek Orthodox Theological Review*, XXV-3 (1980), 301.
[329]   Homily Fifty-Six, 464.
[330]   *Ibid.*

this sense surpasses the most powerful form of union in daily human experience. In the Saint's presentation of Baptism, we see that the whole person – intellect, soul and body – is healed through the celebration of the sacrament. Analogously, the Christian is completely united to Christ in the Eucharist. The joining of only the body or the spirit to Christ would be insufficient, since it would not represent the healing of the entire human person. Of course, union in this case does not suggest a kind of absorption that leads to extinction. According to Saint Gregory's teaching, we will never participate in God's essence.[331] He teaches instead that there is no dimension of the human person that remains unaffected by the therapeutic, eucharistic union with Christ. Part of our ascetic endeavour, therefore, is to open up more and more aspects of our person to Christ for healing.

CHRIST AS BROTHER, FATHER AND MOTHER

Saint Gregory takes three examples of intimate relationships from the human experience of the family to describe how we are joined to Christ through the sacraments. These three illustrations are only approximations, of course, but they are nevertheless adequate for the presentation of three different modes of relationship that the Christian enjoys with Christ. In the first instance, Christ is our brother by joining Himself to our flesh and blood. In the second, He is our Father through Baptism. In the third, He feeds us like a mother with His Blood, Body, and the Holy Spirit.[332] As our Father, Christ has given us new life in Baptism. Like our mother, He is continually nourishing us with His Body and Blood in the Eucharist, and with the Holy Spirit. In joining us to Himself and uniting us to His deified humanity, He has made us one with Him and, in this, He has become our brother.

Saint Gregory stresses that participation in the Eucharist is a means of deification. By partaking in the Eucharist, we become not only in God's image, but gods ourselves.[333] This is a very important point because it illustrates the radical nature of deification. The restoration of God's image, the image we received in Creation, is definitely part of the therapy that

[331] Palamas, *The One Hundred and Fifty Chapters*, c. 78.
[332] Homily Fifty-Six, 464.
[333] *Ibid.*, 465.

we experience in the Church. It is, however, insufficient. We are called to go beyond what the first Adam once had. Saint Gregory states this forcefully because of his strong belief in the deifying encounter that the Church experiences with the Lord in the Eucharist. We have already seen that Christ feeds us like a mother through Holy Communion. The image is particularly graphic because Saint Gregory adds to it the expression "with His own breasts."[334] Christ imparts to us not something "other" to Him, not something created by Him outside of Himself, but instead, His own life. A mother does not mix or create the milk from her own breast. It comes rather from her own organism, and it is therefore "alive." Of course the feeding engenders growth, and the growth must be oriented towards a particular goal: deification. It is not difficult to see, then, why Saint Gregory would not content himself with the restoration and purification of the image as the only effect of the encounter with Christ in the sacraments: it would be an inadequate way of characterizing the eucharistic life. It would represent a kind of defeat for the Church and a minimizing of its therapeutic life, since it is precisely in the Church that a Christian experiences not only the renewal of the image of God but also the emergence of the fullness of God's likeness.

As we are nourished by Christ in the Eucharist with His own life, we learn to commune in His virtues and His suffering.[335] This brings us back to the link that Saint Gregory forges between the two sacraments of Baptism and Eucharist, and the ascetic life. Partaking in the life of Christ must mean taking on His character. It is clear from the context in Homily Fifty-Six that the Saint has more in mind than simple imitation. In fact, he does not use the word "imitate," but says rather that we should "pay heed to ourselves and be very much on our guard, that we might stay aloof from the passions and proclaim the virtues of Him who has graciously deigned to dwell in us on account of the likeness to Him in virtues which has come to light within us."[336] He says, "pay heed" because he is aware that this is a process. He says that the virtues "dwell in us" because this is far more meaningful than "imitate." To imitate is in some fashion to reproduce. Saint Gregory does not exhort us simply to

[334]   *Ibid.,* 464
[335]   *Ibid.,* 466.
[336]   *Ibid.*

reproduce the virtues of Christ, but to commune in them, which means to let them become our life. His emphasis on growth in the ascetic life after receiving Communion is as strong as his stress on a proper preparation before receiving Communion.[337]

TWO TWENTIETH-CENTURY COMMENTATORS

Several twentieth-century Orthodox theologians have examined the works of Saint Gregory Palamas and have contributed to a revival of hesychastic theology. Not all of them, however, have taken an interest in the "sacramental theology" of Saint Gregory. Among those who have, I have chosen two contemporary Greek Orthodox theologians as sources of further commentary on the Saint's teachings: Professor Georgios I. Mantzaridis and Metropolitan Hierotheos Vlachos.

1) Professor Georgios Mantzaridis

Professor Mantzaridis analyzes the relationship between Baptism and Eucharist in Saint Gregory's writings. He remarks that, in the teachings of the Father, the "image" is purified in Baptism, whereas in the Eucharist, an advance is made towards the "likeness."[338] Baptism thus appears as a pledge or a betrothal given in promise of a fuller spiritual reality.[339]

Looking at the eucharistic union with Christ in Saint Gregory's teaching, Mantzarides comments that the latter is more than a moral union, but not a communion in the divine nature.[340] As I noted earlier, it is more than imitation, but does not entail a loss of identity. Mantzarides contrasts the eucharistic theology of Akindynos with the sacramental teaching of Saint Gregory. Akindynos believes that, in the Eucharist, we participate in Christ's created body and uncreated nature. Saint Gregory Palamas teaches that the Eucharist is a communion in the deified human nature of Christ.[341] As we can see from

---

[337] Ibid., 465.
[338] Georgios I. Mantzarides, *The Deification of Man.* trans. Liadain Sherrard (Crestwood, NY: St. Vladimir's, 1984), 51.
[339] Ibid., 48.
[340] Ibid., 53.
[341] Ibid., 54.

Mantzarides's analysis, Saint Gregory defends the Orthodox position, which on one hand entailed a rejection of pantheism but included an affirmation of deification. Here we find an Orthodox *apologia* to those who misinterpret deification and present it as the doorway to polytheism or pantheism. We can never become God because we can never participate in His nature. On the other hand, we have here a defence of the therapeutic tradition of Orthodoxy, in which the deepest pathologies of human nature are brought to the fore, diagnosed, and treated. In this therapeutic treatment, ailing humanity is cured by participating in Christ's deifying human nature.

2) Metropolitan Hierotheos Vlachos

Metropolitan Hierotheos of Nafpaktos stresses the connection in Saint Gregory's writings between Baptism and obedience. He understands obedience to be a basic form of asceticism.[342] He also avers that the combination of sacraments and asceticism, held in balance, represents the catholic doctrinal position of Orthodoxy.[343] Saint Gregory, according to the Metropolitan, rejected two contemporary heresies: Messalianism and Barlaamism.[344] Messalians embraced asceticism and devalued the sacraments; Barlaam and his sympathizers recognized the importance of the sacraments, but rejected the hesychastic ascetic tradition.

Metropolitan Hierotheos has singled out the major identifying characteristic of Saint Gregory Palamas's teaching on Baptism and Eucharist: a perfect balance between the sacramental/ecclesial dimension and the ascetic dimension.[345] What is remarkable in Saint Gregory's *Homilies* is his continual movement between these two dimensions with the goal of maintaining the balance between them. Indeed, the second the reader of the *Homilies* begins to think that the ascetic side is receiving too much attention, the saintly author instinctively turns to the sacramental/ecclesial side, and *vice versa*. So careful is Saint Gregory to preserve the equilibrium between asceticism

[342] Hierotheos, *Orthodox Spirituality*, 67-68.
[343] *Ibid.*, 69.
[344] *Ibid.*, 68-69.
[345] *Ibid.*, 69-71.

and the sacraments that we might say he speaks of one single reality, sacramental asceticism, which he sees quite simply as the Orthodox Christian spiritual life.

A second observation that must be made about Saint Gregory's teaching is that the sacramental asceticism he describes has a therapeutic character. The goal of the sacramental and ascetic life is healing from corruption, sin, and the passions. Metropolitan Hierotheos describes this in plain language when he says, "Man is cured by the sacramental and ascetic life."[346] That Saint Gregory locates healing from corruption in the Eucharist is clear from the following exhortation: "Let us mingle our blood with God's, in order to remove the corruption from our own, for in this blood there is great benefit past telling."[347] The therapeutic character here is rather obvious, but so is the Saint's enduring commitment to the Eucharist as a source of the spiritual life. Thus it is entirely appropriate, in my view, to present Saint Gregory Palamas as a defender of the unity of the spiritual life in both its eucharistic and ascetic dimensions.

---

[346] Metropolitan Hierotheos of Nafpaktos, *St. Gregory Palamas as a Hagiorite*. trans. Esther Williams (Levadia, Greece: Birth of the Theotokos Monastery, 1997), 372.
[347] Homily Fifty-Six, 465.

CHAPTER SEVEN
THE WITNESS OF THREE IMPORTANT AND INTER-RELATED FATHERS

Returning, now, to the beginning of this book and the contention of Zizioulas that Saint Maximos[348] is responsible for the synthesis of

---

[348] Among Saint Maximos the Confessor, Saint Symeon the New Theologian, and Saint Gregory Palamas, it is Saint Maximos who has been receiving the most attention from Orthodox dogmatic theologians of late. Metropolitan John Zizioulas used an academic symposium dedicated to Saint Maximos as the occasion to present a restatement of his own theological position using Maximos's teaching on the will as a point of departure: Metropolitan John (Zizioulas) of Pergamon, "Person and Nature in the Theology of St. Maximus the Confessor." *Knowing the Purpose of Creation through the Resurrection: Proceedings of the Symposium on St. Maximus the Confessor*, Bishop Maxim (Vasiljevic), ed. Alhambra, CA: Sebastian Press, 2013, 85-113. Zizioulas was also using the opportunity to answer several of his critics, among them Jean-Claude Larchet and Father Nikolaos (Nicholas) Loudovikos. Loudovikos has responded to Zizioulas' comments from the symposium in an article in which he also makes use of texts of Saint Maximos to critique Zizioulas' interpretation of person and will in the writings of the same Father: Fr. Nicholas Loudovikos, "Possession or Wholeness? St. Maximus the Confessor and John Zizioulas on Person, Nature and Will." *Participatio*, 4 (2013), 267-295. Larchet responded to Zizioulas with an article demonstrating that *hypostasis, prosopon* and *atomon* are all used more or less interchangeably in Maximos's writings : Jean-Claude Larchet, "Hypostasis, person and individual according to St. Maximus the Confessor, with reference to the Cappadocians and St. John of Damascus." *Personhood in the Byzantine Christian Tradition : Early, Medieval and Modern Perspectives*, Alexis Torrance and Symeon Paschalidis, eds. London and New York: Routledge, 2018, 47-67. In an article published prior to Larchet's chapter in *Personhood*, Julija Vidovic comes to the conclusion that the difference between Zizioulas' and Larchet's positions is not profound. She suggests

the eucharistic and monastic streams in Christian spirituality, I would like to make a few remarks based on the content of Chapter Four, which is on the *Mystagogy*. First of all, there does appear to be a synthesis of the eucharistic and ascetic or monastic aspects of Christian spirituality in this great commentary on the Divine Liturgy. Saint Maximos does indeed position asceticism in a eucharistic context. It is also probable that the saintly author is addressing, as part of his audience, certain monks who may have been undervaluing the place of the Liturgy in the monastic life. From here it is possible to formulate the hypothesis, as Zizioulas does, that the Maximian synthesis represents a watershed in the history of Christian spirituality. Zizioulas, however, does not supply us with the historical proof that this is actually the case, which in any case would be a monumental task. Furthermore, it would be reading too much into the text of the *Mystagogy* itself to draw such a conclusion. From the historical point of view, one would have to demonstrate that Saint Maximos is doing something new in the *Mystagogy* when he keeps the eucharistic and ascetic dimensions in close relationship to each other. Loudovikos posits, as I noted in Chapter Three, that Saint Dionysios the Areopagite forged a synthesis of the eucharistic and therapeutic dimensions prior to Maximos in an ecclesiology that combined the institutional and the spiritual.[349] If this is true, Saint Maximos may well have received the synthesis from Saint Dionysios. In any case, we do not have an exhaustive historical study from Zizioulas that examines this particular question. It would not be too much to say, however, as I did in Chapter Four, that the particular synthesis of older sources and the selection and development of the particular theological themes that we find in the *Mystagogy* are unique to Saint Maximos.

It is important to note, I think, that the ascetic dimension that Saint Maximos develops in the *Mystagogy* has retained its original character. What Saint Maximos does is to place it in relationship to the Church, the

that the former works from the *Logos* towards the *logoi* in his thought, while the latter works from the *logoi* towards the *Logos* : Julija Vidovic, "L'anthropologie de saint Maxime le Confesseur revisitée : le débat nature-personne entre Mgr Jean Zizioulas et Jean-Claude Larchet." *Contacts*, 258 (2017), 153-177. It remains to be seen if Larchet would be willing to accept Vidovic's position.

349 See Chapter 1, n. 161 and 162.

Divine Liturgy, and eschatology. He still uses the language of the ascetic tradition. He refers to the body, soul, and mind in the human person. He speaks about the development of inner prayer. Asceticism in his thought is still linked to purification. Ascetic activity or *praktikē* is still, for him, the beginning of the spiritual life. All these things permeate his commentary on the Divine Liturgy and, although this particular work was not integrated into the *Philokalia*, many of Maximos's other works were. In fact, there is more material from Maximos in the *Philokalia* than from any other Father. The reason for this is that the compilers of the *Philokalia* almost certainly did not sense any dissonance between Saint Maximos and, for example, Saint Gregory of Sinai or Saint Gregory Palamas. One can take the position, as Zizioulas does, that Saint Maximos has endowed asceticism with a special character by placing the emphasis on the struggle against *philautia*,[350] but this does not mean that ascetic practice in Maximos is not still focused, at least in part, on purification, inner struggle, attainment of the vision of God, and so on. Metropolitan John might well have concurred with this himself, but I believe that he could have strengthened his own position by stating the following in unambiguous terms: It is not possible to reduce asceticism in Saint Maximos to the struggle against individualism alone. To do so would make Saint Maximos serve the interests of theological personalism, which would be both inaccurate and anachronistic. It would also remove Maximos from the broader ascetic tradition in Orthodox spirituality, of which he remains an integral part and an exemplary representative. I understand that Zizioulas wishes to distinguish Saint Maximos[351] from Evagrios and Origen – such a distinction can indeed be defended and is accepted by many Orthodox theologians – but this distinction does not allow us to christen Maximos the patron of the struggle against individualism and, by extension, the champion of the theology of communion and otherness, as it is being articulated by the venerable Metropolitan.

In summary, I believe that it is entirely legitimate to locate in the *Mystagogy* a strong and enduring relationship between the ascetic dimension and the Eucharist. It also seems reasonable to call that

[350] Zizioulas, *Communion and Otherness*, 84.
[351] Zizioulas, *Communion and Otherness*, 22. See also *Lectures*, 122-124.

relationship a synthesis, even if it would be difficult to prove historically that Saint Maximos was creating a synthesis both consciously and intentionally. It is also clear that Saint Maximos has invested that synthesis with a creative and dynamic connection with ecclesiology, anthropology, and eschatology. There is no doubt that what he has achieved is particular to him, not in the sense of his having created something novel without theological precedent, but by his having combined what was already in the existing tradition in a creative and compelling way. Given Maximos's prominence as a Father and a Confessor and not simply as a spiritual master, it seems reasonable to accept that the *Mystagogy* had a substantial impact on subsequent Fathers. Whether this is because Saint Maximos appeared at a time of crisis in the history of Christian spirituality and effectively steered it toward the full integration of the ascetic and eucharistic dimensions, or whether such an assumption was already present in much of Christian thought and he was simply reiterating it in a powerful way, the question remains the topic of further historical research. Clearly, the notion of the relationship between the ascetic and the eucharistic dimensions that appears in the *Mystagogy* remains a guiding principle in the *Ethical Discourses* of Saint Symeon the New Theologian and the *Homilies* of Saint Gregory Palamas. Thus, whether or not the *Mystagogy* was a defining moment in the history of Christian spirituality, the legacy of Maximos, or at a minimum his essential theological assumptions on this matter, appear to have remained.

Metropolitan John Zizioulas has called for a study of Saint Symeon the New Theologian and Saint Gregory Palamas with a view to establishing their clear eucharistic orientation.[352] I believe that the Metropolitan can rest assured that his basic intuition is correct. Beginning with Saint Symeon, we can see that he distinguishes himself in the *Ethical Discourses* as a true theologian of the eucharistic life. Recovering from Scripture the theme of marriage between Christ and the Church, Symeon develops a very potent ecclesiology based on the Eucharist. Christians become flesh of Christ's flesh and bone of His bones. There is no separation between Christ and His Body. Although

---

[352]   Zizioulas, *Lectures*, 124.

the Saint does not develop this concept to the extent that Zizioulas does in his ecclesiology (Zizioulas would go so far as to state that there is no Christ without His Body), there is little doubt that, for Symeon, the connection between the two is both permanent and far-reaching.

Saint Symeon grounds his eucharistic teaching in the Incarnation and gives it a very clear eschatological character. In this sense, he is a true disciple of Saint Maximos. What is also evident in the *Ethical Discourses* is the extent to which the Father ties the Eucharist to deification. Indeed, the Eucharist really becomes in his writings both the means and the assurance of deification. Deification emerges in the text as the *telos*, or final goal, and the Eucharist serves as both its promise and revelation. Participation in the Eucharist is, for Symeon, not surprisingly, a *sine qua non* of the spiritual life. The important question, however, is: What kind of participation is required?

Here the ascetic dimension takes on prominence in Symeon's work. The Eucharist is not, according to Symeon, apprehended through the senses. One has to move from sensory perception to intellection. Of course, Saint Symeon has the illumination of the *nous*, or intellect, in mind here, and this connects us with the ascetic tradition again. Since the Eucharist is, as we saw in Chapter Five, a way to receive the Holy Spirit, it becomes apparent that asceticism and the Eucharist have the same goal. But, as Saint Symeon states, "It is the Spirit Who really purifies us and makes us partake worthily of the body of the Lord."[353] Thus, while the Spirit is received in the Eucharist, it is the same Spirit Who makes us ready to receive the Eucharist worthily. The Spirit Who is received through ascetic discipline and acquisition of the virtues makes us ready for the reception of the Spirit in the Eucharist.

This is an important moment in Symeon's work: it shows that there is a Pneumatological and therefore Trinitarian basis to his spirituality. In the spiritual life, it is the Spirit Who initiates, it is the Spirit Who completes. The ascetic and eucharistic dimensions are inextricably linked together by Pneumatic activity. This connection would indicate that, from Saint Symeon's point of view, the whole discussion of the ascetic and eucharistic aspects of the spiritual life really points to one reality:

[353] Third Ethical Discourse, 134.

the reception of the Spirit. Therefore, the question of the synthesis of the two aspects, while important, does not exhaustively describe the spiritual life. It is an entry-level discussion that must necessarily lead to another level, and that is the level of Pneumatology. The ascetic and eucharistic dimensions held in balance, it would seem, guard the Pneumatological core. Disturbing the balance between the two dimensions makes it more difficult to reach the desired end of acquiring the Holy Spirit. This is the real reason why the synthesis of the ascetic and eucharistic dimensions is important. It would be a tragic exercise in missing the point, however, to make the synthesis itself the sole object of theological enquiry.

Turning now to Saint Gregory Palamas, we see that he, like Saint Symeon, places great emphasis on the Eucharist as a means of deification. The Eucharist and Baptism are both interpreted in therapeutic terms. Baptism is the way in which corruption within humanity is cured and the image of God is restored. The Eucharist is the way in which the Christian is brought to full perfection by becoming one body and one spirit with Christ. Baptism requires a thorough preparation through repentance and the catechumenate. The Eucharist also requires its own preparation through confession of sins and repentance. In the Eucharist, we are not only united to Christ, we are divinized. Saint Gregory puts it in a very powerful way when he writes that, in the Eucharist, we become not only God's image, but gods ourselves.[354]

If deification is the goal of participation in the Eucharist, it also is the goal of asceticism. In the writings of Palamas, we see a correspondence between the vision of God, or *theoria*, and deification. They are two different expressions of the same reality. Saint Gregory gives asceticism a strong eschatological orientation precisely by making *theoria* its objective. The latter can be understood as the experience of "the coming of the Kingdom in power." The three Apostles Saints Peter, James, and John entered into this experience at the Transfiguration. Saint Gregory links asceticism and the sacraments, not only by making deification and *theoria* their common objectives, but also by associating the communion in the Body and Blood of Christ with a communion in His virtues and sufferings. It is understood that one of the purposes of asceticism is

---

[354] Homily Fifty-Six, 465.

the acquisition of the virtues. For Palamas, however, the acquisition is a direct participation in the virtues. What we have is therefore not an imitation, but a reception of the very life of Christ. It is through His life that we become gods, not in some vague pseudo-mystical sense, but as gods *in Christ*.

Saint Gregory states that we need *to learn* to commune in Christ's virtues, and this learning is suggestive of a process. It is here that we can see the progressive character of asceticism. There is a discipline to learning, and that discipline represents a kind of school of asceticism for Palamas. The fact that asceticism leads to the Eucharist is undeniable. The tight relationship between the two can be described as a sacramental asceticism.

Metropolitan John Zizioulas states:

> Saint Gregory Palamas has been commonly portrayed as representative of the ecclesiology in which the divine Eucharist is less important than individual spirituality. Nevertheless, I believe that, taken together, his treatises, doctrinal essays and sermons show that Palamas is in agreement with Maximus in regarding the Eucharist as central. We are still waiting for studies that will show us where the other significant representatives of the Patristic tradition, in particular Saint Simeon the New Theologian, stand on this issue.[355]

There would appear to be no doubt that Saint Gregory regards the Eucharist as central. If the Eucharist deifies, it is central to the Christian life. What we see in the *Homilies*, however, is that the deifying Eucharist requires an ascetic preparation. The inherent difficulty in Zizioulas' position appears to be his assumption that eucharistic spirituality and individual spirituality are *necessarily* in conflict with each other. The two expressions appear to be so tightly woven together in the thought of Palamas that the idea of identifying them as two competing dimensions of spirituality simply does not enter his mind. Perhaps this is because Saint Gregory both received and integrated the Maximian synthesis into

---

[355] Zizioulas, *Lectures*, 124.

his own theological work. Perhaps he simply adopted this approach of integration from the prevailing spiritual tradition, since it is clear that Saint Symeon works from the same premise. In any case, separating the two dimensions in Saint Gregory and declaring either one of them central, to the exclusion of the other, seems to be untenable. The Eucharist is central *and* it requires an ascetic context.

This does not in any way diminish the majesty and centrality of the Eucharist; it rather speaks to the need for the Eucharist to be received on a personal level. Whether this would have been problematic for the Metropolitan is not entirely clear. We are left to infer that it might have been. The fact of the matter is that Palamas relates to both expressions of spirituality with great ease. He does not seem vexed by the possibility that asceticism practised on a personal level will necessarily cause a reindividualization of a Christian – a kind of reversion to pre-baptismal categories. The question of the transformation of an individual, or biological *hypostasis*, into a person in communion is not a preoccupation for him. It is not that we cannot interrogate his texts for clues as to how he might relate to such a question; it is more a question of determining the patristic author's own concerns first and foremost.

In the *Homilies*, one of the Archbishop's overriding concerns would appear to be how to open the Christian spiritual life in all its dimensions to every member of his flock. The appeal to every Christian to fast and pray and the impressive *apologia* that Saint Gregory formulates both testify to his desire to initiate his flock into the ascetic life. It is impossible to say that he meant to do this on the corporate level alone. For Palamas, private prayer and liturgical prayer are inseparable. He is very clear in his position that corporate, liturgical prayer without personal prayer is insufficient for the spiritual life: "If someone only wants to pray when he attends God's Church, and has no concern at all for prayer at home, in the streets or in the fields, then even when he is present in church, he is not really praying."[356] In fact, Saint Gregory is stating not only that liturgical and personal prayer are inseparable, but also that the absence of the latter causes the former to be completely ineffective. It is this relationship between personal and liturgical prayer that is not treated

[356] Homily VII.

in Zizioulas' main works. The approach of the Metropolitan restricts the Church to the Eucharist, and this assumption is problematic, as Father Calinic Berger points out. Berger indicates that Father Dumitru Staniloae had a much wider view of the Church and was able to include within his ecclesiology in essence the prayers, the work, and the ascetic life of all Christians. Father Calinic has correctly observed that this is an ecclesiological question, and what we are left to infer from the *Homilies* and the work of Metropolitan John is that the latter does not share all the ecclesiological assumptions undergirding the former.

SECTION C:
TWO REPRESENTATIVE CONTEMPORARY ORTHODOX THEOLOGIANS

CHAPTER EIGHT

FATHER ALEXANDER SCHMEMANN ON THE SPIRITUAL LIFE

INTRODUCTION

Father Schmemann was a prominent Orthodox theologian of the late twentieth century. He embraced eucharistic ecclesiology early in his academic career, likely under the influence of his professor at the Saint Sergius Orthodox Theological Institute, Father Nicholas Afanasiev. Zizioulas places Schmemann beside Afanasiev when he critiques the early representatives of eucharistic ecclesiology in his first work, *Eucharist, Bishop, Church*.[357] Schmemann continued his academic career to become a prominent liturgical theologian with a strong interest in history, ecclesiology, and spirituality. Petros Vassiliadis, in his article on therapeutic and eucharistic spiritualities, relies on Schmemann's first major work, *Introduction to Liturgical Theology*, as an important source for the history of liturgy and more specifically for an analysis of the development of the Divine Liturgy.[358] Schmemann posits in his work that the liturgical understanding of the early Church was altered, first by mysteriological piety and then by monastic worship.[359] Schmemann describes this process as a double synthesis involving three initially

[357] John D. Zizioulas, *Eucharist, Bishop, Church*, trans. Elizabeth Theokritoff (Brookline, MA: Holy Cross Orthodox Press, 2001), 17.
[358] Petros Vassiliadis, "Eucharistic and Therapeutic Spirituality," n. 49.
[359] Alexander Schmemann, *Introduction to Liturgical Theology* (Leighton Buzzard, Beds.: The Faith Press, 1975), 86-113.

distinct layers,[360] although his description suggests a kind of absorption or even displacement of the primary layer.[361] The primary layer in this case is one in which the Eucharist defines the ecclesiology and liturgical consciousness of the early Christian community. Schmemann's dramatic description of the evolution of Orthodox liturgical worship and piety leads, nevertheless, to a very conservative conclusion.[362] It would seem, however, that the description itself, along with its logical implications, captured the theological imagination of Vassiliadis to a greater extent. Schmemann's work is significant in that he treats explicitly of the monastic and eucharistic expressions of liturgical piety and begins to address the question of their interrelationship. In this chapter, however, I will not be making extensive use of *Introduction to Liturgical Theology* as a primary source, but will be relying instead on his books *Of Water and the Spirit*, *The Eucharist*, and *Great Lent*. These are richer sources for spiritual theology.

RESERVATIONS: WHAT SPIRITUALITY IS NOT

In contemporary culture, the meaning of the word "spirituality" is so elastic as to include virtually anything connected to religion, philosophy, or the "metaphysical." There is little doubt that Father Alexander Schmemann considered many of the attitudes, objectives and phenomena emerging from this broad category to be misleading and even harmful. It comes as no surprise to discover that he viewed the whole area of spirituality with great scepticism. For this reason, the word "spirituality" frequently appears in quotation marks in Father Schmemann's writings. Thus, before examining Father Schmemann's understanding of what spirituality *is*, it seems appropriate to present his convictions regarding what it *is not*.

Father Schmemann was a keen observer of the culture of his day. He was very much aware of the rising interest in "spirituality" in the society that surrounded him:

> There is taking place today a significant revival of interest in, and of a search for, "spirituality" – this word covering an

360   *Ibid.*, 116-117.
361   *Ibid.*, 86-101.
362   Schmemann, Introduction to Liturgical Theology, 162-167.

incredible and precisely spiritual confusion which, in turn, generates a great variety of dubious spiritual "teachings" and "recipes." We have a world affirming spirituality ("celebration of life") and a world denying spirituality ("the end of the world"), the ecstatic "Jesus movement" and the ecstatic "charismatic movement," the multiplication of "elders" and "gurus" of all kinds, "transcendental meditation," the "gift of tongues," "Oriental mysticism," rediscovery of the Devil and "witchcraft," obsession with "exorcisms," etc.[363]

Father Schmemann knew that the plethora of spiritual options available to the contemporary person could only engender confusion. How could a person examining this eclectic list of often contradictory and sometimes even mutually exclusive "spiritualities" determine what is true? This is the *first* problem that Father Alexander identifies in his writings with the very word and modern phenomenon of "spirituality."

A *second* major problem that Schmemann associates with "spirituality" in our time is its emergence in our society as a thing in itself somehow disconnected from Christian life and faith as a whole:

> And the main danger, the main deficiency of this whole phenomenon is that too many people today – including the seemingly most traditional "dispatchers" of spirituality – seem to view "spirituality" as a kind of entity in itself, almost disconnected from the entire Christian view and experience of God, world and men, from the totality of Christian faith.[364]

Worse yet, but not surprisingly, "spirituality" is making the transition from an entity in itself to a religion in itself. This is especially true, Schmemann notes, in spiritual approaches that involve a denial of the world and a retreat towards individualism.[365]

---

[363] Alexander Schmemann, *Of Water and the Spirit* (Crestwood, NY: St. Vladimir's Seminary Press, 1974), 72.
[364] *Ibid.,* 73.
[365] Alexander Schmemann, "Liturgy and Eschatology" in *Liturgy and Tradition,* Thomas Fisch (ed.) (Crestwood, NY: St. Vladimir's Seminary Press, 1990), 93.

A *third* major problem that Father Schmemann identifies with the current expression of "spirituality" is that it has been emptied of its Christological content. This permits the reduction of Christian spirituality to the level of non-Christian spiritual disciplines. Symptomatic of this problem is the transformation of the Jesus prayer into the "Jesusprayer."[366] The Jesus prayer in this instance ceases to be a means of communion with Christ and becomes instead a simple mantra. Schmemann's concern in this area is shared by Saint Sophrony (Sakharov), who touches on this problem in his classic work on prayer *His Life is Mine.*[367] For Father Alexander and Saint Sophrony, the idea of a "spirituality" that excludes Christ is nonsensical. The fact that the word "spirituality" is frequently used in this context in contemporary culture demonstrates the need for the Church to recover and reclaim its own terminology and to restore to it its original content and meaning. This is clearly one of Schmemann's primary objectives in his works, not only with regard to the term "spirituality," but also concerning many other terms that have lost the significance they had in the early Church.

SPIRITUALITIES OF CAPITULATION OR RETREAT

Father Schmemann believes that we are living in a post-Christian era. Characteristic of this era is the tendency among Christians to gravitate to one of two types of spirituality: a *spirituality of capitulation* or a *spirituality of retreat.* The reference point for these two types of spirituality is the world, and the two types of worldviews emerging from them reflect either an uncritical acceptance of the world's spiritual agenda or a radical rejection of the world itself.[368] Contemporary "spiritualities" tend to be cast in one of these two moulds. This, according to Schmemann, presents yet another problem with "spirituality" as we encounter it,

---

[366] *Ibid.*, 93.

[367] Archimandrite Sophrony, *His Life is Mine*, trans. Rosemary Edmonds (Crestwood, NY: St. Vladimir's Seminary Press, 1977), 115. St. Sophrony is particularly uncomfortable with the equation of the Orthodox practice of the Jesus prayer with yoga and transcendental meditation.

[368] Schmemann, "Liturgy and Eschatology," 93-95.
Schmemann, *Of Water*, 86-87, 91.

since the two worldviews offered to us are essentially false. He proposes a "third way" to approach the world that both affirms it and goes beyond it.[369] This frees the word "spirituality" from its usual attachment to two fundamentally unchristian approaches.

WHAT SPIRITUALITY IS

Having discussed his reservations with regard to the term "spirituality," we can now proceed to what Schmemann feels spirituality *is*. For the sake of convenience, I have divided this section on spirituality into three parts: a) baptismal/chrismal, b) personal/ecclesial, and c) eucharistic/ eschatological. These parts in no way represent separate categories; on the contrary, there is very substantial overlap between the three.

1) Baptismal/Chrismal

Schmemann states that "Christian life and spirituality have their source in baptismal regeneration" and that "spirituality is above all the fulfillment by men of the gift received in Baptism ...."[370] Spiritual life is therefore essentially baptismal life. Baptism is not simply the beginning of spiritual life, but the source that both energizes it and nourishes it.

A Positive View of Creation

Baptismal spirituality implies a positive approach both to the world and to humanity. It is to be distinguished from a prevalent negative "spirituality" that is identified by its "negation, apocalypticism, fear and a truly Manichean 'disgust' for the world."[371] While affirming the essential goodness of the world, baptismal spirituality does not suggest naïveté. This is not the radical "yes" of what Father Schmemann terms "activism." The "yes" of baptismal spirituality is an affirmation of creation's original goodness and a conviction of its glorious vocation in Christ, with an accompanying deep awareness of its need for redemption. This theological conviction is contained and communicated by the liturgy of Baptism, in which water is consecrated and exorcised. The fact that water is brought for the celebration of the sacrament

---

369   Schmemann, "Liturgy and Eschatology," 93-95.
370   Schmemann, *Of Water,* 83.
371   *Ibid.,* 84.

reflects the Church's belief in the fundamental goodness of the water. The consecration of the water manifests the Church's belief that water has a place in the Kingdom of God. The exorcism of the water exhibits the Church's knowledge of the need for water's liberation from its fallenness. These three elements reveal the positive and yet realistic orientation of baptismal spirituality. The Church denies neither the goodness of creation nor the illness that afflicts it.

An Exalted View of Humanity in Christ

The positive orientation of baptismal spirituality extends not only to creation in general but to humanity specifically: "Man was created as the king of creation: such then is the first and essential truth about man, the source and the foundation of Christian 'spirituality.'"[372] Man was invested with his kingship by God. His kingship is part of the original "image and likeness" given him at creation. The Church knows the same truth about man that she knows about creation: that he is fallen. Nevertheless, the fallen king was truly a king originally, and this positive statement about humanity needs to be made first, before any other statement is made. This is part of what Schmemann terms the "anthropological maximalism"[373] of the Orthodox Church, which is an essential part of baptismal spirituality.

In addition to being a *king*, the human person is also a *priest* and a *prophet*. These three spiritual identities comprise the chrismal or pentecostal dimension of baptismal spirituality. Schmemann sees these three facets of baptismal spirituality as essential to understanding Christian spirituality in general.[374] As a king, man has a God-given authority to act as benefactor for all creation. As a priest, man is called to offer himself and all of creation back to God. As a prophet, man discerns the will of God and speaks His word to creation.[375] I should note that Father Schmemann has not taken these three motifs from the text of the rite of Baptism and Chrismation; instead, he has taken his inspiration from biblical and patristic sources.[376]

---

[372]   *Ibid.*, 82.
[373]   *Ibid.*
[374]   *Ibid.*, 75.
[375]   *Ibid.*, 81-103.
[376]   Schmemann, *Of Water*, 75. *Cf.* Bishop Kallistos Ware, *The Orthodox Way*

All three of these chrismal ministries were distorted by sin. Through sin, man ceases to be a benefactor and becomes an oppressor and an exploiter. He refuses to act as priest and therefore fails to offer himself and creation back to God as an acceptable sacrifice and reasonable worship.[377] He loses his ear to hear God and can no longer see the world through God's eyes. He seeks "prophetic powers" in the paranormal and the occult, and in so doing, becomes a false prophet.[378] Baptism and Chrismation restore man to his original innocence and renew in him the three pentecostal ministries given to him in the beginning.[379]

The Cross

Since Baptism is an immersion into the death and resurrection of Christ, it is only natural that Father Schmemann identify one aspect of baptismal spirituality as being centred on the Cross. For Schmemann, the Cross is an absolutely indispensable part of Christian spirituality, since only in it are the two reductionist "spiritualities" of escapism and activism exposed as false. Only in it is the apparent contradiction between two affirmations resolved: 1) God loves the world and has set man over it as king and benefactor; 2) The kingdom of God is not of this world.[380] Only in Love Crucified, as Saint Philaret of Moscow calls Christ, can we discover the world condemned but redeemed, rejected but loved, denied but affirmed. Only in Christ's self-emptying love is the apparent contradiction transformed into a life-changing truth: "this world" has been buried in Christ's death so that the renewed world can be made manifest in His resurrection.

(Crestwood, NY: St. Vladimir's Seminary Press, 1996), 53-55. Only the motifs of man as king and priest are mentioned here. Bishop Kallistos does not include the theme of man as prophet. He cites Saint Leontios of Cyprus as a source from the patristic tradition. Paul Evdokimov speaks in detail about all three ministries – king, priest, and prophet – in Paul Evdokimov, *Woman and the Salvation of the World* (Crestwood, NY: St. Vladimir's Seminary Press, 1994) 108-111, and in Paul Evdokimov, *The Sacrament of Love* (Crestwood, NY: St. Vladimir's Seminary Press, 1995), 87-92. The main patristic source for Evdokimov's reflection on this topic is Saint Makarios, *Homily XVII*.

[377] Schmemann, *Of Water*, 96-97.
[378] *Ibid.,* 100-101.
[379] *Ibid.,* 75.
[380] *Ibid.,* 86-87.

2) Personal and Ecclesial

The Cross-centred characteristic of Christian spirituality as presented by Father Schmemann requires a response: the Cross of Christ must be appropriated by the individual believer. Otherwise, the teaching on the Cross "remains an antinomy, a mere 'doctrine.'"[381] It is clear that Father Alexander reserves a very special place in his understanding of spirituality for the personal. The personal is not submerged into the ecclesial only to be lost, nor is it subsumed under the generic category "humanity." Rather, it remains essential to the Orthodox Christian worldview and understanding of salvation described by Schmemann, in which "the world is not an 'idea,' an abstract and impersonal 'totality,' but always the unique gift to a unique human being ...."[382] The Cross is personally received when the Christian chooses to be crucified to the world, and it is through this that the world is saved, since "it perishes or is saved in each man."[383]

Father Schmemann points to the secularistic reduction of the human person as one of the main spiritual challenges that Orthodoxy faces in North America.[384] In his discussion, he provides us with a key to understanding the importance of the person in Christianity: "For in a very real sense no general 'man' – be he American or any other – no 'society,' no 'culture' has at any time truly *accepted* Christianity .... But at all times and in all 'cultures' there were *persons* who did accept it and did live by it ...."[385] He even remarks that, "in a sense, a sinful Christian does not belong to the Church ...."[386] He does, however, speak favourably about the emergence of Orthodox nations.[387] Nevertheless, he insists that *persons* in those nations received Christianity, and that "in every Saint the world is *saved* and it is

[381] *Ibid.*, 91.
[382] *Ibid.*, 91-92.
[383] *Ibid.*, 92.
[384] Alexander Schmemann, "Problems of Orthodoxy in America III: The Spiritual Problem" in *St. Vladimir's Theological Quarterly* 9 (1965), 177.
[385] *Ibid.*, 179.
[386] *Ibid.*, 178.
[387] Alexander Schmemann, "The 'Orthodox World,' Past and Present" in *Church, World, Mission* (Crestwood, NY: St. Vladimir's Seminary Press, 1979), 25–66. Alexander Schmemann, "The Missionary Imperative" in *Church, World, Mission*, 216.

fully saved in the one totally fulfilled Person: Jesus Christ."[388]

The attention that Schmemann pays to the personal dimension may seem surprising to those who have a superficial understanding of liturgical theology and eucharistic ecclesiology. Does eucharistic ecclesiology not refer to the gathering of the assembly? Does liturgical theology not refer to the common work of the people? Are liturgical theology and eucharistic ecclesiology not connected more to the collective than to the individual? And if, as Vassiliadis suggests, Father Schmemann is a proponent of "eucharistic spirituality," does his emphasis on the personal not represent a temporary lapse in his theological thinking that leads directly back to a more individualistic and therefore "therapeutic" spirituality? I would propose two answers to these questions, questions that in themselves represent a kind of caricature of liturgical theology and eucharistic ecclesiology. We will see in these two instances that Father Schmemann's understanding of the personal dimension serves to strengthen his connection with eucharistic ecclesiology.

In the *first* place, we must, as mentioned above, distinguish the Church from a society into which persons are incorporated based on traits, characteristics, ethnic or racial background, or geographical location. Persons who find themselves counted as members of such a collective may not have exercised their choice to be so. Someone else has made the decision to include them in a particular group based on certain criteria. A distinguishing characteristic of the Church is that it is formed of persons who have chosen to be part of it.[389] In other words, they have personally appropriated their Baptism and have chosen to grow spiritually in the context of the Church, which becomes for them the place in which they can discover the true meaning of their personhood in Christ. While truly a community, the Church is in no way an impersonal collective, because rather than imposing some artificially selected characteristics on a person, it provides the opportunity, as Zizioulas points out, for personhood to be received in Baptism and experienced in its eucharistic life.[390] Therefore, ecclesial community and personhood are

---

[388]   Schmemann, "Problems," 178.
[389]   *Ibid.*
[390]   John D. Zizioulas, *Being as Communion* (Crestwood, NY: St. Vladimir's Seminary Press, 1985), 19, 53.

not contradictory, but profoundly complementary.

Secondly, we need to have a second look at Schmemann's use of the word "person." A common assumption about the word "person" is that it can be understood as a synonym of the word "individual." Schmemann is careful to speak of the "person" rather than the "individual," and his choice of words is likely deliberate. It is possible also that his choice of words here may reflect a certain understanding of the uniqueness of the "person" and its irreducibility to the level of "individual." This particular understanding is a rather prominent feature of the second generation of proponents of eucharistic ecclesiology and may be present in Schmemann's thinking in its seminal form. Metropolitan John Zizioulas in *Being as Communion* posits that the patristic understanding of the person necessarily includes the aspect of communion.[391] Thus, he concludes that there is an essential difference between "individual" and "person," since the aspect of communion is not intrinsic to the former.[392] It should be noted, however, that this understanding has been contested by at least one contemporary Orthodox theologian.[393]

The Relationship Between the Personal and the Ecclesial

Having clarified the meaning and established the uniqueness of "Church" and "person" in Schemann's thought, we can proceed to explain the relationship he perceives between the two: "There can be no doubt that in the 'spirituality' of early Christianity the 'communal' reinforced the 'personal,' and the 'personal' was impossible without the 'communal.'"[394] It is evident here that a balanced and full Christian spirituality, according

---

[391]   *Ibid.*, 113.

[392]   *Ibid.*, 164.

[393]   Lucian Turcescu, "Person' versus 'Individual,' and Other Modern Misreadings of Gregory of Nyssa," *Re-thinking Gregory of Nyssa*. Sarah Coakley (ed.) (Oxford: Blackwell Publishing, 2003), 97-109. This article was first published in *Modern Theology* 18 (2002), 527-539. See Zizioulas'response in John D. Zizioulas, *Communion and Otherness* (London: T. & T. Clark, 2006), 171-177. See also Aristotle Papanikolaou, *Being With God: Trinity, Apophaticism, and Divine-Human Communion* (Notre Dame, IN: University of Notre Dame Press, 2006), 154-161.

[394]   Alexander Schmemann, *The Eucharist* (Crestwood, NY: St. Vladimir's Seminary Press, 1988), 241.

to Father Schmemann (he took the spirituality of early Christianity as the ideal expression of Christian spirituality), is always both personal and communal. The communal does not limit or suppress the personal; on the contrary, it provides its only possible condition for its wellbeing.

Returning to one of the first premises of Father Schmemann, that Christian spirituality is fundamentally baptismal, we are led to the inescapable conclusion that spirituality is also inherently ecclesial, since Baptism is an entrance into the Body of Christ. Of course, in keeping with what we have already seen, we are able to perceive the personal side of Baptism, since we know it to be a gift that must be personally appropriated. Schmemann is very explicit in exposing what he knows to be the content of the personal/communal ecclesial life:

> But then, where is this true spirituality, this total vision of man, of his nature and his vocation, better revealed than in the Sacrament whose purpose is precisely to restore in man his true nature, to bestow upon him the new life by regenerating him "by Water and the Spirit"?[395]
>
> The fruit of Baptism, its true fulfillment, is a new life; not simply a better, more moral or even more pious life, but a life *ontologically* different from the "old" one. And this difference, the very content of this "newness," is that it is *life with Christ* ....[396]

One way of describing the gift of baptism, and an important characteristic of ecclesial life is, simply stated, "newness." The essence of this "newness" is life with Christ. Because Baptism is, according to Father Schmemann, intrinsically connected to Pascha,[397] we know that the newness of life found with Christ in the Church is also profoundly paschal: "This indeed is what the paschal joy is about: it is in this world that the Kingdom which is 'not of this world' is revealed, manifested, inaugurated as new life ...."[398] For Schmemann, true spirituality has an ecclesial reference: it is the life of the Church. Every person is invited to take part in the life of the Church,

[395]   Schmemann, *Of Water*, 74.
[396]   *Ibid.*, 120.
[397]   *Ibid.*, 7-8, 12-13, 109-115.
[398]   *Ibid.*, 90.

but no one is entitled to select his own spirituality any more than he may choose his own plan of salvation. The life of the Church is precisely a gift to humanity and to the entire world. This is one of the underlying principles of all Schmemann's work. It is for this reason that he concerns himself entirely with the content of the life of the Church as embodied in, and articulated by, the worship of the Church.

The radical ecclesiocentric approach of Father Schmemann precludes the possibility of any "spirituality" that is completely detached from the Church. In addition, it takes for granted that the whole life of the Church constitutes its "spirituality." By this I mean that Scripture, Church history, ethics, dogmatic theology, and so on, are all part of the spirituality. In Schmemann's point of view, there can be no fuller and more integrated expression of all these facets of spiritual life than the Church's liturgy. This is the clear implication of Father Schmemann's affirmation that the *lex orandi* of the Church is the source of its *lex credendi*.[399]

3) Eucharistic and Eschatological

Reflecting on the theology of the early Church, Schmemann observes that, in the first centuries, the corporate led to the ecclesial, and the fullness of the ecclesial was realized in the Eucharist.[400] When early Christians assembled as the Church, they did so with the express intention of celebrating the Eucharist. The early Christian assembly was not a static gathering of people; it had a certain intrinsic movement or dynamic, and that movement found its final fulfillment in the eucharistic celebration.

Turning to the sacrament of Baptism, we discover that it, like the early Christian assembly, found its fulfillment in the Eucharist:

> Baptism, we are told, *integrates* us into the Church. But if the Church's ultimate being and essence are revealed in and through the Eucharist, if Eucharist is truly *the sacrament of the Church* and not only one of the Church's sacraments, then of necessity to enter the Church is to enter into the Eucharist, then Eucharist is indeed the fulfillment of Baptism.[401]

[399] Schmemann, "Theology and Liturgy," *Church, World, Mission*, 143.
[400] Schmemann, *The Eucharist*, 11.
[401] Schmemann, *Of Water*, 117-118.

This leads us to the conclusion that baptismal spirituality, which is so seminal for everything in the Christian life, finds its meaning and *telos* in the Eucharist. It is easy to see why Professor Vassiliadis would lead us to believe that Father Schmemann is a proponent of "eucharistic spirituality." Certainly, Schmemann's understanding of the relationship between person and *ecclesia*, his great interest in the spirituality and ecclesiology of the early Church, and his emphasis on the Eucharist as the context for true spiritual experience, all point in that direction. One could add to this his position that the Eucharist is not simply one of the sacraments but *the* sacrament of the Church, which is one of the basic tenets of eucharistic ecclesiology.[402]

Are Eucharistic Ecclesiology and Eucharistic Spirituality the Same?

While we can, without reservation, see Schmemann as a proponent of eucharistic ecclesiology, we should be careful, in my view, to avoid casting the theologian as an exponent of "eucharistic spirituality." In Father Schmemann's case, it is clear that he is interested in *all* the liturgical worship of the Church, in which, of course, the Eucharist occupies a very special place. Thus, while Schmemann understands the Eucharist to be the "fulfillment of Baptism," he nonetheless dedicates an entire book to the study of Baptism and Chrismation (*Of Water and the Spirit*) and speaks at length about "baptismal spirituality." His book *Great Lent* is not focused on the Eucharist exclusively, but rather takes into account all of the different liturgical aspects of the season as well as its ascetic dimensions. The premise that the rule of faith of the Church is both found in and made explicit by the worship of the Church provided the impetus for Schmemann to develop his argument for liturgical theology. While allowing for the theological critique of liturgy, he nevertheless places his greatest emphasis on the liturgy *as* theology. Following the contours of his argument for liturgical theology, it might seem more accurate to say that Schmemann embraces a "liturgical spirituality" rather than a "eucharistic spirituality." However, were

---

[402]   *Cf.* Paul Evdokimov, "Eucharistie – Mystère de l'Église," *La Pensée orthodoxe*, 1968 (2), 53.

Schmemann alive today, he would likely consider the term "liturgical spirituality" redundant, thinking instead that it should be subsumed under the term "liturgical theology." What Schmemann would have had to say about the relationship between the sacramental and ascetic dimensions of Orthodox spirituality is another question. If anything, he might have been inclined to use the word *synthesis*[403] to describe the relationship between the sacramental and ascetic aspects of the Church's *one* spirituality, but this is only speculation.

Eschatological Spirituality

The spirituality espoused by Schmemann has a very important defining characteristic, the omission of which would seriously compromise any study of his life and work: eschatology. Schmemann defines the Eucharist as "the sacrament of the kingdom."[404] Indeed, so much of his thought is grounded in eschatology. It is the eschatological dimension that provides the true Christian alternative to the two false options frequently offered in the contemporary world: these are activism (the radical "yes") and escapism (the radical "no").[405] As I mentioned earlier in this chapter, it is the pervasiveness of these two false alternatives in Christian circles that compromises the very use of the term "spirituality." Eschatological spirituality reveals the bankruptcy of these two false alternatives and presents a Christian response that is both cosmic (affirming of the world) and prophetic (pointing to the transforming presence of the Kingdom in the world).

Schmemann is so committed to eschatological spirituality that he is willing to point to it as *the* defining characteristic of Byzantine monastic spirituality.[406] However, he goes on to say: "There is nothing 'exclusively' monastic about that eschatological spirituality because every Christian and the entire Church have their true life 'hidden with Christ in God'

---

[403] Fr. Schmemann already uses this term to describe the encounter of parish worship (which was itself a synthesis of early Judaeo-Christian and what the author terms "the new liturgical piety") with monastic worship. See Alexander Schmemann, "The Byzantine Synthesis," *Introduction to Liturgical Theology*, trans. Asheleigh E. Moorhouse (Leighton Buzzard, Beds.: The Faith Press, 1975), 116-167.

[404] Schmemann, *The Eucharist*, 27.

[405] Schmemann, "Liturgy and Eschatology," 93-95.

[406] Alexander Schmemann, "Current Spirituality I: Orthodoxy," *The Study of Spirituality*, Cheslyn Jones *et al.* (eds.) (New York: Oxford, 1986), 522.

(Col. 3:3)."[407] He posits that the Orthodox world collapsed precisely because it rejected its eschatological worldview, which had been its original foundation.[408]

Eschatological spirituality, according to Father Schmemann, can be compromised by those who substitute the apocalyptic for the eschatological and whose spirituality is essentially escapist in orientation. On the other hand, the eschatological dynamism of Orthodox spirituality can be challenged by those "who tr[y] to 'reinterpret' the Orthodox spiritual tradition in typically secularist terms of 'help' and 'therapeutics.'"[409] Here we might ask what Schmemann's attitude would have been towards what Professor Vassiliadis terms "therapeutic spirituality" and what I would call the ascetic tradition.

Two Types of Therapy

In answering this question, we need first to distinguish between the two types of "therapy" that Schmemann mentions in his works. The first type of "therapy" has its roots in secularism. Schmemann is speaking of this type of "therapy" when he discusses the radical "yes" option that is frequently offered to Christians in our post-Christian era. Schmemann writes: "We develop a therapeutical theology, because our world is therapeutic."[410] In this case, Christians are simply trying to catch up with the secular world. One becomes or remains a Christian only insofar as Christianity "guarantees happiness."[411] Such "therapeutic Christianity" has no room within it for the possibility of renouncing a profoundly unchristian worldview that has entered the minds and hearts of Christians unnoticed. Schmemann sees this as diametrically opposed to the dynamic implicit in the rite of Baptism, which includes a renunciation of Satan and everything connected with him.[412] This particular type of "therapeutic spirituality" and the baptismal spirituality embraced by Schmemann are definitely two mutually exclusive categories.

---

[407] *Ibid.*, 523.
[408] *Ibid.*
[409] *Ibid.*, 524.
[410] Schmemann, "Liturgy and Eschatology," 91.
[411] *Ibid.*
[412] Schmemann, *Of Water*, 29.

On the other hand, in his book *Great Lent*, Father Schmemann speaks of the "holy therapy of fasting."[413] This therapy, which stands in opposition to the most pervasive philosophies of our post-modern world, has its roots in the ascetic tradition, which was brought to the Church by monasticism:

> Quite different are the spiritual connotations of the second type of fasting which we have defined as *ascetical*. Here the purpose for fasting is to liberate man from the unlawful tyranny of the flesh, of that surrender of the spirit to the body and its appetites which is the tragic result of sin and the original fall of man .... The art of ascetical fasting had been refined and perfected within the monastic tradition and then was accepted by the entire Church.[414]

Here Schmemann is hinting at a type of synthesis between the spiritual practices of primitive monasticism and the spiritual ethos of the early Church. The result of this synthesis was that the "holy therapy of fasting" became normative for the entire Church and was absorbed into its spiritual life. The Church had appropriated for itself a very important part of the ascetic tradition. This is not the only place where Father Schmemann presents a positive assessment of the ascetic tradition. In an article on Orthodox spirituality, he states that the ascetic tradition, as exemplified in the *Philokalia*, forms part of the canon of Byzantine spirituality.[415] He also feels that the emphasis on sobriety brought to Orthodox spirituality by the ascetic tradition is of very great importance.[416] Since the ascetic tradition forms the foundation of "therapeutic spirituality," it seems that Father Schmemann was quite open to it, finding in this spiritual expression a genuine type of *holy* therapy and an indispensable aspect of Orthodox spiritual life.

---

[413]   Alexander Schmemann, *Great Lent* (Crestwood, NY: St. Vladimir's Seminary Press, 1974), 51.
[414]   *Ibid.*, 50-51.
[415]   Schmemann, "Current," 519.
[416]   Schmemann, *Of Water*, 73.

CONCLUSION

In my opinion, Father Schmemann would not have felt the need to choose between "therapeutic spirituality" and "eucharistic spirituality;" he likely would have felt that both spiritual emphases were already completely integrated into Orthodox ecclesial life. I believe that he is in fact suggesting this when he outlines the two different types of fasts in the Orthodox Church: the eschatological fast and the ascetic fast. He insists that both fasts have an important place in Orthodox spirituality.[417] Implicit in Schmemann's comments is the idea that a balance between the eucharistic and ascetic aspects of the spiritual life already exists in Orthodox liturgical life, so that the issue is not one of choosing one aspect over the other, but one of affirming liturgical life *as* spiritual life. One can nevertheless not ignore the fact that Father Schmemann could have carved out greater space for the ascetic tradition in his theological work. In his last great work, *The Eucharist*, he left the problem of the integration of asceticism and the Eucharist unsolved.[418] The result is that we know he perceived asceticism, particularly in its monastic expression, to have had a negative impact on the ethos of the Church historically, but we do not know how he would have reconciled the historical reality of the monastic tradition with the current life of the Church. Regrettably, he never had the opportunity to put the finishing touches on his book before he entered the heavenly Kingdom, so we are left to speculate as to what he might have done had he had more time. Such speculation is, however, beyond the scope of this study. While Father Schmemann can be perceived in general terms as a representative of the eucharistic expression of spirituality, Metropolitan Hierotheos Vlachos is identified by Professor Vassiliadis as a representative of "therapeutic," or ascetic spirituality. We examine the understanding of spirituality advanced by Metropolitan Hierotheos in the following chapter.

---

[417]   Schmemann, *Great Lent,* 49-52.
[418]   Alexander Schmemann, *The Eucharist* (Crestwood, NY: St. Vladimir's Seminary Press, 1988), 231.

CHAPTER NINE

METROPOLITAN HIEROTHEOS OF NAFPAKTOS ON THE SPIRITUAL LIFE

INTRODUCTION

The books of Metropolitan Hierotheos (Vlachos) began to appear in English translation over twenty years ago. To date, more than twenty major works of the Metropolitan have been translated into English from Greek, in addition to a catechism for children. English-speaking readers first came to know Metropolitan Hierotheos's works with the publication of *A night in the desert of the Holy Mountain* in translation in 1991. This book has enjoyed great popularity and has been translated into many languages. The first substantial theological work of His Eminence to be translated was *Orthodox Psychotherapy*, which appeared in its first edition in 1994 (while the author was still an Archimandrite). This work is a comprehensive presentation of the author's main thesis that Orthodoxy is essentially a therapeutic science. It includes an exhaustive treatment of all the essential elements of the Orthodox ascetic-therapeutic tradition, as well as important sections on spiritual pathology, spiritual therapy, and the therapeutic character of the three degrees of priesthood. It would be no exaggeration to call *Orthodox Psychotherapy* a classic in the area of Orthodox pastoral theology and spirituality.

In writing this chapter, I have selected passages from nine of Metropolitan Hierotheos's works in translation. I have limited myself to the topic of the relationship between asceticism and the sacraments in the Metropolitan's works, with special reference to Baptism and the Eucharist. It is clear to me that this short chapter is but a modest introduction to the topic and that further study needs to be done in order to obtain a more complete picture of the Metropolitan's theological teaching. Here I am thinking most especially of an analysis of his presentation of the priesthood as an ascetic-therapeutic-liturgical ministry and his strongly ascetic interpretation of ecclesiology.

Finally, I need to draw attention to the fact that Metropolitan Hierotheos writes as a pastor and teacher, and not as an academic theologian. Any student of theology needs to take this into account when reflecting on the Metropolitan's works and to approach them in the right spirit. His Eminence makes no secret of his distaste for the scholastic approach to theology and more generally of academic theological analysis that has no concrete roots in the spiritual life. His reflection is often scholarly, but always aimed at living what he terms "the ascetic life in grace": his is *par excellence* an empirical theology, and I have been careful always to keep this in mind when engaging him through his works.

SPIRITUALITY BOTH SACRAMENTAL AND ASCETIC

In his major work on Saint Gregory Palamas, Metropolitan Hierotheos states that "[m]an is cured by the sacramental and ascetical life."[419] These few words sum up his understanding of the spiritual life. What is clear is that neither the sacraments nor asceticism on their own represent the fullness of man's life in the Church. The question that needs to be explored is that of the relationship between the sacramental life and the ascetic life. In fact, it is the Metropolitan's contention that the Orthodox theological position is precisely the balance or middle road between the two: an overemphasis on either asceticism or the sacraments leads, in his view, to a heterodox position.

Metropolitan Hierotheos refers to the witness of Saint Gregory Palamas in order to illustrate further the need for a balanced sacramental and ascetic life. Saint Gregory, he points out, condemns two heretical positions in his writings: Messalianism and Barlaamism. In Messalianism,

---

[419] Hierotheos, Metropolitan of Nafpaktos, *Saint Gregory Palamas as a Hagiorite*, trans. Esther Williams (Levadia, Greece: Birth of the Theotokos Monastery, 1997), 372.

such an emphasis was placed on the ascetic and devotional life that the sacraments became peripheral to the spiritual life. In Barlaamism, the sacraments were valued to the exclusion of the hesychastic-ascetic life.[420] Both of these heretical teachings, through the imbalance they create, direct the human person away from the fullness of salvation.[421]

Throughout his many works, Metropolitan Hierotheos remains faithful to the teaching of Saint Gregory Palamas on the ascetic and sacramental life, and struggles consistently to present both aspects of the spiritual life, even if it appears that he has reflected more deeply on the ascetic side. The Metropolitan understands the ascetic-hesychastic life to be the presupposition of sacramental life.[422] While he is not marginalizing the sacramental life, he is suggesting that sacraments without asceticism lose their proper significance and therefore cannot have their intended effect. In commenting on the relationship between sacraments and asceticism in Orthodoxy, Metropolitan Hierotheos identifies one of the characteristics intrinsic to it: their interdependence. Asceticism cannot exist for its own sake; it must lead somewhere. The sacramental life, however, requires a context in which it can be fruitful.

ASCETIC PRACTICE BEFORE AND AFTER BAPTISM

If asceticism provides the context for the sacramental life, then the purpose of this context is necessarily connected to preparation. Indeed, Metropolitan Hierotheos notes that, "through ascetic practice ... we prepare the way of God's grace to act therapeutically and redemptively within the heart."[423] Here the Metropolitan reveals the two goals of the sacraments: healing and redemption. The purpose of asceticism is to open the human heart to the grace of God, which is at work in the sacraments in order that their goals can be reached. This particular type of preparation finds its expression in the Orthodox Church in several different ways. It is expressed liturgically and pastorally in the retention since ancient

---

[420]   Hierotheos, *Palamas*, 70. Hierotheos, Metropolitan of Nafpaktos, *Orthodox Spirituality*, trans. Effie Mavromichali (Levadia, Greece: Birth of the Theotokos Monastery, 1998), 68-69.

[421]   Hierotheos, *Palamas*, 370.

[422]   *Ibid.*, 371.

[423]   Hierotheos, *Orthodox Spirituality*, 66.

times of the catechumenate as a formal period of preparation for Baptism. Metropolitan Hierotheos places a great emphasis on the catechumenate precisely because it provides the ascetic and pastoral context in which Baptism finds its greatest meaning and power.[424]

Ascetic practice in the ancient Church was not restricted, of course, to the period preceding Baptism. The Church encouraged all of its members to grow in obedience and holiness, and this growth can be considered the true content of asceticism. Nevertheless, the Church required a way of dealing pastorally with Christians who, after Baptism, returned to a life of sin. It therefore created for them a kind of school of repentance in which four stages could be distinguished.[425] The stages led ideally to the full reintegration of the penitent into the eucharistic community, ending with his or her readmission to the Holy Eucharist. Both the catechumenate and the school of the penitents highlight the essentially therapeutic approach that the Church took toward its members in earlier times. It also shows that the Church understood that an appropriate ascetic context for the celebration of the sacraments is absolutely indispensable.

THE ROLE OF DEACONS, PRIESTS AND BISHOPS IN THE BAPTISMAL CELEBRATION

The Church's understanding of the relationship of asceticism to Baptism was also manifested in the liturgical function of deacons, priests, and bishops.[426] A specific liturgical task was committed to each of the three orders in the baptismal celebration. The tasks reveal the orientation of each of the ministers in the Church. The deacons prepared the baptismal candidate by removing his clothing. The priests anointed the candidate with oil. The bishop performed the Baptism. The ministry of the deacon was thus connected with purification, the ministry of the priest with illumination, and the ministry of the bishop with perfection or completion. Metropolitan Hierotheos highlights the connection between the three classic stages of spiritual growth – purification, illumination,

---

[424]   *Ibid.*, 73-75.

[425]   *Ibid.*, 75.

[426]   Hierotheos, Archimandrite [Metropolitan of Nafpaktos], *Orthodox Psychotherapy,* trans. Esther Williams (Levadia, Greece: Birth of the Theotokos Monastery, 1994), 73.

and *theoria* – and the threefold apostolic ministry that can be found in the writings of Saint Dionysios the Areopagite.[427] The Metropolitan posits that this interpretation of the apostolic ministry was not peculiar to Saint Dionysios, but was shared by the entire Church.[428] Striking in this approach to the ordained ministries is its ascetic orientation. No less significant is the idea that Baptism contains within itself all three stages of spiritual growth and therefore communicates to the newly baptized the fullness of the spiritual life. Since, however, the catechumenate is associated to a great extent with purification, it is significant to note that an entire ministry was essentially committed to it. The notion of preparation, it seems, was so fundamental to the understanding of the Church that there needed to be a significant place for it in its theology of ministry and pastoral praxis.

In stating that asceticism provides the context for the celebration of the sacraments, Metropolitan Hierotheos does not mean to suggest that it is connected with preparation alone. In fact, asceticism plays an equally important role after the celebration of the sacraments through the safeguarding of the grace that has been received.[429] Thus the divine energies of God that are received in the sacraments require not only a context in which they can be received, but also a context in which they can continue to be operative. The Metropolitan states this succinctly: "Thus God operates and man co-operates."[430] This co-operation or *synergeia* is not an abstract doctrine that reveals the position of the Church on the free will of man; rather, it is a description of the practical response of the human person to the grace of God. In this sense, asceticism, obedience, and *synergeia* can all be equated.

ASCETICISM AS A MEANS TO REKINDLE THE GRACE OF BAPTISM

In addition to preparing for and safeguarding the grace of God in the sacraments, ascetic practice plays a key role in the rekindling of the grace received in Baptism but buried, as it were, by sin. Metropolitan Hierotheos writes:

427   *Ibid.*
428   Hierotheos, *Orthodox Psychotherapy,* 73.
429   Hierotheos, *Orthodox Spirituality,* 66.
430   *Ibid.,* 67.

Through the "rite of birth in God", holy baptism, man's nous is illuminated, freed from slavery to sin and the devil, and is united with God. That is why baptism is called illumination. But after that, because of sin, the nous is again darkened and deadened. The patristic writings make it clear that every sin and every passion deadens the nous.[431]

Commenting on the role of asceticism, he states: "When we act according to the desires of the flesh, the grace of God which has been in the depths of our spiritual heart since baptism, is hidden by the passions, so our effort is to try to uncover this grace through living an ascetic life in grace."[432] Ascetic practice involves a patient stripping away of the layers of interference caused by sin that are found in the heart. As they are removed, the grace of God is exposed and is released as a great energy throughout the entire person. It is rekindled more in the sense of being released than in the sense of being brought to life. Metropolitan Hierotheos is careful to say that the grace is "hidden" rather than "extinguished." God's grace never "dies," but its activity can be severely restricted by sin and the passions. God's grace does not act in a coercive fashion on man's will, but requires man's active co-operation. The uncovering of the grace of Baptism is in part a process of growth in *synergeia*. The more man chooses to co-operate, the more God is free to work graciously in the heart without doing violence to the human will.

It can be argued that uncovering the grace of Baptism and growing in obedience or *synergeia* is itself a therapeutic process, since it necessarily includes the healing of the human will and heart from the wounds of sin and the passions. I believe that Metropolitan Hierotheos is addressing this particular point when he uses the expression "living an ascetic life in grace."[433] He is acknowledging that the path to the healing of the heart and the discovery in it of the grace of Baptism cannot be followed without God's grace. Asceticism is not simply human effort directed toward a desired "mystical" experience. In Orthodox theology, the ascetic life is itself gracious and therefore mystical. Orthodox spirituality knows no

[431] Hierotheos, *Orthodox Psychotherapy*, 37-38.
[432] *Ibid.*, 160-161.
[433] *Ibid.*, 161.

157

sharp division between "ascetic" and "mystical" theology.

Establishing the gracious character of the ascetic life is of great importance for several reasons. First of all, it provides an answer for those who see the Orthodox ascetic tradition as a thinly veiled form of Pelagianism. Secondly, it makes explicit the biblical roots of Orthodox asceticism and thereby differentiates it from non-Christian forms of asceticism. Thirdly, it greatly enhances the relationship between asceticism and the sacraments by preventing the creation of a false dichotomy between asceticism and grace, and by attributing to the ascetic context, both before and after the celebration of the sacraments, a gracious character.

BAPTISM AS A SOURCE OF THE ASCETIC LIFE

Returning to the Metropolitan's presentation of Saint Dionysios the Areopagite's ascetic interpretation of the threefold apostolic ministry, we see two things: Baptism represents the end or objective of an ascetic process; Baptism contains within it the three stages of the spiritual life and can therefore be considered a source of the ascetic life. Baptism brings to an end the ascetic process of the catechumenate, which in the ancient Church lasted from one to three years.[434] At the same time, Baptism inaugurates an entirely new process of growth in grace by imparting to the newly illumined Christian full potential to experience purification, illumination, and perfection. These three stages of the spiritual life are mediated to the baptismal candidate through three significant moments of the baptismal liturgy, celebrated in order by the three orders of priesthood: the diaconate, the presbyterate, and the episcopate.[435] Since these three stages describe the progression of the "ascetic life in grace," it would be entirely consistent with the Metropolitan's presentation of Saint Dionysios's teaching to identify both Baptism and the priesthood as sources of ascetic life.

In his work *Life after death*, Metropolitan Hierotheos elucidates in greater detail how, in effect, Baptism acts as a source of the ascetic life. Explaining the reasons why we baptize infants, he states:

This is how we understand the baptism of babies. We baptise them so that they may become members of the Church,

---

[434] Hierotheos, *Orthodox Spirituality,* 74.
[435] Hierotheos, *Orthodox Psychotherapy,* 73.

members of the Body of Christ, that they may pass over death, overcome the garments of skin, decay and mortality. That is to say that as they grow, whenever the nous becomes darkened by passions and the darkness of the surroundings, they may have the ability to conquer death in Christ, to overcome the passions and to purify the noetic part of their souls once more.[436]

While the context for the Baptism of an adult is different, the same spiritual dynamism is imparted. Through Baptism, we are granted the ability "to overcome the passions and to purify the noetic part of [our] souls." This is a very clear reference to the ascetic struggle that pertains to the first stage of the spiritual life: purification. Considerable self-discipline and self-denial are required to win the war against the passions, but this necessary human effort is propelled by the grace of God received in Baptism.

Metropolitan Hierotheos continues his discussion of Baptism by indicating that, "through holy Chrism, illumination of the nous is received."[437] We can infer from what he writes in *Orthodox Psychotherapy* that, while the nous is darkened by sin after baptism, the grace of illumination originally received in Chrismation can, through the "ascetic life in grace," be uncovered and reactivated.[438] Chrismation, therefore, can also be considered a gracious source of ascetic life.

Commenting on the Baptism of adults, but addressing the theme of Baptism in general, the Metropolitan writes:

> Furthermore, through holy Baptism they become members of the Church and, being united with Christ and participating in the sacraments, they acquire the power to defeat death and attain deification. The deepest purpose of Baptism for both infants and adults is to attain deification, which is achieved only in Christ and the Church.[439]

---

[436] Hierotheos, Metropolitan of Nafpaktos, *Life after death*, trans. Esther Williams (Levadia, Greece: Birth of the Theotokos Monastery, 1996), 101-102.
[437] Hierotheos, *Life after death*, 102.
[438] Hierotheos, *Orthodox Psychotherapy*, 161.
[439] Hierotheos, *Life after death*, 102.

Here we discover a reference to the third stage of the spiritual life, which is described here as the defeat of death and the attainment of deification. Of particular interest is the means by which death is defeated and deification is attained: union with Christ and participation in the sacraments. Here again there is a sacramental source for the ascetic life. We have seen already that the sacraments have a therapeutic and redemptive character. Now we see the *telos* of the sacraments: deification and the defeat of death. This *telos* is more than just a description of the third stage of the ascetic life; it has a very strong eschatological orientation. By eschatological I do not mean something restricted to the distant future, but a reality currently experienced by the Church that nevertheless gives a foretaste of a future fullness. The implications of what Metropolitan Hierotheos writes are very powerful: the ascetic and the eschatological are one single reality, and the marriage of the two represents a continuation of the dynamic eschatological asceticism that characterized the Church in the apostolic period.[440] The "ascetic life in grace" still initiates the Christian into the experience of the heavenly. So strong is this ascetic-eschatological dynamism that it has become a hallmark of Orthodox ecclesial life. Since all of the sacraments operate as sources of this dynamic asceticism, we can conclude that they have an ascetic and eschatological orientation that is intimately connected to their therapeutic and redemptive character.

EUCHARIST AS A SOURCE OF THE ASCETIC LIFE

The references to the Eucharist in Metropolitan Hierotheos's work reveal his conviction that this sacrament plays an indispensable role in the life of a Christian. There is, however, an ambiguity that can be detected in his presentation of the nature and place of that role in the "ascetic life in grace." Sometimes, he appears to place the Eucharist outside of the therapeutic and ascetic process, preferring instead to reserve it as a goal of asceticism. On other occasions, he gives the impression that the Eucharist is very much a part of man's therapy, leading the reader to infer that the Eucharist is a source of the ascetic life. In *Orthodox Psychotherapy*, he writes:

[440] For a description of the eschatological asceticism practised by the apostolic Church, see Jordan Aumann, *Christian Spirituality in the Catholic Tradition*, (San Francisco: Ignatius Press, 1989), 25-27.

It may well be regarded as a shortcoming that we have not also listed Holy Communion within therapeutic treatment. But we must underline and lay great stress on the fact that we regard the Eucharist, the communion of the Body and Blood of Christ as indispensable for man. The Lord emphasised: "Unless you eat the flesh of the Son of Man and drink of his blood, you have no life in you" (Jn. 6, 53). But it is well known that holy Communion is preceded by purification and preparation. If the therapy about which we are speaking here does not come first, then the receiving of the Body and Blood of Christ is "unto judgement and condemnation". Ecclesiology and eschatology cannot be understood without therapeutic training. So we are not undervaluing the Holy Eucharist, but by emphasising the value of ascetic practice and therapy we are exalting the great gift of the Eucharist. On the other hand, the aim of what we have written is mainly to make clear the precise path which ends at the altar, so that Holy Communion may become light and life.[441]

In this passage, the Eucharist is quite separate from "ascetic practice and therapy." The latter is seen as the path that leads to the former. The Metropolitan feels that "by emphasising the value of ascetic practice we are exalting the great gift of the Eucharist." This is clear, but must the two be considered two separate moments, with one leading to the other? Or can the ascetic path "which ends at the altar" not also be intersected by it along the way?

In Metropolitan Hierotheos's reflection on the Eucharist, we find an overriding pastoral and theological concern: proper preparation is required for the Eucharist to be redemptive. This is a well-established principle of Orthodox spiritual practice. Having acknowledged it, however, can we not allow a place for the Eucharist in the therapeutic process? Can we not say that the "ascetic practice and therapy" that precede the Eucharist are also in fact nurtured by it? Indeed, the encounter with Christ in the Eucharist becomes the source of the desire to know Him and be known by Him. It provides a true impetus and direction for asceticism. It would seem that

[441]   Hierotheos, *Orthodox Psychotherapy*, 54-55.

the Metropolitan's position on the Eucharist and asceticism would in no way be weakened by admitting the Eucharist into the therapeutic process so long as the integrity of the ascetic preparation were fully retained. "Ascetic practice and therapy" provide the indispensable context for the Eucharist, but they are in turn nourished by the Eucharist, which is itself therapeutic. In this way, the Eucharist, taken in its ascetic context, is both a source and a goal of the ascetic life.

In another passage on the Eucharist, Metropolitan Hierotheos adds a dimension to his teaching that is not visible in the first quotation. Commenting on the basic qualities of the priest as therapist, he writes:

> Through the Eucharist we may enter into holy humility and acquire that sacrificial way of life. Therefore in celebrating the Divine Liturgy we are not simply looking for the bread and wine to be transformed into the Body and Blood of Christ but seeking to acquire Christ's way of life. And this is humility. We seek to clothe ourselves in the spirit of the Eucharist, which is self-emptying.[442]

Here the Eucharist is an entrance into the life of Christ and a means of acquiring His "holy humility." What Hierotheos is describing pertains to deification and certainly seems to be connected to the therapeutic process. In this instance, we do not acquire humility through ascetic discipline; rather, we enter into it through the Eucharist. This stands in contrast to several other references to humility in *Orthodox Psychotherapy* in which we see humility as a virtue gained through ascetic struggle.[443] We may conclude from this that humility is acquired both through living the ascetic life and through participation in the Eucharist. In the first case, it is the fruit of patient and persistent obedience and self-sacrifice; in the second, it is a gift graciously received through the eucharistic celebration. The former does not contradict the latter; both represent essential aspects of the spiritual life. We do find here, however, an example of how the Eucharist can be a source, and not only a goal, of the ascetic life.

[442]   Hierotheos, *Orthodox Psychotherapy,* 85.
[443]   *Ibid.,* 240, 285, 291, 294, 306, 308.

ORTHODOX SPIRITUALITY AND PIETISM

In his work *The Person in the Orthodox Tradition*, Metropolitan Hierotheos stresses the uniqueness of Orthodox spirituality and differentiates it from what he describes as pseudo-pietism:[444]

> Pietism is a movement which developed in the protestant domain and is inspired by external acts of piety, which have no reference to the inner domain. In Orthodoxy when we speak about movement from the image to the likeness and about man's union with God, which is achieved through the sacraments and asceticism, and especially through partaking of the Body and Blood of Christ, when we look at this teaching within the teaching of our deified saints, this is not pietism.[445]

Hierotheos reiterates a theme found in his earlier works regarding asceticism and the sacraments with one important addition: "*especially* through partaking of the Body and Blood of Christ ...." The Metropolitan is ascribing a primacy to the Eucharist that is not always apparent in other places where he discusses the essential elements of the Orthodox spiritual life.[446]

METROPOLITAN HIEROTHEOS'S MORE RECENT WORKS

Metropolitan Hierotheos continues to develop the themes of ascetism, hesychasm, and the sacraments in his more recent works. His book on the twelve major feasts gave him the opportunity to ground his theological

[444] The Metropolitan's description does not correspond to the character of classical Protestant pietism. Spener, Francke, Zinzendorf, and other pietists placed a great emphasis on an inner transformation that they connected to a personal experience of conversion and a conscious awareness of the presence of God in the heart of the believer. It would be helpful to know what exactly the Metropolitan has in mind – a decadent form of Puritanism, perhaps?

[445] Hierotheos, Metropolitan of Nafpaktos, *The Person in the Orthodox Tradition*, trans. Esther Williams (Levadia, Greece: Birth of the Theotokos Monastery, 1998), 149–150.

[446] *Cf. Palamas* 372 and *Orthodox Spirituality* 66, where the sacraments and asceticism are presented as important aspects of Orthodox ecclesial-spiritual life without any special emphasis on the Eucharist.

work in the liturgical tradition of the Church.[447] This was a significant development for several reasons. *First*, it allowed him the chance to move away from ascetic literature and turn his attention to Holy Scripture and liturgical texts. *Second*, it permitted him to ground his theological work in the Incarnation by discussing in detail the liturgical texts associated with the Nativity, Circumcision, and Baptism of Christ. *Third*, it opened the door to a substantial study in Christology. *Fourth*, and rather significantly for this study, it provided him with a logical context in which to discuss the sacraments at greater length. Baptism in particular receives detailed treatment in this particular work. None of these things changed the direction of his writing in a major way, but they certainly afforded him the possibility of opening up a greater breadth in his theological work. If, as Metropolitan John Zizioulas says, Christology is inseparable from ecclesiology and vice versa, Metropolitan Hierotheos has, intentionally or not, laid the foundation for further discussions in ecclesiology.

In his sequel to *Orthodox Psychotherapy*, *The Science of Spiritual Medicine*, Metropolitan Hierotheos outlines practical applications of the material discussed in his earlier book. As the title of the latter book suggests, its focus is on Orthodox theology and spiritual life as therapy and cure. The sacraments and asceticism play the main roles in the therapy, as we have already seen. Here the author expands somewhat on his earlier teaching on the sacraments. He does this by setting his thought in an ecclesiological context. The Church in this case is presented as a therapeutic community.[448] He lists the sacraments of Baptism, Chrismation, Holy Communion, and Confession. He then notes that they must be combined with asceticism and prayer. To this he adds the following: "The second point is that, although the grace of the Triune God effects this healing through the sacraments, the experienced guide – the spiritual father and teacher – assists in this process."[449]

---

[447] Metropolitan of Nafpaktos, Hierotheos, *The feasts of the Lord: An introduction to the twelve feasts and Orthodox Christology*, trans. Esther Williams (Levadia, Greece: Birth of the Theotokos Monastery, 2000).
[448] Metropolitan of Nafpaktos, Hierotheos, *The Science of Spiritual Medicine: Orthodox Psychotherapy in Action*, trans. Sister Pelagia Selfe (Levadia, Greece: Birth of the Theotokos Monastery), 252.
[449] *Ibid.*, 253.

Spiritual fatherhood has an important place in the therapeutic process. Here again, Hierotheos links three sacraments – Baptism, Chrismation, and Eucharist – with the three stages of the spiritual life and the three degrees of priesthood. His conclusion is that the Church is a spiritual hospital.[450] The conclusion is hardly new, but there is a slight broadening of the sacraments to include Confession, and a systematic integration of sacraments, asceticism, prayer, and spiritual fatherhood.

Metropolitan Hierotheos dedicates a chapter in his book *Hesychia and Theology* to the Divine Liturgy. The Liturgy is presented as an ascent to Mount Sinai, the Upper Room of the Mystical Supper, Gethsemane and Golgotha, a descent into Hades, an ascent to the Upper Room of Pentecost, an experience of the Cross and Resurrection, and a participation in the eschatological Kingdom.[451] One might say that the Metropolitan presents it as a dynamic *anamnesis*. This general perspective of the Eucharist forms a preface to his remarks regarding the hesychastic elements of the Divine Liturgy. The intent of the author is to demonstrate how the outward celebration of the Eucharist must be joined with an inner Liturgy. Simple participation in the Eucharist on the corporate level is not enough. Indeed, the Metropolitan suggests that a penetration into the deeper meaning and power of the Liturgy is not possible unless the two Liturgies, eucharistic and noetic, are joined together.[452] It is from this perspective that he goes on to analyze several moments and characteristics of the Liturgy. He then draws the following conclusion:

> We can, therefore, conclude that the Divine Eucharist is at the centre of ecclesiastical and spiritual life, but is not independent of the hesychastic tradition. The Divine Eucharist must be preceded by a hesychastic way of life; it must be celebrated in a hesychastic and neptic atmosphere; and afterwards this hesychastic and neptic life carries on.[453]

[450]   Hierotheos, *The Science of Spiritual Medicine*, 253.
[451]   Metropolitan of Nafpaktos, Hierotheos, *Hesychia and Theology: The Context for Man's Healing in the Orthodox Church*, trans. Sister Pelagia Selfe, (Levadia, Greece: Birth of the Theotokos Monastery, 2007) 430-435.
[452]   *Ibid.*, 438.
[453]   *Ibid.*, 449.

The Eucharist is at the centre of ecclesiastical and spiritual life, but it can never be separated from the hesychastic tradition, which supplies its context. If the Eucharist is thus conditioned by the hesychastic tradition, it is clear that the latter is also at the centre of ecclesiastical and spiritual life. The reason for this in the Metropolitan's thinking is quite clear: they both have the same goal of deification. [454]

CONCLUSION

Metropolitan Hierotheos has made a significant contribution to twentieth and twenty-first-century Orthodox theological reflection in several important ways. In his many books, he has presented a very compelling argument from patristic sources that the main hallmark of the Orthodox ascetic tradition is its therapeutic character. He has done this without marginalizing the sacramental life; rather, he has convincingly articulated the relationship between asceticism and the sacraments, which is intrinsic to Orthodox spiritual life. The nature of that relationship has perhaps not yet been fully explored in the Metropolitan's works available in English translation, and one might argue that a greater emphasis on the corporate aspects of the Eucharist would be a fine complement to his detailed analysis of the subject. The author has, however, done a very thorough study of the Fathers in order to provide us with a summary of their teaching on the ascetic life. He has also argued very convincingly that the sacraments need an ascetic context in order to be fruitful. Further explication of liturgical sources would serve to broaden the scope of the Metropolitan's sources and provide more integration of the patristic and liturgical dimensions of his work. He has already demonstrated how credibly he was able to do this in his book *The feasts of the Lord*. A sequel focused on the Lenten liturgical cycle would doubtless yield impressive results. Having said this, I believe it is quite evident that Metropolitan Hierotheos has already established a considerable legacy and that any study of asceticism in Orthodox theology will need to take his substantial theological work into account.

This chapter is adapted from an article by Maxym Lysack first published in The Greek Orthodox Theological Review, Volume 44 (1999).

[454] Metropolitan of Nafpaktos, Hierotheos, *The mind of the Orthodox Church*, trans. Esther Williams, (Levadia, Greece: Birth of the Theotokos Monastery, 1998), 111-113.

CHAPTER TEN

TWO IRRECONCILABLE EXTREMES OR TWO REPRESENTATIVES OF ONE GREATER THEOLOGICAL ENTERPRISE?

Father Alexander Schmemann and Metropolitan Hierotheos have two somewhat different theological legacies. In addition, they are not contemporaries, Father Schmemann having left this world forty years ago. Metropolitan Hierotheos is still writing, and his theological work is thus still in the stage of development. Father Schmemann died having just been able to bring his great work *The Eucharist* to a basic level of completion. More importantly, he never had the time to draw out the implications of many of his observations on the effect of asceticism on the life and worship of the Church. What we have are some strong statements about the historical role of monasticism and the latter's impact on the spiritual thinking and eucharistic participation of the faithful. In the closing pages of his last work, Schmemann writes:

> Asceticism, often in its extreme form, constituted the moral ideal of Christian society, and while not always observed, it proved to have an enormous influence. And the decline of the secular or "white" clergy – as witnessed, for example, in the canons of the Council *In Trullo* (691) – led to the leadership of church life passing over to monasticism. It is impossible for us to dwell here on the causes and forms of this many-sided process.

167

What is important is that it gradually led to *clericalization* of
the Church, to a great distancing of clergy and laity from each
other.[455]

The above could certainly be interpreted as a critique of the ascetic
tradition, but Schmemann, in fact, has another concern in mind here:
he wants to identify the processes by which the Church ceased to be an
eschatological community centred on the Eucharist. More specifically, he
wants to highlight the change from corporate participation to individual,
and indeed optional, participation in the Eucharist. In his words, "The
whole 'atmosphere' of the Church changed."[456] The symptoms, or
manifestations, of this change were the clericalization of the Church and
the shift in eucharistic participation. Schmemann's main preoccupation
is to derive a theology from the liturgical tradition of the Church that
would enable the Church to recover its original eucharistic praxis.

Metropolitan Hierotheos does not share this concern of
Schmemann's and does not consistently use the liturgical life of the
Church as a source of theology. An exception to this is Hierotheos's
engaging study *The Feasts of the Lord*. Nevertheless, the difference
between Schmemann and Hierotheos is not to be found exclusively
in their sources for theology, since, when Hierotheos does access the
liturgical tradition of the Church, he is doing it with a different objective
in mind. For the Metropolitan, the feasts are a rich source of dogmatic
theology. He uses them in a catechetical way, locating his dogmatic
presentation squarely in the context of the theology of deification. He
positions himself more as a dogmatic theologian, whereas Schmemann
is clearly a liturgical theologian, deriving his theology from the content,
structure, and ethos of the liturgy. For Hierotheos, the liturgical worship
of the Church is to be interpreted theologically. On the contrary, for
Schmemann, liturgy itself *is* the theology. It is not surprising, therefore,
that the two theologians have different emphases in their work. It is
certainly true that Schmemann may be placed quite legitimately beside
Afanasiev and other early representatives of eucharistic ecclesiology. It

---

[455] Alexander Schmemann, *The Eucharist*, (Crestwood, NY: SVS Press, 1988),
231-232.
[456] *Ibid.*, 232.

168

is also true that Hierotheos can be seen as a theologian of the ascetic tradition. Should we conclude that the two represent fundamentally different poles in Orthodox spirituality that would be hard to reconcile? I do not think so. We can say that there is a divergence between the two theologians, both from the point of view of what they use as sources for theology and from the point of view of their objectives. Both, however, can and should, from my point of view, be seen as representative of the Orthodox spiritual and theological tradition.

Schmemann never exploited the riches of the ascetic tradition to do theology. We do not find in his works an analysis of the writings of the *Philokalia*. Of course, if his primary interest was the liturgical life of the Church, it is not surprising that he would not have found the *Philokalia* to be germane to his area of enquiry. The more relevant question would be: Did he view it with antipathy? I think that the answer to this question is "no." There is no question, however, that he was opposed to people who felt that spirituality could be carved out of the broader Christian tradition and made an entity unto itself. He was also opposed to those who made of the ascetic tradition a world-denying spirituality. He made his position on these matters clear in his work *On Water and the Spirit*, and I have explicated his position in Chapter Eight. As I also noted in the same chapter, Schmemann's explanation of the two fasts, eschatological-eucharistic and ascetic, indicates that he was willing to accept the synthesis in Orthodox spirituality between the ascetic and the eucharistic dimensions. Moreover, his use of the expression "the holy therapy of fasting" shows an openness to the ascetic tradition. Naturally, he would have needed to reconcile himself to the therapy of fasting to enter fully into the ethos of the Lenten cycle of services, the proof of which was more than adequately displayed in his admirable book *Great Lent*.

So what exactly was Schmemann opposing when he made the comments about asceticism at the end of his work *The Eucharist*? He was opposing, as he indicated, the advent of clericalization into the Church. He was taking a position against what he felt was a "pious" but incorrect interpretation of worthy and unworthy participation in the Eucharist. Both of these phenomena, however, may be considered symptoms of a greater change in the "atmosphere" of the Church. What concerned

Schmemann was the displacement of the Eucharist by individual piety, by a kind of privatized asceticism that reduces the great events of the liturgy to moments of individual sanctification. On a theological level, he was concerned with the reduction of the Divine Liturgy as an eschatological event *par excellence* to an allegory for the purposes of individual salvation. In short, Schmemann was opposed to any interpolation into Christian life or theology that made the Eucharist anything less than the Sacrament of the Kingdom. Does this set Schmemann in opposition to the ascetic tradition? No, it does not. Instead, it is an indication that he was opposed to an incorrect interpretation of it. It is possible that Saint Maximos himself saw similar dangers emerging from the monastic movement of his time and that this occasioned the writing of his brilliant work the *Mystagogy*. The difference here is that the Saint united the eschatological and ascetic interpretations into one whole. Regrettably, Father Schmemann did not live long enough to do the same, and the question of a balanced asceticism as an essential part of the spiritual tradition never received the treatment it needed in his work. We are therefore left with fairly clear indications of what he found objectionable, without having the benefit of knowing in detail what he might have embraced. In short, we do not see in Schmemann's work the clear parameters of an asceticism that would both undergird and even enhance the reality of the Eucharist as the Sacrament of the Kingdom. I would contend, however, that such an asceticism does indeed exist.

Metropolitan Hierotheos comes from the generation of theologians after Father Schmemann. Clearly influenced by Father John Romanides, who was his teacher, the Metropolitan theologizes within well-established limits. His main interest is patristic dogmatic theology, with a focus on spirituality, anthropology and ecclesiology. He is unabashedly anti-scholastic and a strong opponent of much of what one would find in post-Augustinian Western theology. True to his mentor, he is an advocate of the therapeutic, non-forensic interpretation of soteriology and a champion of Saint Gregory Palamas. Not surprisingly, he does not position himself with the supporters of eucharistic ecclesiology and is not a personalist of the likes of Christos Yannaras or Metropolitan John Zizioulas. He is clearly not, as we have seen, a liturgical theologian either in terms of his approach to the sources of theology or his established objectives. To say that he interprets Orthodox theology at all times with a view to deification would not be an exaggeration.

Having positioned him on the map of contemporary Orthodox theology, we might be tempted to infer that Hierotheos is an unqualified supporter of the therapeutic-ascetic tradition, radically different from, if not in actual opposition to, supporters of eucharistic ecclesiology. Not only would such an assessment be simplistic, it would also be incorrect. Metropolitan Hierotheos's own appraisal of Metropolitan John Zizioulas' theology of the person – a theology formulated on the basis of eucharistic ecclesiology – is, in fact, quite sympathetic. Hierotheos terms Zizioulas' approach "ecclesiological" and recognizes its fundamental validity. He goes on to qualify it somewhat by suggesting that a third approach, which he names "hesychastic," provides the ascetic context for the ecclesiological approach to the person, thereby bringing it to completion.[457] The fact that Metropolitan Hierotheos's more recent approach to Metropolitan John Zizioulas has been somewhat less irenic is noteworthy, but does not, I hope, invalidate his earlier assessment of Zizioulas' basic theological work on the person and its roots in eucharistic ecclesiology. Opposing Hierotheos to Schmemann or even Zizioulas on the basis of a perceived split between eucharistic spirituality and ascetic-therapeutic spirituality is not immediately informative in this case. All three of them speak of asceticism and the Eucharist; one needs to understand the dynamics, underpinnings, and objectives of their theological work to gain a more nuanced perception of the divergences between them.

If we restrict ourselves to Schmemann and Hierotheos for the moment, we see that the former, as has been noted already, takes the liturgy as the source of theology, while the latter, for the most part, does not. Hierotheos perceives salvation and the spiritual life in therapeutic terms. Schmemann, while not denying the therapeutic aspect, is not especially concerned with it. He is interested instead in the Eucharist as the Sacrament of the Kingdom. Eschatology therefore features prominently in Schmemann's thought. While the eschatological is not absent in Hierotheos's thought, it does not inform it beyond the contours of the

---

[457] Hierotheos, *Hesychia and Theology*, 149-150.

theology of deification. Schmemann begins his theological reflection on the Eucharist with an essay on the Sacrament of the Assembly. His starting point is the Church, and one could argue quite forcefully that his liturgical theology is really an extension of ecclesiology. In this sense, his transition from canonist and church historian to liturgical theologian early in his academic career may not be as dramatic as it might first appear. In fact, he continued his work in ecclesiology, but in a slightly different form. Hierotheos is certainly interested in ecclesiology, but one could not say that it forms the foundation of his thought. The Metropolitan begins his theologizing with the need for establishing an accurate therapy. The Church emerges in his thought as the spiritual hospital, the place for healing. It is still the assembly, the *ekklesia*, but it has been conditioned completely by its purpose: healing with a view to deification. Orthodox Christianity is the science of spiritual medicine. This places the Church in a limited theological framework.

Both Schmemann and Hierotheos are profoundly interested in theological anthropology. Both acknowledge humanity as fallen. For Schmemann, this means that man has turned away from his first vocation, which is to worship and, more specifically, to offer the world back to God. Baptism and Chrismation restore to man his original liturgical calling, making him prophet, priest and king.[458] For Hierotheos, the effect of the Fall is the darkening of the *nous*.[459] Therapy is required for its illumination, and the healing takes place through asceticism and the sacraments. While Father Schmemann does not often frame his soteriology in terms of deification, the concept is clearly not foreign to him, and he is able to place it with ease within a sacramental context.[460] It is not so much, therefore, that Schmemann and Hierotheos are opposed to each other, but more that each one follows the contours of his theological vision – Father Schmemann the Sacrament of the Kingdom, and Metropolitan Hierotheos deification.

Alexander Schmemann perceives all of the spiritual life as a gift. The gift of Baptism is Christ, or more specifically incorporation into

---

[458] Schmemann, *Of Water*, 75-103.
[459] Hierotheos, *Orthodox Spirituality*, 41-45.
[460] Schmemann, *Of Water*, 80.

Christ and His Body. The gift of Chrismation is the Holy Spirit.[461] The Church itself is a gift. The Divine Liturgy is a gift. The Kingdom into which we enter in the Liturgy is a gift. All of life is a gift. This is why Father Schmemann finished his life with a sermon that was in essence a litany of thanksgiving. "Thank you, Lord," is repeated nine times.[462] Father Alexander saw the returning of thanks as the essence of the spiritual life. There is nothing to suggest that Metropolitan Hierotheos would not perceive deification as a gift, but the spirit of his theological work would tend to suggest more that deification is the end of a journey of great effort. The journey is punctuated by great moments of grace, but deification does not come without *askesis*. The deep experience of grace is at the end. Of course, by the "end," Hierotheos has in mind deification in this life and not a beatific vision after death.

If we return to Petros Vassiliadis's thesis that Schmemann represents "eucharistic spirituality" and Hierotheos "therapeutic spirituality," we can see that Vassiliadis's categories are definitely not without merit. The question that must be posed, however, concerns the obvious need for the integration of these two trends and the clear advantages it would have for contemporary Orthodox theology. As we come to understand Schmemann and Hierotheos as representatives of these two trends, does it not become evident that the two approaches need to be integrated, not simply because it would reflect a synthesis hypothetically effected by Saint Maximos in the seventh century, but because it would allow Orthodox theology to be true to its scriptural and patristic sources while reflecting its genuine liturgical ethos and vision?

Metropolitan John Zizioulas does not style himself a liturgical theologian. Nevertheless, there is no question that he approaches the liturgy as a source for theology. The difference between Schmemann and Zizioulas is that, while the former theologizes based to a great extent on the *ordo*, the shape, and the content of the liturgy, the latter places the liturgy into a very broad framework that references not only ecclesiology, but also Christology and Pneumatology. The theological

---

461   *Ibid.*, 79.
462   See Juliana Schmemann, *My Journey with Father Alexander* (Montreal: Alexander Press, 2006), 99-100.

horizons of Zizioulas' thought are broad. He asks the questions that are implicit in Schmemann's work but not always explored. Furthermore, he makes an attempt, even if it is a limited one, to address the ascetic dimension in Orthodox theology. This, together with his encyclopedic approach to theology and keen interest in contemporary philosophical problems, makes him an imposing figure in modern Orthodox theology. It is to Metropolitan John Zizioulas that we now turn in the last chapter of this book.

Section D:
Metropolitan John of Pergamon: Spirituality and Its Underpinnings

CHAPTER ELEVEN

METROPOLITAN JOHN OF PERGAMON ON THE SPIRITUAL LIFE: AN ANALYSIS

Having started with Metropolitan John Zizioulas at the beginning of this study, we now return, as we approach the end of this book, to a discussion of his spirituality. If, as Zizioulas posits, Saint Maximos the Confessor was responsible for effecting a synthesis of monastic and eucharistic spiritualities, to what extent can that synthesis be perceived in Zizioulas' own theological work? As I noted in Chapter One, the ascetic dimension in the Metropolitan's thought is wanting. It is not absent, but it is restricted. In this chapter, I would like to highlight some of the areas that could be further developed in Zizioulas' thought.

THE ANTECEDENTS IN ORTHODOX THEOLOGY

As I noted in Chapter One, Father Boris Bobrinskoy observed that Father Dumitru Staniloae was perhaps the first among contemporary Orthodox theologians to locate the synthesis between the hesychastic tradition and the Eucharist in the *Philokalia*.[463] The key is that Staniloae discovered it there: he was not required to effect the synthesis anew. This allowed Father Staniloae to articulate a theology based on the teachings of Saint Mark the Ascetic and Saints Kallistos and Ignatios that is squarely in the ascetic tradition but shows all the characteristics of balance and synthesis that Zizioulas could find quite admirable. The

[463]   Chapter 1, 8.

Liturgy of the Heart is precisely the place where the two dimensions, ascetic and eucharistic, converge. This inner liturgy represents the point of intersection of the Eucharist with asceticism. Staniloae was able to demonstrate this with great precision and simplicity. If Saint Maximos was one of the first to forge a synthesis between monastic and eucharistic spiritualities, he was clearly not the last. As I have only begun to demonstrate in the chapters on Saint Symeon the New Theologian and Saint Gregory Palamas, this synthesis was articulated by these two prominent Fathers of the Church after the time of Saint Maximos. Zizioulas knows intuitively that these Fathers are theologians of the Eucharist *par excellence*, but he does not follow his intuition to explore their writings in detail. It is clearly a missed opportunity for the Metropolitan, and the failure to pursue his solid intuition led him to articulate a theology that does not always exhibit a true sensitivity to the ascetic dimension.

In addition, even some of the Fathers much loved and frequently referenced by Zizioulas worked with therapeutic themes, but this fact does not seem to have convinced him to give their ascetic works an authoritative place in his thought. As a result, we know what Saint Basil's contribution was to the Second Ecumenical Council, but we do not hear anything about his decisive role in the organization of monasticism. We read about Saint Gregory of Nyssa's teaching on the *imago dei* and freedom, but we are not exposed to his spiritual thought as expounded in *The Life of Moses*. We are presented with Saint Gregory Nazianzen as a brilliant theologian, but we do not discover him as a spiritual master. While it is normal for a dogmatic theologian such as Zizioulas to confine himself to those writings of the Fathers that prove most salient to his work, he must nonetheless maintain an awareness of the scope of the witness of those Fathers and incorporate something of that richness and depth into any exposition of their thought. Zizioulas relies heavily on what he argues is the decisive contribution of the Cappadocians to the Christian understanding of *hypostasis* as person. His presentation is very compelling. Taking into account, however, the profound interest that the Cappadocians had in the spiritual life and their fundamental commitment to monasticism as an indispensable expression of Christian life, how does the Metropolitan then place monasticism, and with it a good part of the ascetic tradition on the periphery of his own theological project?

METROPOLITAN JOHN ZIZIOULAS' EARLIER WORK: BEING AS COMMUNION

For Zizioulas, Christian spirituality is not properly experienced outside of the community; it is inherently corporate.[464] However, purification of the heart, illumination of the *nous* and the vision of God are undergone and experienced by *persons,* not by communities. So we are left with two alternatives: either the activities connected with the three stages of the ascetic life are intrinsically ecclesial, and therefore an extension of the life of the Church lived out on an individual level, or they are outside of the community and therefore not representative of Christian spirituality. For Father Staniloae, it is clearly the former; in the case of Zizioulas, it is unclear. On one hand, Zizioulas does not state that personal prayer and asceticism are not ecclesial; on the other hand, he does not appear to need them for his thought. Indeed, one is struck by the dearth of references to personal prayer and experience in Zizioulas' works. It would appear that the Metropolitan does not have a real place for them in his ecclesiology. They appear to have been eclipsed by his overriding concern for ontology. While there is little in Zizioulas' early work that would clarify his position, we do have a brief statement with a footnote in one of his essays in *Being as Communion.* Having addressed what he feels are the most important aspects of Pneumatology, Zizioulas adds somewhat parenthetically:

> Now there have been also other functions attached to the particular work of the Spirit in Christian theology, e.g. inspiration and sanctification. The Orthodox tradition has attached particular significance to the latter, namely sanctification, perhaps because of the strong Origenistic influence that has always existed in the East. This is evident in Monasticism as a form of what is normally called "spirituality." But Monasticism – and the notions of "sanctification" and "spirituality" that lie

---

[464] Zizioulas, *Early,* 27.

behind it – has never become a decisive aspect of *ecclesiology* in the East. Ecclesiology in the Orthodox tradition has always been determined by the liturgy, the eucharist; and for this reason it is the first two aspects of Pneumatology, namely *eschatology* and *communion* that have determined Orthodox ecclesiology.[465]

Sensing perhaps that his statement required further explanation or justification, Zizioulas provides the following qualification in a footnote to the text:

> In saying this I do not wish to undermine the importance of individual sanctification, especially as this is understood by Monasticism. Orthodox monasticism is, in any case, tied up with eschatology so closely that it becomes in this way deeply related with ecclesiology. What I wish to underline, however, is that no "spirituality" is healthy and truly Christian unless it is constantly dependent on the event of ecclesial communion. The eschatological community *par excellence* is to be found in the Eucharist, which is thus the heart of all ecclesiology.[466]

The Metropolitan is prepared to acknowledge that sanctification is a work of the Holy Spirit, and he is very much aware that *individual* sanctification figures prominently in Orthodox spirituality, but he refuses to give it a place of significance. It is partially dismissed with the label "Origenistic" and then neatly disposed of by stating that monasticism and its notions of spirituality and sanctification have never been determining factors for ecclesiology in the East. Then, in a moment of apparent ambivalence, he partially rehabilitates it by stating that it had a strong connection with eschatology in any case, so it can fit into the model of Pneumatology that he both espouses and prescribes. Zizioulas' fundamental reservations about monasticism never seem to disappear in his work, but his willingness to engage the topic of asceticism appears to increase with time.

[465] John D. Zizioulas, "Christ, the Spirit and the Church" in *Being as Communion*, (Crestwood, NY: SVS Press, 1985), 131.
[466] *Ibid.*, n. 19.

METROPOLITAN JOHN ZIZIOULAS' LATER WORK: COMMUNION AND OTHERNESS

In his work *Communion and Otherness*, Zizioulas addresses the role of asceticism in ontology. It is clear that he became convinced of the necessity of including it in his work. *Communion and Otherness* represents a completion of what the Metropolitan wrote in *Being as Communion* and, in my view, a progression in the author's theological reflection on spirituality. In Zizioulas' own words, the Church "is in fact founded on martyrdom and asceticism,"[467] a statement he clearly accepts from the historical point of view but does not seem to integrate fully into his ecclesiology. Nevertheless, it would be unfair to dismiss his position entirely. The venerable theologian attempted to bring more balance into his theological analysis, and it should be received on that level. I believe that there is much in *Communion and Otherness* to suggest that Zizioulas was in the process of rethinking his position. The fact that he explicitly connects asceticism to ontology in his later work demonstrates that the author is prepared to give the former serious consideration within the framework of an ontological study. Since it could be argued that Zizioulas has framed his whole theological work within the context of ontology, it means that asceticism has gained a meaningful, albeit not central place in his theological vision.

Zizioulas states: "The ascetic life, therefore, is not concerned with the inner psychological experiences of the individual. Its ground is ontological: one is truly oneself in so far as one is hypostasized in the Other while emptying oneself so that the Other may be hypostasized in oneself."[468] The Metropolitan is placing asceticism in an ontological framework and is insisting that it must be understood in that context alone. Asceticism, when properly understood, leads to communion. The process required to reach communion is self-emptying. Asceticism is therefore to be considered intrinsically kenotic. The corollary here is that everything that seeks to pass itself off as asceticism but is not kenotic and does not aim at communion is in fact not asceticism at all. This seems, at least on the surface, to be a legitimate qualification of

---

[467] Zizioulas, *Communion and Otherness*, 78.
[468] *Ibid.*, 85.

Christian asceticism. The critique of expressions of Christian mysticism that are focused on the inner experiences of the person rather than on the turning of the whole person towards God and others is very welcome. By placing asceticism in an explicitly theological context, Zizioulas gives it a true *raison d'être*. The risk here, however, is that the rejection of all inner experiences as psychological and potentially dangerous, at least from the point of view of an ontological framework, could lead not only to a loss of subjectivity, but to a loss of the subject.[469] While it is clear that Zizioulas has built many safeguards into his thought that would militate against this loss – the author is in fact very insistent that the true *hypostasis* emerges from this communion – it might serve Zizioulas well to make a more nuanced assessment of inner experiences so that they are not all rejected in the name of ontology. Having said this, I think that we can go along with the Metropolitan's basic premise here and continue with a presentation of his understanding of asceticism.

Transferring Evil from the Other to the Self

For Zizioulas then, asceticism is fundamentally ontological. What shall we say then of the moral dimension? Is it lost in Zizioulas' ontologically oriented asceticism? Perhaps the author would argue that it is not lost so much as surpassed. Clearly, however, Zizioulas sees the moral approach as essentially obstructive of the ontological.[470] Here is where he might reconsider some aspects of his position, since the implicit weakness would appear be a refusal to take seriously the devastating effects of sin on the human person and on humanity in general. The moral aspect *does have* a certain immediacy that should not be overlooked. In any case, Zizioulas' argument is engaging, if incomplete: if a person,

[469] Father Nicholas Loudovikos argues this point in his article "Person Instead of Grace and Dictated Otherness: John Zizioulas' Final Theological Position." For a cogent argument that Zizioulas is at risk of sacrificing the particularity of persons in his theological thought, see Miroslav Volf, *After Our Likeness: The Church as the Image of the Trinity* (Grand Rapids, MI: Wm. B. Eerdmans Publishing Co., 2008), 87, 182.

[470] See Pantelis Kalaitzidis, "New trends in Greek Orthodox theology: challenges in the movement towards a genuine renewal and Christian unity." *Scottish Journal of Theology* 67 (2014), n. 22, 145.

even an evil person, is to be known on the basis of what he does or has done alone, that person is condemned to non-existence. The person is marked as evil and, since evil is outside of God, the person would have no chance for communion, and therefore no chance for survival. Nevertheless, Zizioulas knows that evil is a reality to be reckoned with, and realizes that it cannot be ignored. Here the theologian proposes a striking solution: the evil should be transferred from the other to the self. The Desert Fathers, according to Zizioulas, were shining examples of this ascetic feat: "No one has taken evil as seriously as they have .... Yet in a remarkable way they insisted that the Other should be kept free from moral judgment and categorization. This they achieved not by disregarding evil but by *transferring it from the Other to the Self.*"[471]

However, transferring evil from the other to the self is not all that is required here. Zizioulas goes further, suggesting that what we are observing here is more than a principle of Christian asceticism: "The death of 'self' is the *sine qua non* condition for salvation."[472] This is a strong statement indeed, and it brings us back to a question I posed in Chapter One: Which "self" does Zizioulas have in mind here? Is this the "self" as the autonomous unit, the centre of consciousness? Is this simply the self-centred, self-preserving "self," the "self" in rebellion against God? Perhaps this question might not seem entirely relevant to the Metropolitan's thinking here. The point for him, most likely, is about communion. For real communion to occur, the "self" must die. Without communion, there is no salvation. Salvation refers to ontology. Is it ontology, however, that the Desert Fathers had in mind, explicitly or implicitly? If they are going to be cited in support of this notion, this would be a fair question. I think that Zizioulas would have strengthened his presentation by being more specific here. Are all elements of self-awareness and consciousness excluded from otherness? If so, ontology is placing a heavy burden on anthropology.

Further comment, I believe, should be made about the spiritual dynamics in the transfer of evil from the other to the self. While there must be a sense in which the other is liberated in this movement, the main thrust

---

[471] Zizioulas, *Communion and Otherness*, 82.
[472] *Ibid.*

of the action affects the one who makes the transfer. In this ascetic feat, the self is liberated through self-accusation. Pride is crushed and, through humility, the true self emerges. This true self places itself in the posture of communion with the other, but this does not mean that full communion occurs. The other is free, in a perverse sense, to refuse it. Communion cannot be dictated any more than the transfer of evil to the self can be required. Curiously, they have to carry the possibility of failure to have the opportunity for success or completion. This does not mean, of course, that a Christian ought not to offer forgiveness unilaterally or seek the transfer of evil from the other to the self unconditionally. It means simply that communion cannot be imposed. Zizioulas insists that the transfer of evil to self and the offering of oneself for the other have a firm theological basis in Christology,[473] and he is right. Christ indeed died for us and took our sins to Himself. In this sense, we are saved objectively. Who would insist, however, that Christ's forgiveness is imputed to all without any possibility for refusal? The Resurrection of all will serve as proof that Christ's victory is complete. The experience of that victory will, nevertheless, remain radically different for those who receive it and those who reject it. It is the difference between heaven and hell. To understand salvation in ontological terms, as Zizioulas does, is not a mistake. There is a sound basis for it in soteriology. It seems, however, that Zizioulas has made certain anthropological assumptions regarding the self, and these need to be clarified.

KENOTIC ASCETICISM: SAINT SOPHRONY SAKHAROV

Zizioulas' assertion that asceticism is intrinsically kenotic is supported in his work by references to the *alloquia* of Abba Zosimas, a sixth-century desert Father, and the writings of Saint Sophrony Sakharov, a twentieth-century monastic elder and ascetic theologian.[474] The allusion to Elder Sophrony is interesting, since the former developed a whole theology of the emergence of the *hypostasis* long before the Metropolitan did. A full scientific study of the connection between the two would be enlightening indeed. While there are some clear differences between the two –

---

473   *Ibid.*, 83.
474   *Ibid.*

Saint Sophrony had a very keen sense of the ascetic tradition and was profoundly committed to monasticism – it seems entirely plausible that Metropolitan John may have adopted certain philosophical and theological assumptions from him. That Sophrony emphasizes the kenotic element in Christian theology is very evident, but the important question is: To what end? The Metropolitan cites an authoritative study on the thought of Elder Sophrony by Hieromonk Nicholas Sakharov, the grandnephew of Archimandrite Sophrony: "In its 'positive' aspect, kenosis develops the hypostatic *modus agens* – the entire giving over of the I to the other, and the *modus patiendi* – the receiving of the other in his or her fullness."[475] However, Metropolitan John neglects to state that, according to Father Nicholas, *kenosis* in Father Sophrony's thought is intimately connected to repentance and the death of the 'old man.'[476] The Archimandrite also places his theology of *kenosis* in the context of a highly developed ascetic anthropology, much of which he relates to the monastic life. For Saint Sophrony, *kenosis* is a process, and it is clearly something that the monastic or the Christian living in the world must choose to engage: "Hence, kenosis is linked with the idea of the *amplitude* of Christian experience. The closer one advances one's *ascent* to God, the broader is the diapason of one's being."[477] In other words, Sophrony connects asceticism to ontology: the more one deepens one's self-emptying, the more one enters the reality of a new life in Christ. Here asceticism is a precondition for ontology. For Zizioulas, ontology determines asceticism. For this reason, there is little room for ascetic development, a word which Zizioulas himself eschews.[478] There is also little space for Christian experience, a term which Sophrony, unlike Zizioulas, appears to find neither foreign nor objectionable.

METROPOLITAN JOHN ZIZIOULAS AND SAINT SOPHRONY ON SPIRITUALITY: A COMPARISON

Comparing the spiritual thought of Metropolitan John to that of Saint Sophrony is an informative exercise that serves to highlight

475 Nicholas Sakharov, *I Love Therefore I Am: The Theological Legacy of Archimandrite Sophrony*, (Crestwood, NY: SVS Press, 2002), 107.
476 *Ibid.*, 106.
477 *Ibid.*, 108.
478 Zizioulas, *Communion and Otherness*, 84.

both the similarities with and the divergences from the mainstream of the ascetic tradition in the work of the former. It is, I believe, an appropriate comparison, since Elder Sophrony placed a high value on ontology and was conversant with many of the philosophical and theological currents of the twentieth century that influenced the Metropolitan. The affinities make for a sympathetic comparison. Archimandrite Sophrony reveals his ascetic theology in many of his works, but gives an especially concise exposition in his essay *Principles of Orthodox Asceticism*. Sophrony states the following at the beginning of his essay:

> The ascetic continually endeavours to attain perfection. But the perfection which we have in mind is not contained in the *created* nature of man, and so cannot be achieved by developing the potentialities of this nature, as such, with its limitations. Our perfection is in the Divine Being, and is the gift of the Holy Spirit.[479]

We can see in this passage the affinity that Metropolitan John would appear to have for Saint Sophrony's position. The latter is saying that perfection means transcending created nature and entering the Divine Being. Sophrony is clearly presenting perfection in ontological terms, although, as I have noted, asceticism necessarily precedes the ontological for him. Sophrony emphasizes that perfection is the gift of the Holy Spirit, just as Zizioulas insists that "*theosis* is always *granted*, never achieved by the individual."[480] On the surface, the two authors would appear to be saying exactly the same thing. As Sophrony continues to develop his argument, however, the divergences between the former and Zizioulas begin to appear immediately:

> It follows from this that the ascetic concentrates on an effort to merge his life and will with the life and will of God Himself. This he arrives at mainly in prayer, and so prayer is the summit

---

[479] Archimandrite Sophrony, "Principles of Orthodox Asceticism." *The Orthodox Ethos*, A. J. Philippou (ed.). (Oxford, England: Holywell Press, 1964), 259.
[480] Zizioulas, *Communion and Otherness*, 84.

of every ascetic action. Orthodox asceticism reaches its highest
expression in prayer, and the Orthodox ascetic devotes his chief
energies to prayer.[481]

The will, of course, figures prominently in the ascetic tradition, so it is no
surprise that Saint Sophrony introduces it early in his article. The word
"effort" and "merge" are used both because there is a process here and
because that process is arduous. In Zizioulas' statements on asceticism,
there is a paucity of references to process and, as we shall see later, the
role of the will is diminished. While he would concede, I think, that
kenosis is a process, and I am sure that he would agree that it requires
effort, there is nonetheless a different spiritual dynamic at work in his
thinking. Because of his reluctance to engage the will meaningfully,
Zizioulas prescribes a kind of sudden ontological shift: the room is
made for the other; the self must die. How? We do not find the answer
to this question. There is a kind of violence here to the human person
that Zizioulas certainly does not intend, but nevertheless does not seem
to perceive. It is not, however, the violence of the ascetic life, it is the
violence of an imposed ontological programme. It does not address the
ambivalence of the human heart or the weakness of the will, it simply
declares the self dead. Yes, of course, Zizioulas discusses *eros* and *ekstasis*
at length,[482] and it is fair to assume that this somehow includes the will,
since the ecstatic movement is initiated by the Christian in search of
communion with the other. Such is the dynamic of love, but if the
Christian life is, as Saint Maximos states and as Zizioulas proposes[483],
a journey from self-love to pure love, where then is the theology of the
journey? It cannot be subsumed into the ontological programme alone.
It needs a theology of its own, and that theology must, as it does in Elder
Sophrony's writings, set the indispensable precondition for ontology. To
use Zizioulas' own language, ontology must be conditioned by ascetic
theology.

Saint Sophrony continues his exposition of Orthodox asceticism by
stating that the merging of the life and will of the ascetic with the life

[481] Archimandrite Sophrony, "Principles," 259.
[482] Zizioulas, *Communion and Otherness*, 70-75.
[483] *Ibid.*, 84.

and will of God is achieved in prayer. As I have noted earlier, one is hard pressed to find references to personal prayer in the writings of Zizioulas. Of course, there is a continuing reference to the prayer of the eucharistic liturgy. This is clearly not what Sophrony has in mind, however, when he writes about prayer in the ascetic context. Is this simply a question of preference? In my view, it could not be. Sophrony is working from an ecclesiology in which personal prayer and ascetic effort have a meaningful place. Prayer, for Saint Sophrony, is the highest expression of Orthodox asceticism. It is by pure prayer that the ascetic, by the power of the Holy Spirit, enters the Divine Being. It follows, then, that the ascetic must commit his entire life to the achievement of pure prayer. From this, we get the whole theology of the ascetic tradition in all its beauty and power, since ascetics have, in the communion of the Church, been reflecting on the journey to pure prayer for many centuries.

Saint Sophrony writes: "Monasticism above all means purity of the *mind*, which is unattainable without obedience."[484] The Archimandrite returns to this theme and variations on it several times in his essay. In asceticism, the struggle against intrusive thoughts and for the purity of the mind is paramount. Ascetic texts in the Orthodox Church are replete with references to the struggle against thoughts. Indeed, a large part of the struggle against temptation takes place in the mind. Commenting on a passage from Saint Gregory of Nyssa's *On Virginity*, Saint Sophrony summarizes a key imperative in the ascetic tradition this way: "'Let me merely say that the most vital point in this 'art' is the 'preservation of the mind' – the most important rule in this 'feat' is *not to surrender the mind.*'"[485]

This aspect of the preservation of the mind appears to be completely absent from Metropolitan John's presentation of the subject. It is an example of how a purely ontological explanation of asceticism cannot contain all the important elements of the tradition.

Zizioulas does not discuss the will often, but in a rare reference to the will and its place in asceticism, he speaks about the "breaking of one's own will." Freedom from one's own will, he opines, represents the

---

[484] Archimandrite Sophrony, "Principles," 271.
[485] *Ibid.,* 281.

highest form of freedom.[486] This freedom allows a person to enter into the experience of death and the abyss of nothingness found at the depths of the human condition.[487] Zizioulas takes special care to state on several occasions that this is not an individual experience. Everything is placed very deliberately in the context of the corporate.

If we take into consideration what Saint Sophrony says about the subject of the will in the spiritual life, we find a stark contrast. For Sophrony, the essence of the ascetic life lies in the *union* of two natural wills and two natural energies, human and divine.[488] He is very careful to avoid any discussion of the simple breaking of the human will. The monastic life must reflect an obedience that is entirely consensual.[489] The spiritual father must be careful not to destroy the novice's will to make it conform to his arbitrary will.[490] The union of the human will with the divine is the true objective. There is a place for grace, and there is a place for human effort.[491]

What Saint Sophrony is describing reflects very accurately the principles of Chalcedonian Christology. Indeed, the Saint insists that this position reflects the dogmatic tradition of the Church.[492] Metropolitan John is silent about this reality in Orthodox asceticism, and it would seem that the principles of Chalcedonian Christology that he esteems so highly are being applied selectively in his work. When the application of these dogmatic norms does not enhance the collective, they are passed over in silence. Thus we have the Metropolitan quoting with approval the saying of Saint Silouan "Keep thy mind in hell and despair not," but avoiding any discussion of the union of the human will with the divine in the life of a Christian.[493] We could say the same thing about the preservation of the mind. Both of these important aspects of the spiritual life are experienced in individual persons. Saint Silouan and Saint Sophrony are both cited, but many of the riches of

---

[486] Zizioulas, *Communion and Otherness*, 303.
[487] *Ibid.*
[488] Archimandrite Sophrony, "Principles," 281.
[489] *Ibid.*, 274.
[490] *Ibid.*, 275.
[491] *Ibid.*, 281.
[492] *Ibid.*
[493] Zizioulas, *Communion and Otherness*, 83.

their spiritual and theological vision are left untouched. There is no way for humanity to guard its collective mind, at least not from the Christian point of view. Similarly, the union of the human will with the divine, as well as the human energy or activity with the divine, take place in persons, not collectives. The resources of the ascetic tradition are being tapped, but the ascetic tradition itself is not being integrated in its totality. What we have here is clearly not a synthesis of the sacramental and the ascetic dimensions – it is an unequal union. That Zizioulas has given serious consideration to reconciling his theological programme with the Orthodox ascetic tradition is clear and very admirable. What we are witnessing, however, speaks more of an attempt to acknowledge the presence and importance of the ascetic tradition without actually permitting it to establish certain abiding principles for ecclesiology. In this sense, Metropolitan John has not implemented the principles of the Maximian synthesis fully in his own theological work as of yet.

METROPOLITAN JOHN ZIZIOULAS ON ASCETICISM, THEOSIS, AND THE EUCHARIST

What does Metropolitan John have to say about the relationship between asceticism and the Eucharist? We have a clear statement on this question: "The ascetic life culminates in the Eucharist. There is no *theosis* outside the Eucharist, for it is only there that communion and otherness coincide and reach their fullness."[494] The first statement, that the ascetic life culminates in the Eucharist, has clear support from patristic sources, notably the Fathers whose works were treated in this study: Saint Maximos, Saint Symeon the New Theologian, and Saint Gregory Palamas. All three would agree that the Eucharist perfects and completes the ascetic life, but would all of them agree that there is no *theosis* outside the Eucharist? I believe the answer to this question is "no": this would be to drive a wedge between asceticism and the Eucharist. If the *Mystagogy* of Saint Maximos is indeed a work of synthesis, and if, as Zizioulas insists, the principles of Chalcedonian Christology must be applied to dogmatic areas outside of Christology, then clearly the

---

[494] *Ibid.*, 85.

therapeutic or ascetic tradition must not be absorbed into the eucharistic to form a "monophysitic" union of the two. And yet, if asceticism only *culminates* in the Eucharist and does not itself lead to *theosis*, this is indeed the situation. Applying Chalcedonian Christological norms to the relationship between asceticism and the Eucharist should allow us to conceive of both as deifying, even if we still see the Eucharist as the logical completion of asceticism. Saint Gregory Palamas states explicitly that *both* asceticism and the Eucharist have deification as their common goal.

Saint Symeon the New Theologian places a great emphasis on the deifying action of the Eucharist, but insists that the Eucharist cannot be approached without ascetic preparation. In the *Ethical Discourses*, he states that the Eucharist cannot be apprehended by the senses; instead, one must approach the Eucharist through intellection. One reaches intellection only through asceticism, so the end result is that the deifying power of the Eucharist is received by and through asceticism. In this sense, while the Saint does indeed see the Eucharist as deifying, *he does not see it as deifying without asceticism.* This is the nuance that Zizioulas is missing here when he describes the relationship between ascetic practice and the Eucharist. Furthermore, Saint Symeon has placed the whole discussion of the relationship between the ascetic and eucharistic dimensions on a new level by presenting the reception of the Holy Spirit as the objective of both. Perhaps there is indeed a degree of artificiality in discussing the connection between asceticism and the Eucharist without having a wider conversation about the goal of the spiritual life. I will return to this question in the Conclusion of this study.

METROPOLITAN JOHN ZIZIOULAS' FUNDAMENTAL ASSUMPTIONS

By insisting that there is no *theosis* outside the Eucharist, Metropolitan John is making his theological position clear. The reason for this assertion is the author's conviction that communion and otherness reach their fullness only there. Here again, ontology has the place of primacy. There are in fact two basic assumptions here: the first is that ontology is the essence of all theology; the second is that the Eucharist is the *locus* for all ontological activity. One can accept or reject this at face value. Zizioulas

191

has certainly made a convincing case for the revisioning of Christian theology along ontological lines. Recently, he has allowed for more nuance in his thinking,[495] although this may simply represent more of a modest reappraisal of his theological work than an actual softening of his fundamental position. There are basic historical assumptions involved in his thesis, beginning with an analysis of pre-Christian Greek philosophical thought and moving to early Christian thought. There is the assumption that the work of the Cappadocian theologians represents a watershed in the development of Christian theological articulation. There is the assumption about Saint Maximos the Confessor as the chief synthesizer in the history of Christian spirituality. There are assumptions about the development of post-Augustinian thought in the West. There are more assumptions about the development of the self in Western thought and the efforts to free the same thought from an oppressive philosophy of the self. These are just a few of the historical assumptions implicit in Zizioulas' work, and the theological academy awaits studies that would test their actual historical validity.

THE EXCLUSIVE PRIMACY OF THE EUCHARIST IN METROPOLITAN JOHN ZIZIOULAS' THOUGHT

In this study, we have briefly examined the idea of the Maximian synthesis in the spiritual thought of the Christian East. We are concerned here with the theological and more specifically ecclesiological assumption that the Eucharist exercises a kind of primacy in the spiritual life to the exclusion of any other dimension. While this exclusion does not represent a total eclipse of the ascetic dimension, it clearly places the ascetic life, and with it all prayer outside of the context of the Eucharist, in a position of subordination, if not complete absorption. This is not simply, as I have just indicated, an assumption about the history of Christian spirituality or even about the place of individual prayer in the spiritual life; rather, it is an explicitly ecclesiological assumption based on Christology. In assessing the theological legacies of both Cardinal Henri de Lubac and Metropolitan John

[495] Metropolitan John (Zizioulas) of Pergamon, "Person and Nature in the Theology of St. Maximus the Confessor. Knowing the Purpose of Creation through the Resurrection: Proceedings of the Symposium on St. Maximus the Confessor", Bishop Maxim (Vasiljevic), ed., Alhambra, CA: Sebastian Press, 2013, 85-113.

Zizioulas, Father Paul McPartlan authored an impressive study entitled *The Eucharist Makes the Church*.[496] The title seems to be a more than fair appraisal of these two great theologians and summarizes the commonality of their vision. Perhaps, however, with the publication of *Communion and Otherness*, we need to consider the possibility of the title of a new study on the theological vision of Zizioulas himself: *The Eucharist is the Church*. This would seem to be a rather presumptuous title, and one lacking in any nuance. It may, however, be not far off the mark. While Zizioulas prefers a more balanced statement of the relationship between the Church and the Eucharist, and has described that relationship by stating that "the Church constitutes the Eucharist while being constituted by it," [497] he nevertheless comes to the conclusion that "Church and Eucharist are interdependent; they coincide, and are even in some sense identical."[498] Thus, while the Church can be distinguished from the Eucharist on certain levels, and while there are a few senses in which the Church constitutes the Eucharist – by gathering as one people, by possessing the Spirit, and by receiving the priestly ministry – the Church and the Eucharist, in the end, are one reality. Here communion, otherness, Eucharist, Church, and even Christ all converge. It is no small wonder that asceticism in Zizioulas' thought has lost virtually everything that does not pertain to the Eucharist directly. The Maximian synthesis, alas, is undone by its very expositor and advocate. What is left of the ascetic tradition has not only been repositioned, it has been reconditioned and redefined. The altar of the Eucharist remains, but the altar of the heart has been rendered superfluous. The vision of Saints Kallistos and Ignatios of prayer as a eucharistic sacrifice, so eloquently expounded by Father Dumitru Staniloae, has been relegated, in effect, to the realm of Orthodox piety. Zizioulas' unquestionably brilliant and sweepingly comprehensive attempt at synthesis of the dimensions of the spiritual life has been partially unsuccessful.

Should we understand the Church in strictly eucharistic terms,

---

[496]   Paul McPartlan, *The Eucharist Makes the Church: Henri de Lubac and John Zizioulas in Dialogue* (Edinburgh, Scotland: T & T Clark, 1993).
[497]   John D. Zizioulas, "Ecclesiological Presuppositions of the Holy Eucharist." *The One and the Many: Studies on God, Man, the Church, and the World Today*, Fr. Gregory Edwards (ed.). (Alhambra, CA: Sebastian Press, 2010), 68.
[498]   *Ibid.*

as Zizioulas would seem to do, or should we grasp it in wider terms that include, of course, the Holy Eucharist, but also all of the efforts and experiences of the People of God across human history? The latter appears to better represent the theological vision of Father Dumitru Staniloae. When Saint Maximos the Confessor wrote in his *Mystagogy* that, at the time of the closing of the doors in the eucharistic assembly, the doors of history are closed, did he mean this to the exclusion of all ascetic efforts, personal prayers, and lived experiences of Christians outside of the eucharistic liturgy? Could he possibly have meant anything close to this if he was writing as a monk? If he indeed placed the ascetic life in a eucharistic context, was he not also retaining the ascetic life in all its integrity? Clearly he was. Maximos articulated asceticism in a eucharistic context *while keeping the former dimension intact*. Zizioulas has not received the ascetic tradition in this way.

As I noted earlier, Zizioulas' insistence that all *theosis* takes place in the Eucharist is not by chance but by plan. Church and Eucharist have been so tightly connected that it becomes difficult to distinguish one from the other. It is, in fact, as if Zizioulas has located the totality of the Church in the Eucharist, with Baptism acting as a point of entry to it. That said, it is clear that the Metropolitan is aware that Orthodox ecclesiology has two sources: "The Orthodox take their account of the Church from two sources. The first of these is the divine Eucharist, the liturgical experience that all Christians share. The second is the experience of the Christian life and the ascetic tradition of the Church."[499] The question that remains is: Why does Zizioulas not provide a meaningful and enduring place for asceticism in his ecclesiology when he recognizes the former's importance as one of the latter's sources? The words "take their account" are somewhat ambiguous, but they suggest at a minimum that asceticism has been of great importance for the Orthodox narrative of the Church.

METROPOLITAN JOHN ZIZIOULAS' UNDERSTANDING OF ASCETICISM

The answer, I believe, is in Zizioulas' understanding of asceticism. The theologian perceives asceticism as a struggle against evil. Most importantly,

[499]   Zizioulas, *Lectures*, 121.

he links it with the Cross. To Zizioulas' mind, this connection with the Cross makes it part of the Church, *but not part of the ultimate purpose of the Church*. Zizioulas explains his position in this way:

> The Church is the foretaste and realisation of the Kingdom of God, so the spiritual and ascetic life by which we participate in suffering and the cross do not represent the ultimate purpose of the Church. The ascetic life is part of the Church, and the Christian who bears the marks of his participation in the cross of Christ on his person is assuredly a part of the life of the Church. However, when we put on the gold vestments of the eucharistic liturgy, we are looking forward to the kingdom of God. The Church is constituted by the resurrection and so has travelled past the cross and broken through into that new creation which is filled with the uncreated life of God.[500]

Zizioulas' position may be summarized as follows: Asceticism is part of the life of the Church, but linked to the Cross. This grounds it in the Church's life *currently*. Since the Church has passed the Cross, however, and has entered the new life based in the Resurrection, the Church has passed asceticism as well. This is why Zizioulas states that *theosis* occurs in the Eucharist alone. To be deified is to participate in the new life. To Zizioulas' mind, asceticism can help lead one there, but not take one in. Zizioulas eschews any ecclesiology that finds its goal and purpose in the Cross.[501] He speaks of "some Lutherans,"[502] by which he almost certainly means Jürgen Moltmann. He also refers to "those Russian theologians who also see the life of the eternal as bound to suffering and the cross."[503] Here he likely has Father Sergius Bulgakov in mind.[504] The unnamed theologians are dismissed in a paragraph without any real appeal to scriptural exegesis or the tradition as a whole. We are simply left with Zizioulas' contentions

---

[500]   Zizioulas, *Lectures*, 134-135.
[501]   Ibid., 134.
[502]   *Ibid.*
[503]   *Ibid.*
[504]   Zizioulas criticizes both theologians for introducing "kenoticism" into the immanent Trinity. See n. 145, *Communion and Otherness*, 63.

that the Liturgy is eschatologically grounded and that many ecclesiologies stand in need of liberation from their Cross-centredness.

If we accept Zizioulas' first contention, we are still left facing an apparent contradiction within Zizioulas' own work: the exclusion of monasticism and its associated "spirituality" from ecclesiology. The author states in *Being as Communion* that monasticism in the Orthodox tradition, and presumably asceticism together with it, is very closely tied to eschatology.[505] For this reason, one would have thought that monasticism and asceticism ought to be constitutive of ecclesiology. Nevertheless, just as Zizioulas rejected that possibility in *Being as Communion*, he also in his *Lectures* refuses to allow asceticism to participate in the Church's eschatological character even as he admits that monasticism is itself informed by eschatology. The result is that asceticism and spirituality are part of the Church, but not part of its destiny. Since Zizioulas insists, however, that the Church as we experience it is an image of the eschatological Church projected backwards into history,[506] asceticism and monasticism can be seen as provisional at best. While at first glance such a position may seem entirely plausible, when one includes spirituality under asceticism, as Zizioulas does, one is left with the inescapable conclusion that the entire life of inner prayer as we know it in the Church is for this age and is passing away so that the Eucharist alone will remain. While Zizioulas does not draw this conclusion explicitly, there is really no other logical alternative. Asceticism and spirituality therefore find their place in history, while the Eucharist finds its place in the Kingdom. Despite Zizioulas' admirable attempt to link history with eschatology[507] – a needed synthesis that should resolve the problem by including asceticism and spirituality firmly in the vision and identity of the Church both now and in the future – the Eucharist retains a primacy in his thought to the exclusion of all else. Such an inclusion, I believe, could only enhance the articulation of Metropolitan John's theological thought and place it unambiguously within the lived tradition of the Church.

---

[505] John D. Zizioulas, "Christ, the Spirit and the Church" in *Being as Communion*, (Crestwood, NY: SVS Press, 1985), 131.

[506] Zizioulas, *Lectures*, 137.

[507] *Ibid.*, 153-164.

CONCLUSION

As this study comes to a close, we return to the assertion of Metropolitan John (Zizioulas) of Pergamon that Christian spirituality represents a synthesis of the monastic and eucharistic dimensions, with a view to summarizing the observations that have been made in the preceding chapters. I have noted that Zizioulas has provided a limited but nonetheless credible historical basis for his hypothesis. He has successfully placed the discussion of the nature of Christian spirituality in a wider context of the history of the early Church, the theology of personhood, and communion, ecclesiology and Christology. Despite the Metropolitan's emphasis on synthesis, he does not demonstrate a complete balance in his work between the ascetic or monastic and the eucharistic dimensions of spirituality. Instead, the eucharistic aspect exercises a primacy in the synthesis that tends in the direction of either the subordination of the ascetic aspect or its ultimate exclusion. Although the Metropolitan references the ascetic tradition on several occasions, he has chosen only select features of the latter in developing his thesis. Zizioulas presents a compelling appeal for the revisioning of contemporary theology along ontological lines. Nevertheless, he has not succeeded fully in placing Orthodox spirituality in that context without altering its content or dynamics.

CHALCEDONIAN PRINCIPLES NOT FULLY APPLIED TO SPIRITUALITY AND ECCLESIOLOGY

Zizioulas' spirituality is an extension of his ecclesiology. Since his ecclesiology is very strongly identified with the Eucharist, almost to the exclusion of other aspects of ecclesial life, there is no possibility for the emergence of a completely balanced synthesis in his spiritual theology without at least a partial reworking of his ecclesiology. Such a reworking, however, would have to include a reappraisal of the assertion that *theosis* occurs in the Eucharist alone. In addition, the merging of Christ, Church, and Eucharist in Zizioulas' thought provides little space for the articulation of a broader and more inclusive ecclesiology. While Zizioulas places a clear emphasis on Pneumatology, he does not apply it to ecclesiology in a way that would create a significant opening for the ascetic dimension. To be fair to Zizioulas, we should acknowledge that he did not undertake to explore Christian spirituality in depth. The focus of his theological work is personhood and communion in the Church. Christology has been brought alongside, it seems, to enhance his ecclesiology. While Zizioulas shows a noticeable interest in Christology, he does not appear equally interested in all the aspects of the Christological debates of the first millennium. The retrieval of the concept of *hypostasis* from the Second Ecumenical Council is, of course, central to his thought. Zizioulas gives ample attention to the notion of the balance of Chalcedonian Christology. Regrettably, however, he does not draw out the implications of Chalcedonian thought in order to apply them to spirituality and ecclesiology. In the end, the ascetic dimension does not retain its full integrity when combined with the eucharistic dimension in his spirituality and ecclesiology. The Chalcedonian principle of "without division" has been safeguarded, but its associated principle of "without confusion" has not.[508] In this case, spirituality has been conditioned by ontology, but ontology has not been conditioned by asceticism. The result is a spiritual theology that serves as a *product of ontology* instead of being an expression of the lived experience of the Church as articulated by both the Eucharist and the ascetic tradition.

THE SYNTHESIS OF THE MYSTAGOGY NOT FULLY RETAINED

While Zizioulas has not applied the Maximian synthesis to his own

[508] See Zizioulas' development of these two principles and his great attention to maintaining a good balance between them in his discussion of the relationship between the uncreated and the created in *Communion and Otherness*, 259-261. Regrettably, the same penchant for balance cannot be observed in the author's treatment of the ascetic and eucharistic dimensions of spiritual theology and ecclesiology.

work in a way that would produce a balance between the Eucharist and asceticism, he has identified an important dynamic in Christian spirituality. A synthesis between the eucharistic and ascetic dimensions can be observed in the *Mystagogy* of Saint Maximos the Confessor, the *Ethical Discourses* of Saint Symeon the New Theologian, and the *Homilies* of Saint Gregory Palamas. Given the prominent place of these Fathers in the Orthodox spiritual tradition, we can reasonably posit that such a synthesis might be found in other Fathers and, indeed, that it might be endemic to the whole tradition. The synthesis that Zizioulas attributes to Saint Maximos seems to have been used quite effectively by the Saint, although its provenance is unknown. The Father of the Church may have elaborated a preexisting synthesis found in the writings of Saint Dionysios the Areopagite, as posited by Father Nikolaos Loudovikos. The exact genesis of the synthesis remains a question for further historical research.

THE UTILITY OF THE MAXIMIAN SYNTHESIS

The Maximian synthesis is a useful paradigm for understanding and evaluating contemporary Orthodox theology. By identifying it and placing it in a plausible historical context, Zizioulas has certainly done a service to Orthodox theology. As the Metropolitan observes, theologians across history can be understood in terms of their position vis-à-vis the synthesis. Problems begin, according to Zizioulas, when a theologian places too much emphasis on either the ascetic or the eucharistic dimension.[509] The synthesis can thus be used as a hermeneutical tool for dogmatic and spiritual theology. Among twentieth-century Orthodox theologians, Father Alexander Schmemann definitely emphasizes the place of the Eucharist in his theological work, although not to the complete exclusion of the ascetic dimension. Metropolitan Hierotheos Vlachos stresses the ascetic aspect of the Orthodox tradition while giving recognition to the importance of the Eucharist. When we look at the ecclesiologies of both theologians, however, we see that Schmemann clearly embraces a eucharistic ecclesiology, whereas Hierotheos develops a vision of the Church that is grounded mainly in asceticism. Indeed,

---

[509] Zizioulas, *Lectures*, 124.

Zizioulas has demonstrated very convincingly that, to be understood theologically, all spirituality must be interpreted ecclesiologically.

THE LIMITS OF THE MAXIMIAN SYNTHESIS

Having demonstrated the utility of the Maximian synthesis, I would be remiss if I did not say a word about its limits. It is an effective paradigm, but it does not exhaust the content of Orthodox spiritual theology or ecclesiology. Neither area of theology can be understood exclusively in terms of its ascetic and eucharistic dimensions. Saint Symeon the New Theologian makes an appeal to Pneumatology, and such an allusion could resolve any polarization between the ascetic and eucharistic dimensions. If indeed the reception of the Holy Spirit is the goal of both asceticism and the Eucharist, any tension between the two aspects is resolved. We would no longer have a dialectic; both dimensions could be said to lead to the same reality. My intent here is to state that Orthodox spirituality and ecclesiology can certainly be understood and expressed in other terms. Nevertheless, the utility of the Maximian synthesis can be demonstrated in the latter's revelation of the components of spiritual theology and ecclesiology, as well as their interrelatedness. If we accept its limits, the synthesis becomes a useful lens for understanding spirituality and ecclesiology and their historical development within the Christian tradition.

MONASTICISM AS THE ENDURING PROBLEM?

Zizioulas has made use of the Maximian synthesis to evaluate certain expressions of spirituality both within and without the Orthodox Church. I have noted his use of "Augustinian" and "Western" as somewhat ambiguous epithets when he critiques forms of spirituality in the Orthodox Church that he finds objectionable. He reserves his most pointed critique, however, for monasticism in the Orthodox Church. It seems that, in Zizioulas' understanding, monasticism is the threat to be contended with, the problem to be resolved, the contradiction to be explained, and the blemish on the image of Orthodox eucharistic ecclesiology. Perhaps what the venerable theologian fears most is that "the individual charismatic holy man, purified of all passion and selfhood,"[510] will become the normative image of the Church in Orthodoxy. Indeed, according to Zizioulas, spiritual elitism manifests itself in monasticism in the Orthodox Church and in spirituality disconnected from the Church in the Christian West.[511] It seems that Zizioulas is trapped in an existential struggle to save Orthodox ecclesiology from monasticism and its two corollaries, spirituality and asceticism. He references the history of the Church and points to what he feels are two competing ecclesiologies – one eucharistic and eschatological, the other cosmological and based on individual spirituality.[512] While he believes that Saint Maximos was able to reconcile these two ecclesiologies theologically by reorienting the latter toward the former, Zizioulas is nevertheless convinced that the contradiction has not been completely resolved in practice. He fears that monastics will judge the episcopate as being unspiritual and reject the institutional aspects of the Church.[513]

The problem, however, is not monasticism, and certainly not personal prayer, spirituality or asceticism. The problem is the temptation that monasticism faced throughout Christian history and struggled against: non-Christian asceticism, either in the form of Messalianism or a *spirituality of retreat*, as Father Schmemann calls it. We might also think of the latter as an expression of asceticism disconnected from the Eucharist and all its implications. We have a good idea from Christian history about the theological dimensions of Messalianism. What, however, might be the actual characteristics of an asceticism detached from the Eucharist? Here we are not discussing a movement that has occurred in history; we are discussing a *temptation*. I have tried, although very imperfectly, to construct it precisely by describing its possible tendencies.

What are the characteristics of non-eucharistic asceticism? We might start with legalism and formalism. Disconnected from the Eucharist, which is itself the highest form of thanksgiving, non-eucharistic asceticism renders the spiritual life rigid. There is a preoccupation with doing everything correctly. Every departure is suggestive of a betrayal of

---

[510]   Zizioulas, *Lectures*, 123.
[511]   *Ibid.*, 125.
[512]   *Ibid.*, 129-130.
[513]   Zizioulas, *Lectures*, 130.

Orthodoxy. Daily life is not lived in a spirit of thanksgiving to God, but in a fear that the type of asceticism practised might itself prove inadequate. More and more severe asceticism is thus called for. A strong dualism between the spiritual and the non-spiritual is introduced. Soon very little in the world can be seen as a sacrament; instead, much of the world is seen as intrinsically evil. There is, in fact, very little to offer back to God when the Eucharist is served within the constraints of this worldview. The world has ceased to be the workshop in which man is placed to work out his salvation, the vineyard of the New Testament,[514] and becomes a dangerous place in which a person may lose his salvation with great facility. Even should a Christian manage to find salvation during his life on earth, he is likely to lose it after death anyway. There is not much joy in this type of asceticism, for reasons that should be abundantly clear. Ascetic practice, however, was never meant to be an end in itself, as it so easily can become when it is detached from the Eucharist.

Non-eucharistic asceticism is quietly suspicious of marriage in the Church, viewing it as intrinsically inferior to celibacy. It confuses chastity with celibacy, seeing marriage as fundamentally unchaste. It demands obedience, but not for the liberation of the will. It separates asceticism from grace, making itself a heresy worse than Pelagianism. It allows for the Eucharist, but marginalizes it, making it the reward for strict asceticism.

If there is a problem about which Metropolitan John should be concerned, it is not monasticism, it is its perversion or, more precisely the distortion of balanced Christian asceticism. It is the defence of monasticism that ought to have captured his imagination, as well as the defence of the simple and balanced Christian asceticism, informed by the Eucharist, that Orthodox faithful ought to practise in the world. Monasticism therefore does not need to be seen as a threat. Happily, the asceticism practised in many parts of the Orthodox world is profoundly different from what I have described above.

As for the "individual charismatic holy man, purified of all passion and selfhood" becoming the normative image of the Church in Orthodoxy, what would be the difficulty if such a man were also

[514] Matt. 21:33

202

a fully eucharistic being? I think, for example, of Saint Porphyrios, a great ascetic, purified of passions, profoundly joyful and loving, but also deeply connected to the Eucharist. It is not that he represents the victory of monasticism over the Eucharist so much as that he represents in the minds and hearts of Orthodox Christians the possibility of a man's being healed of his passions and becoming completely transparent to the grace of God. As for the possibility of such a person's judging the Church and the bishops, we know that it is exactly what Saint Porphyrios taught us not to do.[515] In any case, we ought to be reminded that all of us will be judged: monastics, bishops, priests, deacons, and laity.

The Intrinsic Weaknesses of Eucharistic Spirituality

If the Maximian synthesis can be used as a point of departure to critique expressions of spirituality that tend more to the ascetic side, and especially those that might be disconnected from the Eucharist, it could certainly be used to evaluate spiritual expressions that might be more disconnected from asceticism. A non-ascetic eucharistic ecclesiology emphasizes the structure of the Church at the expense of its lived spiritual life. It allows bishops and priests to exercise authority in the Church without acquiring humility and gentleness. It permits bishops in particular to act without any feeling of accountability to their clergy or their people and thus encourages authoritarian and paternalistic behaviour. It asserts authority with arrogance when questioned; it is not longsuffering and patient. It promotes the liturgical life of the Church on the premise that merely being present at liturgical celebrations is sufficient for the spiritual life. Such an ecclesiology or spirituality does not encourage the healing of the Christian from the passions and thus fails to advance the necessity of acquiring virtue. It cannot tolerate process in the spiritual life and tends to see a resolution to all human needs and problems within the confines of liturgical worship. For this reason, it provides little in the way of pastoral care on a deeper level. It does not confront the reality

---

[515] Elder Porphyrios *Wounded by Love: The Life and Wisdom of Elder Porphyrios*, Sisters of the Holy Convent of Chrysopigi (eds.), trans. John Raffan. (Limni, Evia, Greece: Denise Harvey, 2005), 91.

of sin directly, but refers everything back to eucharistic participation. It therefore leaves the Christian alone in his struggle to find healing.

The supporters of eucharistic spirituality and ecclesiology insist that their position is supported by the recovery of an early Christian eucharistic vision of the Church. Such a recovery played an important role in Orthodox theology in the twentieth century. While much has been learned through the study of the early Church and its worship, some important questions remain unanswered. Is the bishop's mere *position* as the main celebrant of the Eucharist enough in itself to establish his suitability for this ministry, without any reference to his own spiritual life? Why, then, does the canonical tradition of the Orthodox Church call for the candidate for the episcopate to be a monastic? Would this not suggest that the Church requires the candidate to be an experienced practitioner of the ascetic life, thereby grounding the celebration of the Eucharist in it and preserving a perfect balance between the ascetic and eucharistic dimensions? Or does the Church function fully and ideally, simply by virtue of its eucharistic and charismatic *structure*? Metropolitan John does not offer any clear answers to these questions and, more importantly, he does not seem inclined to pose them. These questions do need to be posed, however, because if we can detect a spirituality that is overly individualistic and consequently anti-ecclesial, we can certainly identify an ecclesiology that is triumphalistic and tends towards authoritarianism. Father Gaëtan Baillargeon, who wrote one of the earliest assessments of Zizioulas' ecclesiology from a Roman Catholic perspective, confronts the former possibility in his book *Perspectives orthodoxes sur l'Église-Communion*:

> Does the Church *in via*, the pilgrim Church, not stand in need of conversion? Is there not a difference between the Church recorded in history and the coming Kingdom? Does the Eucharist celebrated by this Church in movement not give only a foretaste of the good things to come, the *eschata*, and even those in a way that is not definitive? [516]

---

[516] Gaëtan Baillargeon, *Perspectives orthodoxes sur l'Église-Communion: L'oeuvre de Jean Zizioulas*, (Montréal, Québec: Les Éditions Paulines, 1989), 256.

While Orthodox theology might place more emphasis on the immediacy of the *eschata*, there is no question that Father Baillargeon has identified one of the weaknesses intrinsic to eucharistic ecclesiology. I have highlighted in previous chapters the Metropolitan's reluctance to take seriously the role of the human will and have pointed to this as one of the dangers of imposed communion. Father Nikolaos Loudovikos has written of a dictated otherness. Father Callinic Berger, informed by Father Dumitru Staniloae's theological work, has stressed the importance of making holiness constitutive of ecclesiology. Aristotle Papanikolaou has called for an integration of the ascetic and eucharistic dimensions in Orthodox ecclesiology. All of this points to the need for greater balance in Metropolitan John's ecclesiology and spirituality.

As we consider the question of the nature and content of Orthodox spirituality, we see how important it is to include the ascetic tradition, and more specifically the tradition and practice of inner prayer, in its articulation. Of course, this articulation should not imply the displacement of the eucharistic life of the Church. Quite on the contrary, *it is entirely appropriate to give the Eucharist a centrality in Orthodox ecclesiology and spirituality.* In so doing, we acknowledge the reality of the continuation of the Incarnation in the Church. We confess the Church to be the Body of Christ, part of the plan of salvation, and the fulfillment of God's plan for the world. We reject the artificial barriers between Christ, the Church, and the Eucharist. At the same time, we are careful to say that they are not exactly the same. While the created and the uncreated are to be found in a relationship "without division," it is also a communion "without confusion."[517] Significantly for the Orthodox spiritual tradition, the Eucharist becomes inclusive of human persons – , Christians – in a way that unites, but without compromising "otherness" in any way. Not only is otherness retained, but it also supports the Eucharist in a way that allows the latter to retain its corporate integrity. What I am suggesting here is not only that personal or inner prayer should not be opposed to the Eucharist, but that such prayer should also be understood as contributing to the sacrament's very celebration. This is the only way to bring about a full integration of Orthodox eucharistic

[517]   *Ibid.*, 257.

205

ecclesiology and the hesychastic tradition, the tradition which stresses the practice of inner prayer. While the Eucharist indeed constitutes the Church and is constituted by it, as Zizioulas insists, it also shapes the inner life of every Christian communicant. The *eucharistic liturgy* engenders what Father Dumitru Staniloae terms the *liturgy of the heart*. The *liturgy of the heart* in turn opens the Christian to the celebration of the *eucharistic liturgy* and ensures that its celebration is continual. Whether Christians are gathered together in one place, *epi to auto*, or separated temporarily by space and daily activities, *the same liturgy continues in two modes*. Is the Holy Spirit not the author of both? The Divine Liturgy both informs and corrects the personal *liturgy of the heart*, ensuring that it does not slip into subjectivism and individualism. The *liturgy of the heart* personalizes the *eucharistic liturgy*, ensuring that the communicants do not take the celebration for granted, receiving the Body and Blood of the Lord "for remission of sins and everlasting life," and "not unto judgment or condemnation."[518]

Why, however, make the Church less than the Church when it is not actively celebrating the Divine Liturgy? Why exclude the non-eucharistic activity of the Church from *theosis*? It seems to me to be a gratuitous step on Zizioulas' part, even if he feels he must take it to protect the primacy of the Eucharist. Asceticism is not competing with the Eucharist; it is creating the preconditions for its celebration. Furthermore, as I mentioned above, the Eucharist is leaving its stamp on personal prayer such that the prayer of each Christian becomes a sacrifice, and the *liturgy of the heart* becomes a reality. Thus, prayer outside of the Eucharist becomes a eucharistic activity. In this sense, *the Church is always celebrating the Eucharist*. The statement that *theosis* occurs in the Eucharist alone is itself a tautology, since the Eucharist can only be celebrated in the Church and the Church is never without the Eucharist. The discussion here is about two modes, and the *liturgy of the heart* should be considered a eucharistic expression of personal prayer. Quite simply, it is the Eucharist on another Holy Table.

Is this reality not in keeping with Saint Maximos the Confessor's assertion that the Church is the image of man? Referring still to the

---

[518]   From the prayer before communion in the Orthodox Divine Liturgy.

Church's temple, he identifies the sanctuary as the type of the soul, the altar as the image of the mind, and the nave as the symbol of the body.[519] Why would a human being have a sanctuary, an altar and a nave and no inner Eucharist? To draw this conclusion is to create a certain void in Christian anthropology: the human being is forced to experience the Eucharist as an exclusively *external* reality when the inner ecclesiastical architecture is, in fact, completely innate to him. If Saint Maximos is the greatest ecclesiologist among the Fathers, as Father Loudovikos insists, and if he is also the primary reconciler of monastic spirituality (read prayer and asceticism) with the Eucharist, as Zizioulas asserts, how can we draw any other conclusion than that man is a little church, fully equipped to assimilate the Eucharist internally and to continue it unceasingly? Unceasing prayer is nothing less than unceasing Eucharist. Can we infer that all prayer is unceasing Eucharist? No, because the human being as a little church needs to be healed, purified, and formed. For this healing, he needs asceticism. He needs to be baptized in order to have his inner ecclesiastical architecture fully assembled. He needs to grow and to fight sin. He also needs the Eucharist itself and is in fact dependent on it to celebrate the *liturgy of the heart*. There is no threat to the centrality of the Eucharist here; there is simply a necessary consistency between ecclesiology and anthropology. The Church and man are intrinsically related, as Saint Maximos points out: the man who is himself a church needs nevertheless to be within the Church. The Church that includes man does so, in part, because it is the image of man. Man is made for the Church because he carries the image of the Head of the Church, Christ Himself. For this reason, he can in no way become fully man without the Church and, consequently, without the Eucharist. Man is fundamentally and immutably ecclesial. The Church, however, cannot be separated from its anthropological dimension, both because of the Incarnation of its Head and the reality of its body. Yes, man is made for the Church. Equally true is that the Church is made for man. This relationship of interdependence makes it clear that Saint Maximos the Confessor did not, strictly speaking, forge a synthesis of monastic

[519] Mystagogy, 189-190.

spirituality (including prayer and asceticism) and the spirituality of the Eucharist. Instead, he revealed their indivisibility. He is not so much a synthesizer of diverging spiritual tendencies or poles as he is a prophet: he has revealed the reality as it is.

THE SYNTHESIS OF THE ASCETIC AND THE EUCHARISTIC DIMENSIONS MUST BE SAFEGUARDED

If we recall the discovery made by Father Dumitru Staniloae of the full synthesis of the hesychastic tradition and the Eucharist in the writings of Saint Mark the Ascetic and Saints Kallistos and Ignatios Xanthopouli, we come to the realization that this synthesis has existed in the Church for a long time. Saint Mark likely lived in the fifth century. Saints Kallistos and Ignatios lived in the fourteenth century. The synthesis perhaps reaches its zenith in the case of the latter two Saints. The point here is not simply to appeal to antiquity, but to establish that key representatives of the hesychastic tradition already saw the need to integrate the tradition of inner prayer with the Eucharist. *We do not need to effect such a synthesis anew; rather, we need to ensure that we do not drive a wedge between the ascetic and eucharistic dimensions in spirituality and ecclesiology.* While the Church has always enjoyed a lived experience of eucharistic ecclesiology, it is only recently that theologians have articulated this ecclesiology afresh, taking into account the insights of new historical research. Such a development can only be welcomed by all theologians, but it has produced perhaps a certain imbalance, in that eucharistic ecclesiology is being articulated without a meaningful reference to the ascetic tradition. Now we have the opportunity to recover the older synthesis – whether it should be attributed to Saint Maximos, Saint Mark or Saint Dionysios – and bring it to the fore of contemporary theology.

WHAT IS ORTHODOX SPIRITUALITY?

In the Introduction, we saw Vladimir Lossky refer to mystical theology, and with it Orthodox spirituality, as spirituality with a doctrinal attitude. We have certainly seen the doctrinal attitude in the preceding pages of this study. It is impossible to speak of spirituality meaningfully in the Orthodox Christian tradition without engaging Christology and ecclesiology. The serious engagement of the two is certainly part of the lasting theological legacy of Metropolitan John Zizioulas. Serious engagement, however, also suggests integration, and it is precisely the greater integration of the ascetic and eucharistic dimensions in Orthodox spirituality that I am proposing. Lossky, however, also speaks of spirituality as union with God. Union with God in the Christian tradition presupposes, as I have tried to demonstrate, a union in which the process of engagement with the spiritual life, what we call asceticism, allows for the retention and active use of the human will. The active use of the will also suggests a level of awareness – not a narcissistic consciousness, but an ascetic awareness. Lossky himself was convinced that such an awareness was an indispensable feature of the spiritual life.[520] Ascetic awareness is associated with knowledge, not with self-love. Without it, we would be blind in the spiritual life.[521] When we discuss the importance of asceticism, it is not only for the sake of maintaining the balance in the time-honoured relationship between asceticism and the Eucharist, the personal and the corporate, it is to protect a fundamental dimension of the human person: the will. Asceticism represents a choice, a free choice, to say "yes" to God and to be in relationship to Him and others who carry His image. It both allows and initiates communion, but it cannot be demanded or imposed; it is an act of love.

Asceticism is a feature of the journey to union with God. Certainly it can never displace the grace of God – we are saved by grace, through faith, Saint Paul writes[522] – and it is not its place to do so. On the contrary, asceticism welcomes grace, gives the gracious activity of the Holy Spirit a place, and promotes the struggle to maintain that place, making the Christian ever more available to God. If the Orthodox tradition stood in defence of uncreated grace, it was precisely to guard the possibility of a personal, unmediated experience of God in the spiritual life. This experience has nothing to do with psychologizing the spiritual life; it speaks instead to the joy and wonder of the encounter with God.

The ascetic dimension of the spiritual life certainly points to the need for all human beings to find salvation and healing in God, but in

[520]   Lossky, *Mystical Theology*, 215.
[521]   *Ibid.*
[522]   Eph. 2:8.

safeguarding human participation in the union with God, it reveals all that is fundamentally *good* in humanity. God did not endow us with a nature that needs to be surpassed; He gave us a nature that, although fallen and bearing the "garments of skin," has been redeemed and renewed. Ours is the nature embraced by the Word of God in the Incarnation. Ours is the nature that has been glorified and has ascended to the right hand of the Father. The power of Christian asceticism is rooted in the Incarnation of the Word. Therefore the human will that is grounded in human nature and expressed hypostatically can be either the sign of brokenness and sin or the sign of redemption and glorification. United with the human natural will of Christ, it has the full potential for sanctification, love and communion.

Metropolitan John has reminded us that humanity is created and therefore vulnerable. The human being is created from nothing and would be vulnerable to death without the intervention of Christ. To be sure, to ensure his survival, the human being needs to be found in Christ's Person. Even so, there is a dimension of Christ's Person that will always be beyond us. It is precisely through assuming our *nature* that Christ gathers us into His Person. He is truly the eschatological Man, the corporate Person, but the Word of God did not assume a human person, He assumed human nature, and His deified humanity renews ours. Orthodox spirituality is the growth into the likeness of Christ, Whose image we carry from creation.

As we pose the question, "What is Orthodox spirituality?" we need to answer it both in reference to the Church and in reference to the Church's living tradition of asceticism and personal prayer. It must be ecclesial, both by affirming the centrality of the Eucharist and by including the whole spiritual life of the Church and its members. Orthodox spirituality is Eucharist and asceticism, Church and spirituality, the *liturgy of the Eucharist* and the *liturgy of the heart*. In this way, it is both profoundly ecclesial and fully personal.

BIBLIOGRAPHY

Afanasieff, Nicolas. "The Church which Presides in Love," trans. Katherine Farrer. *The Primacy of Peter in the Orthodox Church*. Leighton Buzzard, Bedfordshire: The Faith Press, 1973.

Afanasiev, Nicholas. *The Church of the Holy Spirit*, trans. Vitaly Permiakov, Michael Plekon (ed.). Notre Dame, IN: University of Notre Dame Press, 2007.

Alfeyev, Hilarion. *St. Symeon the New Theologian and Orthodox Tradition*. Oxford: Oxford University Press, 2000.

Aumann, Jordan. *Christian Spirituality in the Catholic Tradition*. San Francisco: Ignatius Press, 1985.

Ayres, Lewis. "(Mis)Adventures in Trinitarian Ontology." *The Trinity and an Entangled World: Relationality in Physical Science and Theology*. John Polkinghorne (ed.). Grand Rapids, MI: William B. Eerdmans Publishing Company, 2010, 130-145.

Baillargeon, Gaëtan. *Perspectives orthodoxes sur l'Église-Communion : L'oeuvre de Jean Zizioulas*. Montréal: Les Éditions Paulines, 1989.

Berger, Calinic (Kevin M.). "Does the Eucharist Make the Church? An Ecclesiological Comparison of Stanilaoe and Zizioulas." *St. Vladimir's Theological Quarterly*, 51: 1 (2007), 23-70.

Berger, Kevin M. "An Integral Approach to Spirituality: The *Orthodox Spirituality* of Dumitru Staniloae." *St. Vladimir's Theological Quarterly*, 48: 1 (2004), 125-148.

Bolshakoff, Sergius. *Russian Mystics*. Kalamazoo, MI: Cistercian Publications, 1980.

Bouyer, Louis. "Byzantine Spirituality." *A History of Christian Spirituality II: The Spirituality of the Middle Ages*, Dom Jean Leclercq *et al.* (eds.). New York: The Seabury Press, 1968, 547-590.

Bobrinskoy, Boris. *The Compassion of the Father*, trans. Anthony P. Gythiel. Crestwood, NY: St. Vladimir's Seminary Press, 2003.

211

ASCETICISM AND THE EUCHARIST

Bradshaw, David. *Aristotle East and West.* Cambridge: Cambridge University Press, 2004.

Christou, Panagiotis K. "The Monastic Life in the Eastern Orthodox Church," trans. C. Cavarnos. *The Orthodox Ethos,* A. J. Philippou (ed.). Oxford: The Holywell Press, 1964, 249-258.

Clément, Olivier. *Orient-Occident : Deux Passeurs : Vladimir Lossky et Paul Evdokimov.* Geneva: Labor et Fides, 1985.

Collins, Gregory. "Simeon the New Theologian: An Ascetical Theology for Middle-Byzantine Monks." *Asceticism,* Vincent L. Wimbush and Richard Valantasis (eds.). Oxford: Oxford University Press, 1998, 343-356.

Collins, Paul M. *Partaking in Divine Nature: Deification and Communion.* London: T&T Clark, 2010.

_____ *Trinitarian Theology West and East: Karl Barth, the Cappadocian Fathers and John Zizioulas.* Oxford: Oxford University Press, 2001.

Deseille, Placide. *Orthodox Spirituality and the Philokalia,* trans. Anthony P. Gythiel. Wichita, KS: Eighth Day Press, 2008.

Dragas, Protopresbyter George Dion. "The Lord's Prayer : Guide to the Christian Life According to St. Maximos the Confessor." *Ecclesiasticus II Orthodox Icons, Saints, Feasts and Prayer.* Rollinsford, NH: Orthodox Research Institute, 2005.

_____ "What is the Church? Saint Maximus' Mystagogical Answer." *Ecclesiasticus I: Introducing Eastern Orthodoxy.* Rollinsford, NH: Orthodox Research Institute, 2004.

Evdokimov, Paul, *Les âges de la vie spirituelle.* Paris : Desclée de Brouwer, 1995.

_____ *Le Christ dans la pensée russe.* Paris: Cerf, 1986.

_____ "Eucharistie–Mystère de l'Église." *La Pensée orthodoxe,* 1968 (2), 53-69.

_____ *L'Orthodoxie.* Paris: Desclée de Brouwer, 1979.

_____ *La prière de l'Église d'Orient.* Paris: Desclée de Brouwer, 1985.

_____ *The Sacrament of Love,* trans. Anthony P. Gythiel and Victoria Steadman. Crestwood, NY: St. Vladimir's Seminary Press, 1995.

_____ *Woman and the Salvation of the World,* trans. Anthony P. Gythiel. Crestwood, NY: St. Vladimir's Seminary Press, 1994.

Fagerberg, David W. *What Is Liturgical Theology?: A Study in Methodology.* Collegeville, MN: The Liturgical Press, 1992.

Florovsky, Georges, "St. Gregory Palamas and the Tradition of the Fathers." *Bible, Church, Tradition: An Eastern Orthodox View, The Collected Works, vol. 1.* Richard S. Haugh (ed.), Vaduz, Europa: Buchervertriebsanstalt, 1987, 105-120. Reprinted from *The Greek Orthodox Theological Review,* V-2 (Winter 1959-60).

Golitzin, Alexander. *St. Symeon the New Theologian On the Mystical Life: The Ethical Discourses, Vol. 3: Life, Times and Theology.* Crestwood, NY: St. Vladimir's Seminary Press, 1997.

Hierotheos, Metropolitan of Nafpaktos. *Hesychia and Theology: The Context for Man's Healing in the Orthodox Church,* trans. Sister Pelagia Selfe. Levadia, Greece: Birth of the Theotokos Monastery, 2007.

_____ *Life after death,* trans. Esther Williams. Levadia, Greece: Birth of the Theotokos Monastery, 1996.

_____ *The mind of the Orthodox Church,* trans. Esther Williams. Levadia, Greece: Birth of the Theotokos Monastery, 1998.

_____ (Archimandrite Hierotheos Vlachos). *Orthodox Psychotherapy,* trans. Esther Williams. Levadia, Greece: Birth of the Theotokos Monastery, 1994.

_____ *Orthodox Spirituality,* trans. Effie Mavromichali. Levadia, Greece: Birth of the Theotokos Monastery, 1994.

_____ *The person in the Orthodox Tradition,* trans. Esther Williams. Levadia, Greece: Birth of the Theotokos Monastery, 1999.

_____ *Saint Gregory Palamas as a Hagiorite,* trans. Esther Williams. Levadia, Greece: Birth of the Theotokos Monastery, 1997.

_____ *The Science of Spiritual Medicine: Orthodox Psychotherapy in Action,* trans. Sister Pelagia Selfe. Levadia, Greece: Birth of the Theotokos Monastery, 2010.

Kalaitzidis, Pantelis. "New trends in Greek Orthodox theology: challenges in the movement towards a genuine renewal and Christian unity." *Scottish Journal of Theology* 67 (2014), n. 22

Keselopoulos, Anestis. *Passions and Virtues According to Saint Gregory Palamas,* trans. Hieromonk Alexis (Trader) and Harry Michael Boosalis (eds.). South Canaan, PA: St. Tikhon's Seminary Press, 2004.

Knight, Douglas H. (ed.). *The Theology of John Zizioulas: Personhood and the Church.* Aldershot, Hampshire, England: Ashgate Publishing Limited, 2007.

Krivocheine, Basil. *In the Light of Christ,* trans. Anthony P. Gythiel. Crestwood, NY: St. Vladimir's Seminary Press, 1986.

_____ (Archevêque Basile Krivochéine). "La spiritualité orthodoxe," trans. Nikita Krivochéine *et al. Dieu, l'homme, l'Église.* Paris: Les Éditions du Cerf, 2010).

LaCugna, Catherine Mowry. *God for Us: The Trinity and Christian Life.* New York: HarperCollins, 1991.

Larchet, Jean-Claude. *La divinisation de l'homme selon saint Maxime le Confesseur.* Paris : Les Éditions du Cerf, 1996.

_____ "Hypostasis, person and individual according to St. Maximus the Confessor, with reference to the Cappadocians and St. John of Damascus." *Personhood in the Byzantine Christian Tradition: Early, Medieval and Modern Perspectives,* Alexis Torrance and Symeon Paschalidis, eds. London and New York: Routledge, 2018, 47-67.

_____ *Personne et nature.* Paris : Les Éditions du Cerf, 2011.

_____ *Thérapeutique des maladies spirituelles.* Paris : Les Éditions du Cerf, 1997.

Letham, Robert. *The Holy Trinity in Scripture, History, Theology and Worship.* Phillipsburg, NJ: R&R Publishing, 2004.

Lison, Jacques. *L'Esprit répandu: la pneumatologie de Grégoire Palamas.* Paris: Les Éditions du Cerf, 1994.

Lossky, Vladimir. *The Mystical Theology of the Eastern Church.* Crestwood, NY: St. Vladimir's Seminary Press, 1976.

_____ "The Palamite Synthesis." *The Vision of God,* trans. Asheleigh Moorhouse. Leighton Buzzard, Bedfordshire: The Faith Press, 1973.

_____ *Orthodox Theology: An Introduction,* trans. Ian and Ihita Kesarcodi-Watson. Crestwood, NY: St. Vladimir's Seminary Press, 1978.

Loudovikos, Nicholas. "*Eikon* and *mimesis* eucharistic ecclesiology and the ecclesial ontology of dialogical reciprocity," *International Journal for the Study of the Christian Church*, 11:2-3, (2011), 123-136.

_____ "Ontology Celebrated: Remarks of an Orthodox on Radical Orthodoxy." *Encounter between Eastern Orthodoxy and Radical Orthodoxy,* Adrian Pabst and Christoph Schneider (eds.). Farnham, Surrey, England: Ashgate Publishing Limited, 2009.

_____ "Person Instead of Grace and Dictated Otherness: John Zizioulas' Final Theological Position." *The Heythrop Journal,* XLVIII (2009), 1-16.

_____ "Possession or Wholeness? St. Maximus the Confessor and John Zizioulas on Person, Nature and Will." *Participatio,* 4 (2013), 267-295.

Loudovikos, Nikolaos. *Analogical Identities: The Creation of the Christian Self: Beyond Spirituality and Mysticism in the Patristic Era.* Turnhout, Belgium: Brepols. Publishers, 2019.

_____ *Church in the Making: An Apophatic Ecclesiology of Consubstantiality.* Yonkers, NY: St. Vladimir's Seminary Press, 2016.

_____ *A Eucharistic Ontology: Maximus the Confessor's Eschatological Ontology of Being as Dialogical Reciprocity.* Brookline, MA: Holy Cross Orthodox Press, 2010.

Lyssack (*sic*), Fr. Maxym. "The Ascetic and Sacramental Dimensions in Metropolitan Hierotheos (Vlachos) of Napata's Theological Work." *The Greek Orthodox Theological Review,* 44: 1-4 (1999), 491-504.

Maloney, George A. *The Mystic of Fire and Light.* Denville, NJ: Dimension Books, 1975.

Mantzarides, Georgios I. *The Deification of Man: St. Gregory Palamas and the Orthodox Tradition,* trans. Liadain Sherrard. Crestwood, NY: St. Vladimir's Seminary Press, 1984.

_____ "Spiritual Life in Palamism" *Christian Spirituality: High Middle Ages and Reformation,* Jill Raitt (ed.). New York: Crossroad, 1997, 208-222.

Matsoukas, Nikos A. *La vie en Dieu selon Maxime le Confesseur.* Nathan: Éditions Axios, 1994.

Maximos the Confessor, Saint. "The Church's Mystagogy." *Maximus Confessor: Selected Writings,* trans. George C. Berthold. Mahwah, NJ: Paulist Press, 1985.

McCall, Thomas H. *Which Trinity? Whose Monotheism: Philosophical and Systematic Theologians on the Metaphysics of Trinitarian Theology.* Grand Rapids, MI: William B. Eerdmans Publishing Company, 2010.

McPartlan, Paul. *The Eucharist Makes the Church: Henri de Lubac and John Zizioulas in Dialogue.* Edinburgh: T&T Clark, 1993.

_____ "Eucharistic Ecclesiology." *One in Christ,* (1986-4), 314-331.

Meyendorff, John. *Christ in Eastern Christian Thought,* trans. Fr. Yves Dubois. Crestwood, NY: St. Vladimir's Seminary Press, 1975.

_____ *St. Gregory Palamas and Orthodox Spirituality.* Crestwood, NY: St.Vladimir's Seminary Press, 1974.

_____ *A Study of Gregory Palamas,* trans. George Lawrence. Leighton Buzzard, Beds.: The Faith Press, 1974.

Meyendorff, Paul. "Introduction." St. Germanus of Constantinople, *On the Divine Liturgy,* trans. Paul Meyendorff. Crestwood, NY: St. Vladimir's Seminary Press, 1984.

Nichols, Aidan. *Theology in the Russian Diaspora: Church, Fathers, Eucharist in Nikolai Afanas'ev, 1893-1966.* Cambridge: Cambridge University Press, 1989.

Palamas, St. Gregory. "The Decalogue of the Law According to Christ, That Is, The New Covenant," trans. Soterios Mouselimas. *The Greek Orthodox Theological Review,* Vol. XXV-3 (1980): 297-305.

_____ *Douze homélies pour les fêtes,* trans. Jérôme Cler. Paris: O.E.I.L./YMCA-Press, 1987.

_____ *The Homilies.* trans. Christopher Veniamin (ed.). Waymart, PA: Mount Thabor Publishing, 2009.

Palamas, St. Gregory. *Treatise on the Spiritual Life,* trans. Daniel M. Rogich. Minneapolis: Light and Life, 1995.

Papanikolaou, Aristotle. *Being with God: Trinity, Apophaticism, and Divine-Human Communion.* Notre Dame, IN: University of Notre Dame Press, 2006.

_____ "Integrating the ascetical and the eucharistic: current challenges in Orthodox ecclesiology." *International Journal for the Study of the Christian Church*, 11: 2-3 (2011).

_____ "Personhood and its Exponents in Twentieth-century Orthodox Theology." *The Cambridge Companion to Orthodox Christian Theology*, Mary B. Cunningham and Elizabeth Theokritoff (eds.). Cambridge: Cambridge University Press, 2008.

Papathanasiou, Athanasios N. "Some Key Themes and Figures in Greek Theological Thought." *The Cambridge Companion to Orthodox Christian Theology*, Mary B. Cunningham and Elizabeth Theokritoff (eds.). Cambridge: Cambridge University Press, 2008, 218-231.

Phan, Cho D. "Evdokimov and Monk Within." *Sobornost* 3 (1981): 53-61.

_____ "Mariage, monachisme et eschatologie: contribution de Paul Evdokimov à la spiritualité chrétienne." *Ephemerides Liturgicae* 93 (1979): 352-380.

Plekon, Michael. "The Church, the Eucharist and the Kingdom: Towards an Assessment of Alexander Schmemann's Theological Legacy." *St. Vladimir's Theological Quarterly* 40 (1996): 119-143.

_____ "The God Whose Power is Weakness, Whose Love is Foolish: Divine Philanthropy, the Heart of Paul Evdokimov's Theology." *Sourozh* 60 (1995): 15-26.

_____ "Interiorized Monasticism: Paul Evdokimov on the Spiritual Life." *The American Benedictine Review* 48 (1997): 227-253.

_____ "A Liturgical Being, A Life of Service: Paul Evdokimov's Gift and Witness to the Church." *Sobornost* 17 (1995): 28-37.

Romanides, John S. *The Ancestral Sin*, trans. George S. Gabriel. Ridgewood, NJ: Zephyr Publishing, 2002.

_____(Protopresbyter John Romanides). *An Outline of Orthodox Patristic Dogmatics*, trans. Protopresbyter George Dion. Dragas (ed.). Rollinsford, NH: Orthodox Research Institute, 2004.

_____ (Protopresbyter John S. Romanides). *Patristic Theology*, trans. Hieromonk Alexios (Trader). The Dalles, OR: Uncut Mountain Press, 2008.

Russell, Norman. *The Doctrine of Deification in the Greek Patristic Tradition*. Oxford: Oxford University Press, 2006.

Sakharov, Nicholas V. *I Love Therefore I Am: The Theological Legacy of Archimandrite Sophrony*. Crestwood, NY: Saint Vladimir's Seminary Press, 2002.

Schmemann, Alexander. *Church, World, Mission*. Crestwood, NY: St. Vladimir's Seminary Press, 1979.

_____ "Current Spirituality." *The Study of Spirituality*, Cheslyn Jones *et al.* (eds.). New York: Oxford University Press, 1986, 519-525.

_____ *The Eucharist*. Crestwood, NY: St. Vladimir's Seminary Press, 1988.

_____ *For the Life of the World*. Crestwood, NY: St. Vladimir's Seminary Press, 1973.

_____ *Great Lent*. Crestwood, NY: St. Vladimir's Seminary Press, 1974.

_____ "The Idea of Primacy in Orthodox Ecclesiology." *The Primacy of Peter in the Orthodox Church*. Leighton Buzzard, Bedfordshire: The Faith Press, 1973.

_____ *Introduction to Liturgical Theology*. Leighton Buzzard, Beds.: The Faith Press, 1966.

_____ "Liturgy and Eschatology." *Liturgy and Tradition*. Thomas Fisch (ed.). Crestwood, NY: St. Vladimir's Seminary Press, 1990.

_____ *Of Water and the Spirit*. Crestwood, NY: St. Vladimir's Seminary Press, 1974.

_____ "Problems of Orthodoxy in America III: The Spiritual Problem." *The Study of Spirituality*, Cheslyn Jones *et al.* (eds.). New York: Oxford University Press, 1986, 171-193.

_____ "Symbols and Symbolism in the Orthodox Liturgy." *Orthodox Theology and Diakonia*. Demetrios J. Constantelos (ed.) Brookline, MA: Hellenic College, 1981.

Skira, Jaroslav Z. "Breathing with Two Lungs: The Church in Yves Congar and John Zizioulas." *In God's Hands: Essays on the Church and Ecumenism in Honour of Michael A. Fahey, S.J.*, Jaroslav Z. Skira and Michael S. Attridge (eds.). Leuven: Leuven University Press, 2006.

_____ *Christ, the Spirit and the Church in Modern Orthodox Theology: A Comparison of Georges Florovsky, Vladimir Lossky, Nikos Nissiotis and John*

Zizioulas. Ph.D. dissertation, University of Toronto, 1998.

Sophrony, Archimandrite. *His Life is Mine,* trans. Rosemary Edmonds. Crestwood, NY: St. Vladimir's Seminary Press, 1977.

_____ "Principles of Orthodox Asceticism," trans. R. Edmonds. *The Orthodox Ethos,* J. Philippou (ed.). Oxford: The Holywell Press, 1964, 259-286.

Sopko, Andrew J. *The Theology of John Romanides.* Dewdney, BC: Synaxis Press, 1998.

Staniloae, Dumitru, "The Liturgy of the Community and the Liturgy of the Heart from the View-point of the Philokalia." *One Tradition,* No. 4 (1980).

_____ *Orthodox Spirituality: A Practical Guide for the Faithful and a Definitive Manual for the Scholar,* trans. Archimandrite Jerome Newville and Otilia Kloos. South Canaan, PA: St. Tikhon's Seminary Press, 2002.

Stead, Julian. *The Church, the Liturgy and the Soul of Man: The Mystagogia of St. Maximus the Confessor,* translated with historical note and commentaries. Still River, MA: St. Bede's Publications, 1982.

Sylvia Mary, Sister. "Symeon the New Theologian and the Way of Tears." *One Yet Two: Monastic Tradition East and West,* M. Basil Pennington (ed.). Kalamazoo, MI: Cistercian Publications, 1976, 95-119.

[St.] Symeon the New Theologian. *The Discourses,* trans. C.J. de Catanzaro. New York: Paulist Press, 1980.

_____ *Hymns of Divine Love,* trans. George A. Maloney. Denville, NJ: Dimension Books (no date).

_____ *On the Mystical Life: The Ethical Discourses, Vol. 1: The Church and the Last Things,* trans. Alexander Golitzin. Crestwood, NY: St. Vladimir's Seminary Press, 1995.

_____ *On the Mystical Life: The Ethical Discourses, Vol. 2: On Virtue and Christian Life,* trans. Alexander Golitzin. Crestwood, NY: St. Vladimir's Seminary Press, 1996.

_____ *The Practical and Theological Chapters* and *The Three Theological Discourses,* trans. Paul McGuckin. Kalamazoo, MI: Cistercian Publications, 1982.

Thunberg, Lars. *Man and the Cosmos*. Crestwood, NY: St. Vladimir's Seminary Press, 1985.

Torrance, Alan J. *Persons in Communion: An Essay on Trinitarian Description and Human Participation*. Edinburgh: T&T Clark, 1996.

Torrance, Alexis. "Personhood and Patristics in Orthodox Theology: Reassessing the Debate." *The Heythrop Journal*. LII (2011), 700-707.

Turcescu, Lucian. "'Person' versus 'Individual' and Other Modern Misreadings of Gregory of Nyssa." *Re-thinking Gregory of Nyssa*, Sarah Coakley (ed.). Oxford: Blackwell Publishing Ltd., 2003.

Vassiliadis, Petros. "Eucharistic and Therapeutic Spirituality." *The Greek Orthodox Theological Review* 42 (1997): 1-23.

_____ "The Eucharistic Perspective of the Church's Mission." *Eucharist and Witness: Orthodox Perspectives on the Unity and Mission of the Church*. Brookline, MA: Holy Cross Orthodox Press, 1998, 49-66.

Vidovic, Julija. "L'anthropologie de saint Maxime le Confesseur revisitée : le débat nature-personne entre Mgr Jean Zizioulas et Jean-Claude Larchet." *Contacts*, 258 (2017), 153-177.

Volf, Miroslav. *After Our Likeness: The Church as the Image of the Trinity*. Grand Rapids, MI: William B. Eerdmans Publishing Company, 1998.

Ware, Kallistos, "Greek Writers from the Cappodocians to John of Damascus: Introduction," *The Study of Spirituality*, Cheslyn Jones *et al.* (eds.) (New York: Oxford University Press, 1986).

_____ "The Hesychasts: Gregory of Sinai, Gregory Palamas, Nicolas Cabasilas." *The Study of Spirituality*, Cheslyn Jones *et al. (eds.)*. New York: Oxford University Press, 1986, 242-255.

_____ *The Orthodox Way*. Crestwood, NY: St. Vladimir's Seminary Press, 1996.

_____ "Symeon the New Theologian." *The Study of Spirituality*, Cheslyn Jones *et al.* (eds.). New York: Oxford University Press, 1986, 235-242.

_____ "The Way of the Ascetics: Negative or Affirmative." *Asceticism*, Vincent L. Wimbush and Richard Valantasis (eds.). Oxford: Oxford University Press, 1998.

BIBLIOGRAPHY

Williams, Rowan. "Bread in the Wilderness: The Monastic Ideal in Thomas Merton and Paul Evdokimov." *One Yet Two*, M. Basil Pennington (ed.). Kalamazoo, MI: Cistercian Publications, 1976, 452-473.

Yangazoglou, Stavros. "Ecclésiologie eucharistique et spiritualité monastique," *L'ecclésiologie eucharistique*, Jean-Marie Van Cangh (ed.). Bruxelles: Éditions du Cerf, 2009.

Zakharias, Archimandrite. *Christ, Our Way and Our Life: A Presentation of the Theology of Archimandrite Sophrony.* So. Canaan, PA: St. Tikhon's Seminary Press, 2003.

Zhivov, V.M. "The Mystagogia of Maximus the Confessor and the Development of the Byzantine Theory of the Image," trans. Ann Shukman. *St. Vladimir's Theological Quarterly,* 31: 4 (1987), 349-376.

Zizioulas, John D. *Being as Communion.* Crestwood, NY: St. Vladimir's Seminary Press, 1993.

_____ *Communion and Otherness,* Paul McPartlan (ed.). London: T&T Clark, 2006.

_____ "The Early Christian Community." *Christian Spirituality: Origins to the Twelfth Century*, Bernard McGinn *et al.* (eds.). New York: Crossroad Publishing Company, 1997.

_____ (Metropolitan John of Pergamon). "The Eucharist and the Kingdom," trans. Elizabeth Theokritoff. *Sourozh,* 58 (1994), 1-12; 59 (1995), 22-38; 60 (1995), 32-46.

_____ *Eucharist, Bishop, Church,* trans. Elizabeth Theokritoff. Brookline, MA: Holy Cross Orthodox Press, 2001.

_____ *The Eucharistic Communion and the World,* Luke Ben Tallon (ed.). London: T&T Clark, 2011.

_____ *Lectures in Christian Dogmatics,* Douglas H. Knight (ed.). London: T&T Clark, 2008.

_____ *The One and the Many: Studies on God, Man, the Church, and the World Today,* Fr. Gregory Edwards (ed.). Alhambra, CA: Sebastian Press, 2010.

_____ "Person and Nature in the Theology of St. Maximus the Confessor." *Knowing the Purpose of Creation through the Resurrection: Proceedings of the Symposium on St. Maximus the Confessor*, Bishop Maxim (Vasiljevic), ed. Alhambra, CA: Sebastian Press, 2013, 85-113.

_____ "Relational Ontology: Insights from Patristic Thought." *The Trinity and an Entangled World: Relationality in Physical Science and Theology.* John Polkinghorne (ed.). Grand Rapids, MI: William B. Eerdmans Publishing Company, 2010, 146-156.

INDEX OF AUTHORS

Afanasiev, Nicholas 14, 16, 17, 25, 36, 39, 42, 135, 168
Akindynos 121
Augustine of Hippo (Saint) 18, 38, 50, 52
Aumann, Jordan 160

Baillargeon, Gaëtan 204
Bairaktaris, Porphyrios (Saint) 202, 203
Barlaam of Calabria 122, 153, 154
Basil the Great (Saint) 178
Berger, Calinic (Kevin M.) 11, 19, 66-69, 132, 205
Bobrinskoy, Boris 31, 177
Buber, Martin 17, 51

Bulgakov, Sergius 195

Cabasilas, Nicholas (Saint) 28, 38
Cappadocian Fathers 124, 178, 192
Chrestou, Panagiotes 111
Cyril of Jerusalem (Saint) 38

De Catanzaro, C. J. (Bishop) 92
De Lubac, Henri 38, 192, 193
Desert Fathers 183, 184
Dionysiatis, Theoklitos 65
Dionysios the Areopagite (Saint) 20, 28, 36, 73, 74, 79, 125, 156, 158, 199, 208
Dragas, George Dion 77, 78, 90

Evagrius 55

Evdokimov, Paul 10, 14, 19, 26, 27, 35-43, 46, 141, 147
Florovsky, Georges 14, 16-18, 69, 108, 109
Francke, August Hermann 163

Gregory Nazianzen (Saint) 92, 178
Gregory of Nyssa (Saint) 54, 144, 178, 188
Gregory Palamas (Saint) 11, 19, 20, 28, 30, 64, 70, 107-124, 126, 127, 129-131, 153, 154, 170, 178, 190, 191, 199
Gregory of Sinai (Saint) 30, 126
Golitzin, Alexander (Archbishop) 93, 95

Ignatios Xanthopoulos (Saint) 31, 32, 177, 193, 208
Irenaeus of Lyon (Saint) 37

John the Apostle (Saint) 92, 129
John Chrysostom (Saint) 37, 38
John Climacus (Saint) 39, 54, 55
John of Kronstadt (Saint) 41, 42
Justin Martyr (Saint) 103

Kalaitzidis, Pantelis 182
Kallistos Xanthopoulos (Saint) 31, 32, 177, 193, 208

Kern, Kiprian 14
Krivocheine, Basil (Archbishop) 10, 19, 26-31, 36

Larchet, Jean-Claude 10, 19, 69-71, 78, 124, 125
Le Guillou, Marie-Joseph 71

Leontios of Cyprus (Saint) 141
Levinas, Emmanuel 17, 51
Lossky, Vladimir 9, 13, 14, 16-18,
    64-66, 69, 109, 209
Loudovikos, Nikolaos (Nicholas) 11,
    16, 19, 20, 55, 56, 71-74, 94, 124,
    125, 182, 199, 205, 207
Lysack, Maxym 9-11

Macarios of Egypt (Saint) 55
Maloney, George 92
Mantzaridis, Georgios 63, 64, 121
Mark the Ascetic (Saint) 31, 34, 35,
    177, 208
Maximos the Confessor (Saint) 10,
    11, 15, 16, 19-21, 25, 26, 38, 44-46,
    48, 56, 59, 62, 70, 74, 75, 77-91,
    124-128, 170, 173, 177, 178, 190,
    192, 194, 199, 207-208
McPartlan, Paul 38, 50, 192, 193
Mersch, Emile 38
Meyendorff, John 55, 109
Meyendorff, Paul 86, 90, 91
Moltmann, Jürgen 195

Neptic Fathers 31, 54
Nikodemos the Hagiorite (Saint) 42
Optina Fathers 42
Origen 15, 54-56, 73, 126, 179, 180

Papanikolaou, Aristotle 11, 16, 19,
    68, 69, 144, 205
Papathanasiou, Athanasios 64
Paul the Apostle (Saint) 49, 52, 58,
    99, 114, 117, 209
Peter the Apostle (Saint) 129
Philaret of Moscow (Saint) 141

Romanides, John 14, 63-65, 170

Sakharov, Nicholas 185
Sakharov, Sophrony (Saint) 138,
    184-189

Schmemann, Alexander 9, 11, 14, 19, 21,
    25, 79, 80, 116, 118, 135-151, 167-
    173, 200, 201
Seraphim of Sarov (Saint) 42
Silouan of Athos (Saint) 189
Spener, Philipp Jakob 163
Staniloae, Dumitru 10, 14, 19, 26, 27,
    31-35, 41, 64, 66-69, 109, 132, 177-
    179, 193, 194, 205, 206, 208
Symeon the New Theologian (Saint) 11,
    19, 20, 27, 28, 30, 91-107, 124, 127-
    129, 131, 178, 190, 191, 199, 200

Theophan the Recluse (Saint) 42
Tikhon of Zadonsk (saint) 42
Tillich, Paul 17
Torrance, Alexis 16, 73, 124
Turcescu, Lucian 144

Vassiliades, Petros 11, 19, 21, 59-64, 66,
    135, 136, 143, 147, 149, 151, 173
Velychkovskyy, Païsiy (Saint) 42
Veniamin, Christopher 111, 112
Vidovic, Julija 124, 125
Vlachos, Hierotheos (Metropolitan) 14,
    19, 21, 63, 64, 84, 121, 122, 151, 152,
    199
Volf, Miroslav 182
Von Zinzendorf, Nicholas Ludwig 163

Ware, Kallistos (Metropolitan) 55, 141

Yangazoglou, Stavros 19, 64-66
Yannaras, Christos 17, 69, 170

Zhivov, V.M. 79, 81
Zizioulas, John (Metropolitan) 9-11,
    14-21, 23, 25-28, 32, 35, 38, 44-63,
    65-74, 77, 91, 92, 108, 124-127, 130,
    131, 135, 144, 164, 170, 171, 173, 174,
    177-201, 203-208
Zosimas (Saint) 184